The Miracle of Theism

The Miracle of Theism

Arguments for and against the existence of God

J. L. MACKIE

*Late Reader in Philosophy
and Fellow of University College, Oxford*

91-2035

CLARENDON PRESS · OXFORD

Oxford University Press, Walton Street, Oxford OX2 6DP

Oxford New York Toronto
Delhi Bombay Calcutta Madras Karachi
Petaling Jaya Singapore Hong Kong Tokyo
Nairobi Dar es Salaam Cape Town
Melbourne Auckland

and associated companies in
Berlin Ibadan

Oxford is a trade mark of Oxford University Press

Published in the United States by
Oxford University Press, New York

First published 1982
Fifth impression 1992

British Library Cataloguing in Publication Data

Mackie, J. L.
The miracle of Theism.
1. God—Proof
I. Title
212'.1   BT102
ISBN 0–19–824682–X (Pbk)

Library of Congress Cataloging in Publication Data

Mackie, J. L. (John Leslie)
The miracle of theism.
Includes index.
1. God—Proofs.   2. Theism.   I. Title
BT102.M244   212'.1   82–3552
ISBN 0–19–824682–X (Pbk).

Printed in Hong Kong

To Joan

Preface

My aim in this book is to examine the arguments for and against the existence of God carefully and in some detail, taking account both of the traditional concept of God and of the traditional 'proofs' of his existence and of more recent interpretations and approaches. While my own view is atheist, I have tried to give a full and fair hearing to the opposing case. In particular, I have tried to present as well as to answer the philosophical arguments for theism given recently by Richard Swinburne in *The Existence of God* and the very different case developed by Hans Küng in *Does God Exist?*

I have discussed this question over many years in various lectures and seminars, but not much of what appears here has been published previously. Chapter 6 is an expanded version of 'Die Ohnmacht moralischer Gottesbeweise', which appeared in *Glaube und Vernunft*, edited by Norbert Hoerster (Deutscher Taschenbuch Verlag, 1979), and Chapter 9 incorporates and develops the arguments of 'Evil and Omnipotence', published in *Mind* 64 (1955) and of replies to several critics of that article. I am grateful to the editors and publishers for permission to use these materials again.

I am particularly grateful to Norbert Hoerster, who has read the whole typescript and has suggested many improvements, and also to Michael Ayers, Robert Gay, John Lucas, Derek Parfit, Gerhard Streminger, Timothy Stroup, and David Wiggins for a number of corrections and suggestions.

J.L.M.

September 1981

Contents

Introduction   1

1. Miracles and Testimony   13
   (a) Hume's Argument—Exposition   13
   (b) Hume's Argument—Discussion   18

2. Descartes and the Idea of God   30
   (a) The Argument of the Third Meditation—Exposition   30
   (b) The Argument of the Third Meditation—Discussion   37

3. Ontological Arguments   41
   (a) Descartes's Proof and Kant's Criticism   41
   (b) Anselm's Ontological Proof and Gaunilo's Reply   49
   (c) Plantinga's Ontological Proof   55

4. Berkeley's God and Immaterial Realism   64
   (a) Berkeley's Theism—Exposition   64
   (b) Berkeley's Theism—Discussion   71

5. Cosmological Arguments   81
   (a) Contingency and Sufficient Reason   82
   (b) The Regress of Causes   87
   (c) Finite Past Time and Creation   92
   (d) Swinburne's Inductive Cosmological Argument   95

6. Moral Arguments for the Existence of a God   102
   (a) A Popular Line of Thought   102
   (b) Newman: Conscience as the Creative Principle of Religion   103
   (c) Kant: God as a Presupposition of Morality   106
   (d) Sidgwick: The Duality of Practical Reason   111
   (e) God and the Objectivity of Value   114

7. The Argument from Consciousness   119

8. Arguments for Design   133
  (a) Hume's *Dialogues*—Exposition   133
  (b) Hume's *Dialogues*—Discussion   137
  (c) Swinburne's Restatement   146

9. The Problem of Evil   150
  (a) Survey of the Problem   150
  (b) Attempts to Sidestep the Problem   156
  (c) The Paradox of Omnipotence   160
  (d) The Free Will Defence   162
  (e) Digression: the Nature of Free Will   166
  (f) The Free Will Defence—continued   172

10. Religious Experience and Natural Histories of Religion   177
  (a) The Varieties of Religious Experience   177
  (b) Natural Histories of Religion   187

11. Belief without Reason   199
  (a) Pascal's Wager   200
  (b) William James and the Will to Believe   204
  (c) Kierkegaard and the Primacy of Commitment   210

12. Religion without Belief?   217

13. Replacements for God   230

14. Conclusions and Implications   240
  (a) The Challenge of Nihilism   240
  (b) The Balance of Probabilities   251
  (c) The Moral Consequences of Atheism   254

Index   263

Introduction

THE topic of this book is theism, the doctrine that there is a god, and in particular a god as conceived in the central tradition of the main monotheistic religions, including Judaism, Christianity, and Islam. It is my view that the question whether there is or is not a god can and should be discussed rationally and reasonably, and that such discussion can be rewarding, in that it can yield definite results. This is a genuine, meaningful, question, and an important one—too important for us to take sides about it casually or arbitrarily. Neither the affirmative nor the negative answer is obviously right, but the issue is not so obscure that relevant considerations of argument and evidence cannot be brought to bear upon it.

The central doctrines of this traditional theism are well summed up by Richard Swinburne: there is a god who is 'a person without a body (i.e. a spirit), present everywhere, the creator and sustainer of the universe, a free agent, able to do everything (i.e. omnipotent), knowing all things, perfectly good, a source of moral obligation, immutable, eternal, a necessary being, holy, and worthy of worship'.[1] In general, I shall follow Swinburne in taking these descriptions fairly literally, though in some places I shall allow reasonable qualifications and flexibilities in interpretation.

It is sometimes doubted whether such descriptions *can* be literally meaningful. But there is really no problem about this. We know, from our acquaintance with ourselves and other human beings, what a person is—a person, as Swinburne explains, in the ordinary modern sense. Although all the persons we are acquainted with have bodies, there is no great difficulty in conceiving what it would be for there to

---

[1] R. Swinburne, *The Coherence of Theism* (Oxford University Press, 1977), p. 2. References to Swinburne are either to this book or to *The Existence of God* (Oxford University Press, 1979).

be a person without a body: for example, one can imagine oneself surviving without a body, and while at present one can act and produce results only by using one's limbs or one's speech organs, one can *imagine* having one's intentions fulfilled directly, without such physical means. Knowing what it is to be present in one place, we can form the concept of a spirit who is present everywhere. Similarly we can form the concept of creating something where there was nothing. The notion of sustaining something in existence can be spelled out in causal and conditional or hypothetical statements. God is thought to sustain the universe in that it continues to exist only because he so wills; if he did not so will, it would cease to exist. And so on. The notion of a necessary being is more difficult, but we shall be considering it in Chapters 3 and 5, and the notion of a source of moral obligation will be considered in Chapter 6. Holiness, too, may be a somewhat obscure notion; but we can say roughly that to be holy is to be the appropriate object of feelings of awe or attitudes of worship of which we have introspective experience.

The main reason why it has been thought that religious language cannot be literally meaningful is that some philosophers—particularly the logical positivists—have embraced a strongly verificationist theory of meaning, supposing that the meaning of any statement is given or constituted by the method or methods by which that statement itself could be verified or confirmed. Then, since it is not easy to say how the existence of a god with such attributes as those listed could be verified or confirmed, or falsified either, doubt is cast on the meaningfulness of the statement that there is such a god, or some different, less literal, meaning is sought for it. But this theory of meaning is itself highly implausible. It is well known that the adoption of it would similarly create serious difficulties for the meaning of many ordinary statements, including all those about past, historical, events, or about the minds, thoughts, and feelings of persons other than oneself. Rejecting it, we can still retain an empiricist or weak verificationist view, that all our terms have to be given meaning by their use in *some* statements that are verifiable or confirmable in our experience; but such terms can then be used to build up further statements for which, perhaps, no direct experiental test is possible. For example, once we are aware of the passage of time, and understand the sentence 'It is raining now', we can derive from these materials an understanding of the sentence 'It was raining an hour ago'; and this understanding, and the meaning thus given to this sentence, are quite independent of any opportunities we have and any methods we might use to check whether it *was* raining an hour ago. Similarly, if I know how a toothache feels to me, I can meaningfully ascribe a feeling of just the same sort to another person, despite the fact that I may have to use ways of finding out whether he is having this feeling which are quite different from the way in which I can tell that I have a toothache.

Correspondingly, a somewhat old-fashioned Christian may believe, literally, that there will be a last judgement. He need not, indeed, suppose that there will be such a scene as that depicted by Michelangelo on the wall of the Sistine Chapel; but he could still believe that each human person will survive, or live again, after the death of his body, and that for each such person (and perhaps for all together) there will come a time when he will be either admitted to a life of heavenly bliss or condemned to something much less pleasant, perhaps in accordance with his conduct in this present earthly life. One can understand the statement that there will be a last judgement as literally entailing this general description without claiming to have any adequate concepts of either the joys of heaven or the torments of hell, just as one can understand the general descriptions listed above as constituting the traditional notion of God without claiming to have an adequate idea of God, that is, to know the whole, supposedly infinite, nature of God.

I am saying only that talk about a last judgement *can* be understood literally. Admittedly, someone may prefer to take it as a metaphor; but then he can surely unpack the metaphor and state explicitly the meaning he intends. I mention this example of talk about a last judgement because this, as we shall see in Chapter 12, is used by some thinkers who argue that religious language must or should be taken in some non-literal, non-factual, way. This view will be discussed further in that chapter. For the present I need say no more about the meaning of religious language, particularly because this is very thoroughly and satisfactorily dealt with by Swinburne, in Chapters 4, 5, and 6 of *The Coherence of Theism*.

It may be thought that this central concern with traditional doctrines, literally understood—even if there is no problem about meaning—is narrow, old-fashioned, and no longer 'relevant'. As Swinburne says, there is, particularly in modern Protestant Christian theology, a strong tendency to play down credal statements, assertions of explicit belief in such doctrines, and to locate the centre of religion rather in 'a personal relationship to God in Christ'. But the

latter makes little sense unless the former are at least presupposed.
If God is not an objective reality but merely an intentional object,
that is, exists only in the believer's mind as do the objects of
imagination or events in dreams, then it is misleading to speak of a
relationship, and all the more misleading to describe the relationship
in terms of 'reliance', 'trust', 'guidance', and 'surrender': how could
one sensibly rely upon a figment of one's own imagination? Those
who are dissatisfied with the old creeds should change them,
not try to do without credal statements. If the other term of the
relation is not God in the traditional sense, then to go on using
the traditional names and descriptions, the familiar religious
language, carries at least a risk of misunderstanding, and, more
importantly, it tempts the believer himself into oscillating between
the views he is really prepared to assert and defend and the
familiar suggestions and connotations of the language he continues
to use.

If it is agreed that the central assertions of theism are literally
meaningful, it must also be admitted that they are not directly verified
or directly verifiable. It follows that any rational consideration of
whether they are true or not will involve arguments. Some of these
may be deductive. For example, several variants of the ontological
proof of God's existence (which will be examined in Chapter 3) are
presented as being deductively valid and as relying either on no
empirical or synthetic premisses at all or only on very obvious and
indubitable ones. On the opposite side, the problem of evil (discussed
in Chapter 9) may be presented as a formally valid disproof of the set
of propositions which constitutes traditional theism, as a demonstration that this set is internally inconsistent, so that these propositions
cannot all be true. But most of the arguments on either side are not
like this: they include important non-deductive elements. Each of
them starts from various pieces of evidence or considerations about
some part of our experience, and in many cases the conclusions
clearly go beyond what is contained, even implicitly, in the premisses.
All such arguments can be seen as resting on one general principle,
or as sharing one basic form and purpose: they are arguments to the
best explanation. The evidence supports the conclusion, it is suggested, because if we postulate that that conclusion is true—or better,
perhaps, that it is at least an approximation to the truth—we get a
more adequate overall explanation of that whole body of evidence,
in the light of whatever considerations are cited, than would be given
by any available alternative hypothesis. It is well known that it is

reasoning of this general form that gives scientific theories and hypotheses whatever support they have, and that makes it reasonable for us to claim truth or verisimilitude for them. It might, then, be supposed that, if we take non-deductive reasoning about God's existence to conform to this model, we are forcing theology into a 'scientistic' mould, or that we are prejudicially adopting a mode of thinking and a criterion of rationality that are peculiar to the age of modern science. But this is not so. On the contrary, this way of thinking is also thoroughly familiar in quite different, non-scientific, contexts. When a detective, in a story or in real life, reaches a conclusion about how the crime was committed, and by whom, he does so precisely on the ground that that conclusion emerges from an account which would explain all the relevant and available evidence better than any other account that anyone has been able to suggest. When a historian offers his own preferred account of how and why things happened in the period he is studying, or of who did what and from what motives, he too is claiming that this account gives a better explanation of all the data—records, reports, memoirs, archaeological traces, and so on—than any rival. Legal reasoning, either on questions of fact or on questions of law, is also of the same general sort. The earliest of the Greek philosophers used, though they did not formulate, this pattern of thought. And there is every reason to believe that this kind of thinking has been and is intelligible to reasonable people at all periods of history and in all cultures. No doubt there have been and still are many who give less weight than we would to arguments of this sort. But not because they cannot understand them or doubt their force; rather because they think they have other sources of information which make arguments of this kind unnecessary. They rely on revelations, intuitive certainties, authoritative traditions, 'what everyone knows'; they may not even raise the *question* whether God exists. However, once we do raise fundamental questions about religion we should be guilty of vicious circularity if we tried to settle them by appealing to the authority of any supposed revelations or traditions or common certainties, for their authority itself is at issue. Hence John Locke rightly insists that revelation needs the support of reason:

Reason must be our last judge and guide in everything. I do not mean that we must consult reason and examine whether a proposition revealed from God can be made out by natural principles, and if it cannot, that then we may reject it; but consult it we must, and by it examine whether it be a *revelation* from God or no; and if *reason* finds it to be revealed from God, *reason* then declares for it as much as for any other truth, and makes it one of her dictates.[2]

Descartes, too, made this point well in the ironic dedicatory letter of his *Meditations*, addressed to the Faculty of Theology in Paris:

... although it is quite true that the existence of God is to be believed since it is taught in the sacred Scriptures, and that ... the sacred Scriptures are to be believed because they come from God ... nevertheless this cannot be submitted to infidels, who would consider that the reasoning proceeded in a circle.[3]

Of course it is not only infidels but Descartes himself and any sensible person who can see that this reasoning is circular, and cannot be used to decide whether there is a god or not. Once that question is raised, it must be examined either by deductive reasoning or, if that yields no decision, by arguments to the best explanation; for in such a context nothing else can have any coherent bearing on the issue.

These considerations radically undermine the attempts, which have been made repeatedly, particularly in the last century or so, to substitute reliance on a revelation, perhaps a biblical tradition, for reasoned discussion of theistic doctrines. This is not to say that there is no place for faith. St. Anselm, who devised the ontological argument which has puzzled and fascinated philosophers for 900 years, spoke of *fides quaerens intellectum*, faith seeking understanding. He started with a belief in God, but hoped to find, and thought he had found, a reasoned support for that belief. This is a thoroughly respectable procedure. In fact, as the American pragmatist and empiricist William James shows, thinkers of all kinds must engage in such a pursuit. We all start with natural and conventional beliefs—for example, in a material world, in the existence of minds other than our own, in some moral principles, and many more. We could hardly survive without them. But it is not enough to leave them just as natural beliefs: as such, they are wide open to sceptical challenges. To rebut scepticism, faith or natural belief must seek understanding, reasoned support. We shall further examine the place of faith and its relation to reason in Chapter 11, with reference to the work both of James and of Kierkegaard.

If it turns out that deductive reasoning, using only analytic or obviously true assumptions, will not settle our questions either way,

[2] J. Locke, *An Essay concerning Human Understanding*, Book IV, Chapter xix, Section 14.
[3] R. Descartes, *Meditations on the First Philosophy*, Dedication.

and we therefore have to rely on non-deductive arguments, this will have an important implication that is often not properly understood. Where several different arguments bear upon the same issue, they may have a cumulative effect. It will not be sufficient to criticize each argument on its own by saying that it does not prove the intended conclusion, that is, does not put it beyond all doubt. That follows at once from the admission that the argument is non-deductive, and it is absurd to try to confine our knowledge and belief to matters which are conclusively established by sound deductive arguments. The demand for certainty will inevitably be disappointed, leaving scepticism in command of almost every issue. But also it will not be sufficient to say, though it may be true, that each argument on its own leaves the conclusion less likely than not, leaves the balance of probability against it. For a set of arguments of each of which, on its own, this adverse comment is true may together make the conclusion *more* likely than not. This is plain in a legal case, where a party may rely on the joint effect of a number of considerations each of which on its own would be too weak to justify a decision in that party's favour, but whose combined effect may justify such a decision. This holds equally in historical and scientific contexts. (The point is well made by Swinburne in Chapter 1 of *The Existence of God*.) It follows that after we have taken several different non-deductive arguments for and against the existence of a god and examined them separately, we must also consider their cumulative effect and decide what conclusion is the better supported by the evidence as a whole. This is done in Chapter 14.

This point might tell in favour of the theistic view; but there is a related point which may tell on the other side. An important anti-theistic consideration is summed up in the title of one of Hume's works, *The Natural History of Religion*. This phrase suggests that there is some adequate natural explanation, in terms which do not depend at all on even the approximate truth of the theistic doctrines, for the whole phenomenon of religious belief and practice. The explanation may be that religion satisfies widespread psychological human needs, or that it fulfils some social function. The availability of such an explanation would not in itself tend to show that the theistic doctrines are false, but it would undermine any presumption of their truth that might otherwise be founded on their widespread acceptance. In any field of inquiry we normally start by taking for granted what is almost universally believed, and revise or discard this only reluctantly and for strong reasons. But if we can show that a certain belief would be almost universally held, even if it were groundless, the issue is made far more open: there is no clear onus of proof on either side. As we shall see in Chapter 10, several different natural histories of religion have been offered. Hume said that religion stems from 'the incessant hopes and fears, which actuate the human mind'; he inferred that the first religions were polytheistic, with many gods representing the many forces that variously help or threaten human life. Feuerbach saw religion rather differently, as a projection of human thoughts, ideals, and relationships. Marx held that religion flourishes because it serves a function in a society divided by class conflict, the function of bolstering the authority of a ruling class, and of taking some of the heat out of class struggles by giving illusory satisfactions and compensations to otherwise deprived and alienated classes. Freud and other psychoanalysts find the source of religion in our repressed and unconscious wishes. At first sight these are rival, mutually exclusive, accounts. But on reflection we see that this is not so. Religion is a complex phenomenon: its various beliefs and even more various practices may well result from the interplay of a number of causal factors, and some of its most central features, such as the ascription of great power to one or more supernatural beings, and feelings of awe towards them, could be causally over-determined. The full causal explanation of religion as a natural phenomenon may well include the factors picked out separately by Hume and Feuerbach and Marx and Freud, and perhaps others as well. What we should weigh in the end is the adequacy of some complete and probably complex natural history of religion.

Since Nietzsche, it has become customary to raise the basic issue in the philosophy of religion by asking 'Is God dead?' But, taken even half literally, this is a silly question. The affirmative answer could mean only that theism as a system of beliefs has died out or is dying out. That is the only sense we could make of the suggestion that God was formerly alive but is so no longer. And that is neither here nor there: the important question is whether these beliefs are *true*. They might well be true even if they were no longer popular; equally, they could continue to be popular even if they were not true. Questions about fashions of belief or disbelief are of interest only to the sociologist or historian of ideas. In fact, even if religious beliefs are false and lack any rational foundation, we should still expect them to continue to flourish and to revive repeatedly after periods of relative decline. This is a consequence of all the suggested natural histories of religion. Religion is likely to survive as long as there are psychological and social forces to maintain it. Hume's theory is no exception. The advance of science may make redundant all super-natural explanations of droughts and floods, earthquakes and dis-ease, and it has given us such effective ways of killing our enemies that it may seem superfluous also to pray for their destruction. Yet in other ways science has increased our insecurity and need for assurance. It has revealed the immense deserts of inter-stellar and inter-galactic space, so that we might be glad of a belief in a universal mind and purpose that would make us feel more at home; and it has focused attention on new problems that seem to call for explanation, like the beginning of life and of the universe itself, and the very existence of natural law. Even the Marxist theory, sensibly applied, would no longer suggest a rapid and permanent decline of religion, for even when class conflicts are supposed to have been abolished they reappear in new forms and disguises.

Hume himself was well aware of the power of religion to persist in the face of rational criticism. In the dialogue which he imagines taking place between Charon and himself on the bank of the Styx, he says:

But I might still urge, 'Have a little patience, good Charon, I have been endeavouring to open the eyes of the Public. If I live a few years longer, I may have the satisfaction of seeing the downfal of some of the prevailing systems of superstition.' But Charon would then lose all temper and decency. 'You loitering rogue, that will not happen these many hundred years. Do you fancy I will grant you a lease for so long a term? Get into the boat this instant, you lazy loitering rogue.'[4]

This book uses few technical terms, and most that are used will explain themselves. But I should perhaps explain my reference to different kinds of probability. A statistical probability is simply a frequency in a finite class or the limiting frequency in an indefinitely extended series—for example, in a series of tosses of a certain coin, the proportion of heads among the results may keep coming closer to some value, say 50 per cent; if so, this would be the limiting frequency or statistical probability of heads in this series. A physical probability or propensity is a measure of the strength of the tendency for an outcome of a certain sort to result from a certain set-up. This may be shown by the frequency of that outcome in instances of that set-up; but the propensity can be ascribed to each single occurrence

[4] Letter from Adam Smith to William Strahan of 9 Nov. 1776; printed in the Supplement to Hume's *Dialogues concerning Natural Religion*, edited by Norman Kemp Smith (Nelson, London and Edinburgh, Second Edition, 1947).

of the set-up, whereas the frequency can characterize only a class or series. The probabilities with which we shall be most concerned are epistemic ones: the epistemic probability of a certain statement relative to some body of information is a measure of the degree of support that that information gives to that statement, or, equivalently, of the degree of belief that it is reasonable to give to that statement on the basis of that information. We often speak of high or low epistemic probabilities where we cannot assign any exact measures to them. But where the only relevant information is that the matter we are interested in is a member of some class or of some series of events in which there is a known statistical probability for items of that sort, or that it would be the outcome of a certain set-up which has a known propensity to produce such an item, we can derive from the statistical or physical probability an epistemic probability of the same value. For example, if tosses of this coin have a 50 per cent propensity to fall heads, and this is all the relevant evidence we have about the result of the next toss, the epistemic probability of heads at the next toss will also be 50 per cent. I shall occasionally use formulae of the form '$P(x/y)$': this is to be read as 'the epistemic probability of x in relation to y', that is, as the degree of support given by the statement represented by 'y' to that represented by 'x'.

One point of orthography should also be explained. I write 'God', with a capital 'G', where this is used as the proper name of an actual or supposed being, but 'god', with a small 'g', where this is a general term, for example, where I speak of the question whether there is a god.

Since this is a fairly long book, I should also explain its plan. Broadly, Chapters 1 to 8 deal with traditional arguments for theism, and Chapters 10 to 14 with more characteristically modern approaches and ways of defending theism, or part of it, in the face of difficulties; Chapter 9 discusses one of the major problems for theism, that of evil. Chapters 1 and 2 are both pilot projects, one introducing the concepts and methods of non-deductive reasoning, the other illustrating the attempt to settle questions by rational, demonstrative, and largely *a priori* argument. Chapters 3, 5, 6, 7, and 8 discuss several variants, both classical and recent, of each of the best-known 'proofs' of God's existence, while Chapter 4 considers Berkeley's immaterialism as a distinctive argument for a god. Chapter 10 considers religious experience both as something that may have value in itself and as the basis of a possible argument for a god (or gods), Chapter 11 deals with recommendations of voluntary decisions in favour of belief, not supported by epistemic reasoning or probability, and Chapter 12 with attempts to explain religion as not necessarily involving the literal assertions discussed in the earlier chapters. Chapter 10 also considers whether religion, including religious and mystical experiences, can be explained in natural terms. Chapter 13 looks at the suggestion that the notion of objective value as itself creative might replace or supplement the concept of a personal god. Chapter 14 criticizes the attempt of Hans Küng to defend theism as a necessary bulwark against the threat of nihilism, and finds many of the earlier themes combined in his recent work. This leads to the final estimate of the balance of probabilities for and against the existence of a god, and a sketch of the contrasting moral consequences of theism and atheism.

A reader whose interest is mainly in distinctively modern approaches might, therefore, start with Chapters 10 to 14, and only then turn back to the earlier parts. But the argument of the book is continuous, and what is said in the later chapters depends to some extent on previous results. In particular, arguments that appear in a rather confused form in Küng can be best understood with the help of earlier, more straightforward presentations, and the clarity and honesty of most of those discussed in the earlier chapters (Swinburne as well as the classical writers) will be a welcome contrast to the evasiveness and oscillations between mutually incompatible views in which some recent theologians have taken refuge from criticism.

I hope, therefore, that readers of this book who are not already familiar with the classical discussions on which it is based will be encouraged to turn to these original writings. For many of the great philosophers—Descartes, Berkeley, Hume, and Kant among others—the existence of a god was a central issue, and their discussions of this problem are often the most accessible and immediately comprehensible parts of their work. And quotations that I have given will show that some of them offer us not only profound and challenging thought but also eloquent and attractive presentation.

Of course my selection of writers to discuss, both classical and recent, has been fairly arbitrary. My purpose is not the impossible one of doing justice to all who have made significant contributions to this subject, but has been rather to use whatever formulations would best help the argument along and illustrate at least the main relevant lines of thought.

Finally, a brief explanation of the title of this book. The word 'miracle' originally meant only something surprising or marvellous, but it now usually means a violation of the laws of nature by the purposive intervention of a supernatural being, and it is sometimes extended to cover any supernatural action upon the natural world, so that the laws of nature themselves, or the very existence of a material world, can be seen as a continuing miracle. In this last, broad, sense, theism is necessarily the assertion of a miracle. Traditional theism is also committed to miracles in the second sense, to particular divine interventions into the natural order—for example, the coming of Christ. But my title also echoes Hume's ironic remark that the Christian religion cannot be believed without a miracle by any reasonable person. Theistic belief in general is no miracle, if (as Chapter 10 will indicate) there can be an adequate natural history of religion. But I hope to show that its continuing hold on the minds of many reasonable people is surprising enough to count as a miracle in at least the original sense.

I

Miracles and Testimony

(a) *Hume's Argument—Exposition*

TRADITIONAL theism, as defined in the Introduction, does not explicitly include any contrast between the natural and the supernatural. Yet there is a familiar, if vague and undeveloped, notion of the natural world in contrast with which the theistic doctrines stand out as asserting a supernatural reality. The question whether and how there can be evidence for what, if real, would be supernatural is therefore one of central significance. Besides, explicit assertions about supernatural occurrences, about miracles or divine interventions which have disrupted the natural course of events, are common in nearly all religions: alleged miracles are often cited to validate religious claims. Christianity, for example, has its share of these. In the life of Christ we have the virgin birth, the turning of water into wine, Christ's walking on the water, his healing of the sick, his raising of Lazarus from the dead, and, of course, the resurrection. The Roman Catholic church will not recognize anyone as a saint unless it is convinced that at least two miracles have been performed by the supposed saint, either in his or her life or after death.

The usual purpose of stories about miracles is to establish the authority of the particular figures who perform them or are associated with them, but of course these stories, with their intended interpretation, presuppose such more general religious doctrines as that of the existence of a god. We can, therefore, recognize, as one of the supports of traditional theism, an argument from miracles: that is, an argument whose main premiss is that such and such remarkable events have occurred, and whose conclusion is that a god of the traditional sort both exists and intervenes, from time to time, in the ordinary world.

Hume, however, in his essay on miracles, Section 10 of his *Enquiry concerning Human Understanding*, makes the bold claim that he has discovered an argument which refutes all such stories about the occurrence of miracles.[1] 'I flatter myself,' he says, 'that I have dis-covered an argument . . . which, if just, will, with the wise and learned, be an everlasting check to all kinds of superstitious delusion, and consequently, will be useful as long as the world endures. For so long, I presume, will the accounts of miracles and prodigies be found in all history, sacred and profane.' (p. 110) In this fairly early work, as in the much later remarks quoted in the Introduction, Hume does not expect the popular belief in the supernatural to die out: it is only with the 'wise and learned' that rational criticism can be expected to carry much weight. But how sound is the argument in which he felt this modest confidence? What is its substance?

We should distinguish the central argument which Hume dis-covered, and which he states in Part I of this section, from various secondary reasons which he gives in Part II for doubting the stories about miracles. Let us run through these secondary reasons first, and then come back to the main argument.

First, Hume says that there are no really well-attested miracles: none, that is, 'attested by a sufficient number of men, of such un-questioned good-sense, education, and learning, as to secure us against all delusion in themselves; of such undoubted integrity, as to place them beyond all suspicion of any design to deceive others; of such credit and reputation in the eyes of mankind, as to have a great deal to lose in case of their being detected in any falsehood; and at the same time attesting facts, performed in such a public manner, and in so celebrated a part of the world, as to render the detection unavoidable' (pp. 116–17). These are high standards. But such high standards are appropriate in an area where deceit, self-deception, and mistake are so easy. Unfortunately, it is a matter of controversy whether they have ever been met. At least Hume's remarks here specify questions that we might well ask when we encounter any reports of alleged miracles.

Hume points out, secondly, that the human mind has a positive tendency to believe what is strange and marvellous in an extreme degree. 'The passion of *surprise* and *wonder*, arising from miracles, being an agreeable emotion, gives a sensible tendency towards the

---

[1] D. Hume, *Enquiries concerning the Human Understanding and concerning the Principles of Morals*, edited by L. A. Selby-Bigge (Oxford University Press, 1902). References in the text are to pages in this edition.

belief of those events from which it is derived.' (p. 117) The willing-ness of many people today to believe accounts of flying saucers and their crews illustrates this tendency: such reports are, paradoxically, made more believable by the very divergence from the ordinary which in fact makes them less worthy of belief.

Thirdly, reports of miracles 'are observed chiefly to abound among ignorant and barbarous nations'. Where they are believed by civilized peoples, these 'will be found to have received them from ignorant and barbarous ancestors', so that the stories will have acquired the authority of received opinions before the nations in question have developed powers of criticism and traditions of rational inquiry. (p. 119)

Fourthly, different religions are in conflict: their claims therefore undermine and destroy one another. The truth of any report of a miracle which would tend to establish the religious authority of Christ or his followers would require the falsity of any report of a miracle which would tend to establish the authority of Mahomet. Thus the miracle reports of any one religion are implicitly or in effect contradicted by the miracle reports of many other religions: it is as if a lawcourt were presented with, say, twenty witnesses, each of whom was denounced as a liar by the other nineteen. (pp. 121–2)

This argument, however, has less force now than it had when Hume was writing. Faced with influential bodies of atheist or scep-tical opinion, the adherents of different religions have toned down their hostility to one another. The advocate of one religion will now often allow that a number of others have at least some elements of truth and even, perhaps, some measure of divine authorization. It is no longer 'The heathen in his blindness . . .', but rather 'We worship the same god, but under different names and in different ways'. Carried far enough, this modern tendency would allow Christian miracles to support, not undermine, belief in the supernatural achievements of stone-age witch doctors and medicine men, and vice versa. It is as if someone had coined the slogan, 'Miracle-workers of the world, unite!'

Fifthly, Hume says, the very fact that a miracle story is used to introduce a new religion or to support an existing one is an additional reason for scepticism. Many people have an intense desire to believe in some religious object, and experience shows that large numbers are constantly deluded by such claims. (pp. 125–6) This is in itself a strong point. But we might add to it the fact that in a religious context credulity is often thought to be meritorious, while doubt or critical caution is felt to be sinful. Consequently, once even a modicum of belief arises in a group of people in communication with one another, it tends to reinforce itself and so develop into total conviction. No doubt this appears to the members of such a group as a virtuous spiral, but it has no valid claim to be regarded as a rational process.

These five points, then, are of unequal force, but between them they certainly provide grounds for a high degree of initial caution and scepticism about every alleged miracle. But they are secondary considerations, additional and subordinate to Hume's main argument.

This main argument rests upon a principle that governs the acceptance of testimony, believing what one is told, about any matter at all. If someone tells you something, you are in general disposed to believe him; but why? Why should you give any credence at all to what he says? Your basic reason must be that it is unlikely that he would have told you this if it were not so. His report—assuming that you have understood it correctly—could be false only in either of two ways: he might be mistaken, or he might be deceiving you. Is it likely that he is mistaken? Is it likely that he is insincere? If both of these are unlikely, then it is unlikely that he would be telling you this if it were not so. Since he *is* telling you this, it is unlikely that it is not so; that is, so far as these considerations are concerned, it is likely that it is so. But these are not the only relevant considerations: you must weigh along with them the intrinsic likelihood or unlikelihood of whatever it is that your informant reports. The less intrinsically likely this is, the more reliable the testimony needs to be, if it is to deserve acceptance. The question to be answered is this: 'Which of these two is the more unlikely as a whole: that he should be telling you this and it not be so—and therefore that he should be mistaken or dishonest—or that he should be telling this and it be so—that is, that the event he reports, despite whatever intrinsic unlikeliness attaches to it, should have happened?' So if the event reported is something intrinsically improbable, the crucial question is whether the reporter's being either deceived or a deceiver is intrinsically more improbable still. Further, the magnitude of each of these unlikelihoods or improbabilities must be determined with reference to the way the world goes on, that is, with reference to the laws of nature so far as we know them. In deciding how the world goes on, we can rely only on past experience: we must reason inductively from what we have observed. Now if the event reported is a miracle, it must be literally contrary to the laws of nature, it must contradict the conclusion of an induction of maximum strength. That is, it must be as unlikely as anything could be. The competing unlikelihood of the reporter's being deceived or a deceiver cannot exceed this, but can at most equal it. Indeed Hume thinks it will never even equal it, for it will not be contrary to a law of nature that your informant should have made a mistake or that he should be dishonest. But if the two unlikelihoods are equal, they will simply cancel one another out: we shall still have, on balance, no positive reason for accepting the report of the miracle.

That, at least, seems to be what Hume is saying. However, at the end of Part I of this Section he hesitates. 'The plain consequence', he says, 'is "That no testimony is sufficient to establish a miracle, unless the testimony be of such a kind, that its falsity would be more miraculous, than the fact, which it endeavours to establish; and even in that case there is a mutual destruction of arguments, and the superior only gives us an assurance suitable to that degree of force, which remains, after deducting the inferior".' (pp. 115-16) This comment seems to allow that the balance of probabilities could be in favour of our accepting the miracle report, though with no very high degree of confidence; it will also entail something that Hume seems not to have noticed, that if the force of testimony is pretty strong, though not strong enough to make it reasonable for us to accept the miracle report, it will significantly lower the degree of confidence with which we reject it.

In fact, Hume's conclusion needs to be tidied up and restated as follows. There are three conceivable cases. In the first, the unlikelihood of the testimony's being false (either mistaken or dishonest) is less than the intrinsic unlikelihood of the miracle's having occurred: in this case, we must reject the miracle report, with a degree of confidence that corresponds to the difference between these unlikelihoods. In the second, the two unlikelihoods are equal: now we must simply suspend our judgement until some fresh consideration tips the balance either way; but in the meantime we cannot rationally accept the report. In the third case the occurrence of the miracle is intrinsically less unlikely than the testimony's being false: in this, we are rationally bound to accept the miracle report, but again with a degree of conviction that corresponds to the difference between the two unlikelihoods. This degree of conviction can never be high, on account of the great intrinsic improbability of the miracle. Where the falsity of the report would itself be a miracle in the sense of a violation

of what we take to be the laws of nature, we must, Hume says, 'weigh
the one miracle against the other', and 'reject the greater miracle'. 'If
the falsity of his testimony would be more miraculous than the event
which he relates; then, and not till then, can he pretend to command
my belief or opinion.' (p. 116)

Thus tidied up, the conclusion of Part I clearly allows, in principle,
cases where the testimony would establish a miracle, at least tentatively, with no great preponderance of rational support, and also
cases where we ought to suspend judgement. But we can now understand the argumentative function of the secondary considerations
offered in Part II. They are meant to show that neither of these two
conceivable cases is ever actually realized, that the unlikelihood that
the testimony brought in favour of a miracle should be false is never
in practice very great, so that it will always in fact be less than the
unlikelihood of the miracle's having occurred.

(b) *Hume's Argument—Discussion*

What Hume has been expounding are the principles for the rational
acceptance of testimony, the rules that ought to govern our believing
or not believing what we are told. But the rules that govern people's
actual acceptance of testimony are very different. We are fairly good
at detecting dishonesty, insincerity, and lack of conviction, and we
readily reject what we are told by someone who betrays these defects.
But we are strongly inclined simply to accept, without question,
statements that are obviously assured and sincere. As Hume would
say, a firm association of ideas links someone else's saying, with
honest conviction, that *p*, and its being the case that *p*, and we pass
automatically from the perception of the one to belief in the other.
Or, as he might also have said, there is an intellectual sympathy by
which we tend automatically to share what we find to be someone
else's belief, analogous to sympathy in the original sense, the tendency to share what we see to be someone else's feelings. And in
general this is a useful tendency. People's beliefs about ordinary
matters are right, or nearly right, more often than they are wildly
wrong, so that intellectual sympathy enables fairly correct information to be passed on more smoothly than it could be if we were
habitually cautious and constantly checked testimony against the
principles for its rational acceptance. But what is thus generally
useful can sometimes be misleading, and miracle reports are a special
case where we need to restrain our instinctive acceptance of honest

statements, and go back to the basic rational principles which deter-mine whether a statement is really reliable or not. Even where we are cautious, and hesitate to accept what we are told—for example by a witness in a legal case—we often do not go beyond the question 'How intrinsically reliable is this witness?', or, in detail, 'Does he seem to be honest? Does he have a motive for misleading us? Is he the sort of person who might tell plausible lies? Or is he the sort of person who, in the circumstances, might have made a mistake?' If we are satisfied on all these scores, we are inclined to believe what the witness says, without weighing very seriously the question 'How intrinsically improbable is what he has told us?' But, as Hume insists, this further question is highly relevant. His general approach to the problem of when to accept testimony is certainly sound.

Hume's case against miracles is an epistemological argument: it does not try to show that miracles never do happen or never could happen, but only that we never have good reasons for believing that they have happened. It must be clearly distinguished from the sugges-tion that the very concept of a miracle is incoherent. That suggestion might be spelled out as follows. A miracle is, by definition, a violation of a law of nature, and a law of nature is, by definition, a regularity—or the statement of a regularity—about what happens, about the way the world works; consequently, if some event actually occurs, no regularity which its occurrence infringes (or, no regularity-statement which it falsifies) can really be a law of nature; so this event, however unusual or surprising, cannot after all be a miracle. The two defini-tions together entail that whatever happens is not a miracle, that is, that miracles never happen. This, be it noted, is not Hume's argu-ment. If it were correct, it would make Hume's argument unneces-sary. Before we discuss Hume's case, then, we should consider whether there is a coherent concept of a miracle which would not thus rule out the occurrence of miracles *a priori*.

If miracles are to serve their traditional function of giving specta-cular support to religious claims—whether general theistic claims, or the authority of some specific religion or some particular sect or individual teacher—the concept must not be so weakened that any-thing at all unusual or remarkable counts as a miracle. We must keep in the definition the notion of a violation of natural law. But then, if it is to be even possible that a miracle should occur, we must modify the definition given above of a law of nature. What we want to do is to contrast the order of nature with a possible divine or supernatural intervention. The laws of nature, we must say, describe the ways in

which the world—including, of course, human beings—works when
left to itself, when not interfered with. A miracle occurs when the
world is not left to itself, when something distinct from the natural
order as a whole intrudes into it.

This notion of ways in which the world works is coherent and by
no means obscure. We know how to discover causal laws, relying on
a principle of the uniformity of the course of nature—essentially the
assumption that there are some laws to be found—in conjunction
with suitable observations and experiments, typically varieties of
controlled experiment whose underlying logic is that of Mill's
'method of difference'. Within the laws so established, we can further
mark off basic laws of working from derived laws which hold only in
a particular context or contingently upon the way in which something
is put together. It will be a derived law that a particular clock, or
clocks of a particular sort, run at such a speed, and this will hold
only in certain conditions of temperature, and so on; but this law will
be derived from more basic ones which describe the regular behaviour of certain kinds of material, in view of the way in which the
clock is put together, and these more basic laws of materials may in
turn be derived from yet more basic laws about sub-atomic particles,
in view of the ways in which those materials are made up of such
particles. In so far as we advance towards a knowledge of such a system
of basic and derived laws, we are acquiring an understanding of ways
in which the world works. As well as what we should ordinarily call
causal laws, which typically concern interactions, there are similar
laws with regard to the ways in which certain kinds of things simply
persist through time, and certain sorts of continuous process just go
on. These too, and in particular the more basic laws of these sorts,
help to constitute the ways in which the world works. Thus there are
several kinds of basic 'laws of working'.[2] For our present purpose,
however, it is not essential that we should even be approaching an
understanding of how the world works; it is enough that we have the
concept of such basic laws of working, that we know in principle
what it would be to discover them. Once we have this concept, we
have moved beyond the definition of laws of nature merely as (statements of) what always happens. We can see how, using this concept
and using the assumption that there are some such basic laws of
working to be found, we can hope to determine what the actual laws

---

[2] The notion of basic laws of working is fully discussed in Chapters 8 and 9 of my
The Cement of the Universe: A Study of Causation (Oxford University Press, 1974 and
1980).

of working are by reference to a restricted range of experiments and observations. This opens up the possibility that we might determine that something *is* a basic law of working of natural objects, and yet also, independently, find that it was occasionally violated. An occasional violation does not in itself necessarily overthrow the independently established conclusion that this *is* a law of working.

Equally, there is no obscurity in the notion of intervention. Even in the natural world we have a clear understanding of how there can be for a time a closed system, in which everything that happens results from factors within that system in accordance with its laws of working, but how then something may intrude from outside it, bringing about changes that the system would not have produced of its own accord, so that things go on after this intrusion differently from how they would have gone on if the system had remained closed. All we need do, then, is to regard the whole natural world as being, for most of the time, such a closed system; we can then think of a supernatural intervention as something that intrudes into that system from outside the natural world as a whole.

If the laws by which the natural world works are deterministic, then the notion of a violation of them is quite clear-cut: such a violation would be an event which, given that the world was a closed system working in accordance with these laws, and given some actual earlier complete state of the world, simply could not have happened at all. Its occurrence would then be clear proof that either the supposed laws were not the real laws of working, or the earlier state was not as it was supposed to have been, or else the system was not closed after all. But if the basic laws of working are statistical or probabilistic, the notion of a violation of them is less precise. If something happens which, given those statistical laws and some earlier complete state of the world, is extremely improbable—in the sense of physical probability: that is, something such that there is a strong propensity or tendency for it *not* to happen—we still cannot say firmly that the laws have been violated: laws of this sort explicitly allow that what is extremely improbable may occasionally come about. Indeed it is highly probable (both physically and epistemically) that some events, each of which is very improbable, will occur at rare intervals.[3] If tosses of a coin were governed by a statistical law that gave a 50 per cent propensity to heads at each toss, a continuous run of ten heads

[3] The distinction between physical and epistemic probability has been drawn in the Introduction; the exact form of statistical laws is discussed in Chapter 9 of *The Cement of the Universe*.

would be a highly improbable occurrence; but it would be highly probable that there would be some such runs in a sequence of a million tosses. Nevertheless, we can still use the contrast between the way of working of the natural world as a whole, considered as a normally closed system, and an intervention or intrusion into it. This contrast does not disappear or become unintelligible merely because we lack decisive tests for its application. We can still define a miracle as an event which would not have happened in the course of nature, and which came about only through a supernatural intrusion. The difficulty is merely that we cannot now say with certainty, simply by reference to the relevant laws and some antecedent situation, that a certain event would not have happened in the course of nature, and therefore must be such an intrusion. But we may still be able to say that it is very probable—and this is now an epistemic probability— that it would not have happened naturally, and so is likely to be such an intrusion. For if the laws made it physically improbable that it would come about, this tends to make it epistemically improbable that it did come about through those laws, if there is any other way in which it could have come about and which is not equally improbable or more improbable. In practice the difficulty mentioned is not much of an extra difficulty. For even where we believe there to be deterministic laws and an earlier situation which together would have made an occurrence actually impossible in the course of nature, it is from our point of view at best epistemically very probable, not certain, that those are the laws and that that was the relevant antecedent situation.

Consequently, whether the laws of nature are deterministic or statistical, we can give a coherent definition of a miracle as a supernatural intrusion into the normally closed system that works in accordance with those laws, and in either case we can identify conceivable occurrences, and alleged occurrences, which if they were to occur, or have occurred, could be believed with high probability, though not known with certainty, to satisfy that definition.

However, the full concept of a miracle requires that the intrusion should be purposive, that it should fulfil the intention of a god or other supernatural being. This connection cannot be sustained by any ordinary causal theory; it presupposes a power to fulfil intentions directly, without physical means, which (as we shall see in Chapters 5 and 7) is highly dubious; so this requirement for a miracle will be particularly hard to confirm. On the other hand it is worth noting that successful prophecy could be regarded as a form of miracle for which there could in principle be good evidence. If someone is reliably recorded as having prophesied at t_1 an event at t_2 which could not be predicted at t_1 on any natural grounds, and the event occurs at t_2, then at any later time t_3 we can assess the evidence for the claims both that the prophecy was made at t_1 and that its accuracy cannot be explained either causally (for example, on the ground that it brought about its own fulfilment) or as accidental, and hence that it was probably miraculous.

There is, then, a coherent concept of miracles. Their possibility is not ruled out *a priori*, by definition. So we must consider whether Hume's argument shows that we never have good reason for believing that any have occurred.

Hume's general principle for the evaluation of testimony, that we have to weigh the unlikelihood of the event reported against the unlikelihood that the witness is mistaken or dishonest, is substantially correct. It is a corollary of the still more general principle of accepting whatever hypothesis gives the best overall explanation of all the available and relevant evidence. But some riders are necessary. First, the likelihood or unlikelihood, the epistemic probability or improbability, is always relative to some body of information, and may change if additional information comes in. Consequently, any specific decision in accordance with Hume's principle must be provisional. Secondly, it is one thing to decide which of the rival hypotheses in the field at any time should be provisionally accepted in the light of the evidence then available; but it is quite another to estimate the weight of this evidence, to say how well supported this favoured hypothesis is, and whether it is likely that its claims will be undermined either by additional information or by the suggesting of further alternative hypotheses. What is clearly the best-supported view of some matter at the moment may still be very insecure, and quite likely to be overthrown by some further considerations. For example, if a public opinion poll is the only evidence we have about the result of a coming election, this evidence may point, perhaps decisively, to one result rather than another; yet if the poll has reached only a small sample of the electorate, or if it was taken some time before the voting day, it will not be very reliable. There is a dimension of reliability over and above that of epistemic probability relative to the available evidence. Thirdly, Hume's description of what gives support to a prediction, or in general to a judgement about an unobserved case that would fall under some generalization, is very unsatisfactory. He seems to say that if *all* so far observed As have been Bs, then this amounts to a 'proof' that some unobserved A will be (or is, or was) a B, whereas if some observed As have been Bs, but some have not, there is only a 'probability' that an unobserved A will be a B (pp. 110-12). This mixes up the reasoning *to* a generalization with the reasoning *from* a generalization to a particular case. It is true that the premisses 'All As are Bs' and 'This is an A' constitute a proof of the conclusion 'This is a B', whereas the premisses 'x per cent of As are Bs' and 'This is an A' yield—if there is no other relevant information—a probability of x per cent that this is a B: they *probabilify* the conclusion to this degree, or, as we can say, the probability of the conclusion 'This is a B' relative to that evidence is x per cent. But the inductive argument from the observation 'All so far observed As have been Bs' to the generalization 'All As are Bs' is far from secure, and it would be most misleading to call this a proof, and therefore misleading also to describe as a proof the whole line of inference from 'All so far observed As have been Bs' to the conclusion 'This as yet unobserved A is a B'. Similarly, the inductive argument from 'x per cent of observed As have been Bs' to the statistical generalization 'x per cent of As are Bs' is far from secure, so that we cannot say that 'x per cent of observed As have been Bs' even probabilifies to the degree x per cent the conclusion 'This as yet unobserved A is a B'. A good deal of other information and background knowledge is needed, in either case, before the generalization, whether universal or statistical, is at all well supported, and hence before the stage is properly set for either proof or probabilification about an as yet unobserved A. It is harder than Hume allows here to arrive at well-supported generalizations of either sort about how the world works.

These various qualifications together entail that what has been widely and reasonably thought to be a law of nature may not be one, perhaps in ways that are highly relevant to some supposed miracles. Our present understanding of psychosomatic illness, for example, shows that it is not contrary to the laws of nature that someone who for years has seemed, to himself as well as to others, to be paralysed should rapidly regain the use of his limbs. On the other hand, we can still be pretty confident that it is contrary to the laws of nature that a human being whose heart has stopped beating for forty-eight hours in ordinary circumstances—that is, without any special life-support systems—should come back to life, or that what is literally water should without addition or replacement turn into what is literally good-quality wine.

However, any problems there may be about establishing laws of nature are neutral between the parties to the present debate, Hume's followers and those who believe in miracles; for both these parties need the notion of a well-established law of nature. The miracle advocate needs it in order to be able to say that the alleged occurrence is a miracle, a violation of natural law by supernatural intervention, no less than Hume needs it for his argument against believing that this event has actually taken place.

It is therefore not enough for the defender of a miracle to cast doubt (as he well might) on the certainty of our knowledge of the law of nature that seems to have been violated. For he must himself say that this *is* a law of nature: otherwise the reported event will not be miraculous. That is, he must in effect *concede* to Hume that the antecedent improbability of this event is as high as it could be, hence that, apart from the testimony, we have the strongest possible grounds for believing that the alleged event did not occur. This event must, by the miracle advocate's own admission, be contrary to a genuine, not merely a supposed, law of nature, and therefore maximally improbable. It is this maximal improbability that the weight of the testimony would have to overcome.

One further improvement is needed in Hume's theory of testimony. It is well known that the agreement of two (or more) *independent* witnesses constitutes very powerful evidence. Two independent witnesses are more than twice as good as each of them on his own. The reason for this is plain. If just one witness says that *p*, one explanation of this would be that it was the case that *p* and that he has observed this, remembered it, and is now making an honest report; but there are many alternative explanations, for example that he observed something else which he mistook for its being that *p*, or is misremembering what he observed, or is telling a lie. But if two witnesses who can be shown to be quite independent of one another both say that *p*, while again one explanation is that each of them has observed this and remembered it and is reporting honestly, the alternative explanations are not now so easy. They face the question 'How has there come about this *agreement* in their reports, if it was not the case that *p*? How have the witnesses managed to misobserve to the same effect, or to misremember in the same way, or to hit upon the same lie?' It is difficult for even a single liar to keep on telling a *consistent* false story; it is much harder for two or more liars to do so. Of course if there is any collusion between the witnesses, or if either has been influenced, directly or indirectly, by the other, or if both stories have a common source, this question is easily answered. That is why the independence of the witnesses is so important. This principle of the improbability of coincident error has two vital bearings upon the problem of miracles. On the one hand, it means that a certain sort of testimony can be more powerful evidence than Hume's discussion would suggest. On the other, it means that where we seem to have a plurality of reports, it is essential to check carefully whether they really are independent of one another; the difficulty of meeting this requirement would be an important supplement to the points made in Part II of Hume's essay. Not only in remote and barbarous times, but also in recent ones, we are usually justified in suspecting that what look like distinct reports of a remarkable occurrence arise from different strands of a single tradition between which there has already been communication.

We can now put together the various parts of our argument. Where there is some plausible testimony about the occurrence of what would appear to be a miracle, those who accept this as a miracle have the double burden of showing both that the event took place and that it violated the laws of nature. But it will be very hard to sustain this double burden. For whatever tends to show that it would have been a violation of natural law tends for that very reason to make it most unlikely that it actually happened. Correspondingly, those who deny the occurrence of a miracle have two alternative lines of defence. One is to say that the event may have occurred, but in accordance with the laws of nature. Perhaps there were unknown circumstances that made it possible; or perhaps what were thought to be the relevant laws of nature are not strictly laws; there may be as yet unknown kinds of natural causation through which this event might have come about. The other is to say that this event would indeed have violated natural law, but that for this very reason there is a very strong presumption against its having happened, which it is most unlikely that any testimony will be able to outweigh. Usually one of these defences will be stronger than the other. For many supposedly miraculous cures, the former will be quite a likely sort of explanation, but for such feats as the bringing back to life of those who are really dead the latter will be more likely. But the *fork*, the disjunction of these two sorts of explanation, is as a whole a very powerful reply to any claim that a miracle has been performed.

However, we should distinguish two different contexts in which an alleged miracle might be discussed. One possible context would be where the parties in debate already both accept some general theistic doctrines, and the point at issue is whether a miracle has occurred which would enhance the authority of a specific sect or teacher. In this context supernatural intervention, though *prima facie* unlikely on any particular occasion, is, generally speaking, on the cards: it is not altogether outside the range of reasonable expectation for these parties. Since they agree that there is an omnipotent deity, or at any rate one or more powerful supernatural beings, they cannot find it absurd to suppose that such a being will occasionally interfere with the course of nature, and this *may* be one of these occasions. For example, if one were already a theist and a Christian, it would not be unreasonable to weigh seriously the evidence of alleged miracles as some indication whether the Jansenists or the Jesuits enjoyed more of the favour of the Almighty. But it is a very different matter if the context is that of fundamental debate about the truth of theism itself. Here one party to the debate is initially at least agnostic, and does not yet concede that there is a supernatural power at all. From this point of view the intrinsic improbability of a genuine miracle, as defined above, is very great, and one or other of the alternative explanations in our fork will always be much more likely—that is, either that the alleged event is not miraculous, or that it did not occur, that the testimony is faulty in some way.

This entails that it is pretty well impossible that reported miracles should provide a worthwhile argument for theism addressed to those who are initially inclined to atheism or even to agnosticism. Such reports can form no significant part of what, following Aquinas, we might call a *Summa contra Gentiles*, or what, following Descartes, we could describe as being addressed to infidels. Not only are such reports unable to carry any rational conviction on their own, but also they are unable even to contribute independently to the kind of accumulation or battery of arguments referred to in the Introduction. To this extent Hume is right, despite the inaccuracies we have found in his statement of the case.

One further point may be worth making. Occurrences are sometimes claimed to be literally, and not merely metaphorically, miracles, that is, to be genuine supernatural interventions into the natural order, which are not even *prima facie* violations of natural law, but at most rather unusual and unexpected, but very welcome. Thus the combination of weather conditions which facilitated the escape of the British army from Dunkirk in 1940, making the Luftwaffe less than usually effective but making it easy for ships of all sizes to cross the Channel, is sometimes called a miracle. However, even if we accepted theism, and could plausibly assume that a benevolent deity would have favoured the British rather than the Germans in 1940, this explanation would still be far less probable than that which treats it as a mere meteorological coincidence: such weather conditions can occur in the ordinary course of events. Here, even in the context of a debate among those who already accept theistic doctrines, the interpretation of the event as a miracle is much weaker than the rival natural explanation. *A fortiori*, instances of this sort are utterly without force in the context of fundamental debate about theism itself.

There is, however, a possibility which Hume's argument seems to ignore—though, as we shall see, he did not completely ignore it. The argument has been directed against the acceptance of miracles on testimony; but what, it may be objected, if one is not reduced to reliance on testimony, but has observed a miracle for oneself? Surprisingly, perhaps, this possibility does not make very much difference. The first of the above-mentioned lines of defence is still available: maybe the unexpected event that one has oneself observed did indeed occur, but in accordance with the laws of nature. Either the relevant circumstances or the operative laws were not what one had supposed them to be. But at least a part of the other line of defence is also available. Though one is not now relying literally on another witness or other witnesses, we speak not inappropriately of the evidence of our senses, and what one takes to be an observation of one's own is open to questions of the same sort as is the report of some other person. I may have misobserved what took place, as anyone knows who has ever been fooled by a conjurer or 'magician', and, though this is somewhat less likely, I may be misremembering or deceiving myself after an interval of time. And of course the corroboration of one or more independent witnesses would bring in again the testimony of others which it was the point of this objection to do without. Nevertheless, anyone who is fortunate enough to have carefully observed and carefully recorded, for himself, an apparently miraculous occurrence is no doubt rationally justified in taking it very seriously; but even here it will be in order to entertain the possibility of an alternative natural explanation.

As I said, Hume does not completely ignore this possibility. The Christian religion, he says, cannot at this day be believed by any reasonable person without a miracle. 'Mere reason is insufficient to convince us of its veracity: And whoever is moved by *Faith* to assent to it, is conscious of a continued miracle in his own person, which subverts all the principles of his understanding ...' (p. 131) But of course this is only a joke. What the believer is conscious of in his own person, though it may be a mode of thinking that goes against 'custom and experience', and so is contrary to the ordinary rational principles of the understanding, is not, as an occurrence, a violation of natural law. Rather it is all too easy to explain immediately by the automatic communication of beliefs between persons and the familiar psychological processes of wish fulfilment, and ultimately by what Hume himself was later to call 'the natural history of religion'.

2

Descartes and the Idea of God

(a) *The Argument of the Third Meditation—Exposition*

ALTHOUGH Hume was joking when he said that religious belief is self-certifying, that the believing itself is a miracle which requires, for its explanation, the truth of what is believed, similar views have been held seriously by other philosophers. Some versions of the ontological proof (which will be the subject of Chapter 3) show one way of developing this view; here we shall consider a simpler and more direct argument, that anyone who has in his mind the idea or notion or concept of God is thereby in possession of something that could have come from no source other than God himself; for anyone who has this idea, therefore, no other proof of the reality of its object is required. Descartes presents, in his Third Meditation, an argument of this sort.[1] He also offers, in the Fifth Meditation, a quite distinct argument which is a form of the ontological proof.

God's existence is not, for Descartes, an optional extra: it plays a central part in his system of knowledge. Being dissatisfied with the state of what passed for learning in his time, he wanted to eliminate doctrines that purported to be knowledge but that had no good claim to this title, and to re-establish what was genuine knowledge on a secure foundation. To this end he pursued his method of doubt, initially calling in question and rejecting anything that could be doubted at all, but hoping eventually to reach some proposition that was proof against scepticism. This he found in his thesis *cogito ergo sum*: 'I think, therefore I exist'. He built on this foundation in several ways. First, from the fact that it was only in thinking that he established his own existence, and that he could coherently doubt the existence of his body whereas he could not coherently doubt the

[1] R. Descartes, *Meditations on the First Philosophy* (published in many editions).

existence of his mind, he inferred that that whose existence he had established was essentially a thinking thing, and that mind, whose essence is thinking, is radically different from body or matter. Secondly, he thought that what made the *cogito* principle itself indubitable was the fact that he clearly and distinctly perceived its truth, and so he inferred that clear and distinct perception would be in all cases a criterion of truth. Thirdly, he argued (not now *from* the *cogito*) that there exists a God who is an infinitely perfect being, who cannot therefore be a deceiver. From this he inferred that he could after all rely upon his sense perceptions to establish the existence of material things, provided that he took care to distinguish what he conceived clearly and distinctly as belonging to those material things as causes of some of his ideas from elements in his perceptions that were confused and obscure, or that could be explained, not as deceptions imposed on him by God, but as defects that arose unavoidably from the physiological mechanisms of perception. Thus the proof of God's existence is, for Descartes, an essential step in the secure reconstruction of human knowledge.

It has often been thought that there is a radical weakness in this order of argument. In his proofs of the existence of a god, Descartes seems to rely on several things that he claims clearly and distinctly to conceive or perceive, but elsewhere he seems to argue for the reliability of his clear and distinct conceptions and perceptions from the premiss that there is a god who, being perfect, cannot be a deceiver. But these two arguments together would constitute a circularity as gross as that which Descartes himself pointed out in the theologians' reliance on scriptural evidence for God's existence.[2]

He has, however, some defence against this charge. His initial position in the Third Meditation is that while the *cogito* argument is conclusive, it can be seen to owe its conclusiveness to the clear and distinct perception that it embodies; it is from this that Descartes derives the general rule that all that is very clearly and distinctly apprehended is true. He then tests this presumption: it is not refuted by the possibility of sensory illusion, for in sensation all that is clearly and distinctly apprehended is that I have certain ideas; and it is not refuted but rather confirmed by the reliability of (careful) mathematical judgements. It is, however, threatened by the possibility of there being a deceitful deity who might make me go wrong even about things that I think I am apprehending with complete clarity. The possible existence of a god has to be investigated, therefore, in

[2] Cf. quotation in the Introduction from Descartes's Dedication.

the first place, as a threat to what would otherwise be, in Descartes's view, a reliable method of discovery. Since clear and distinct perception has an independent authority, derived from the *cogito*, it is not circular to rely on it when inquiring whether there is a deity and, if so, of what sort. Since this inquiry ends, Descartes thinks, in the conclusion that there is indeed a deity but a non-deceitful one, this threat evaporates and clear and distinct perception is vindicated at least by being shown not to refute itself. Yet its independent authority is incomplete, since it is exposed to the threat of a deceitful deity, and that threat is removed only by an argument based on clear and distinct perception itself. Descartes's views, therefore, are not proof against all possibility of scepticism.

There are, however, other grounds on which we might criticize Descartes's line of reasoning. What really gives the *cogito* argument its conclusiveness is the self-refuting character of the supposition that I am not now thinking, which makes incoherent any doubt of my present existence as a thinking thing. But this is something quite different from any clear and distinct perceiving or conceiving that is exemplified in, for example, mathematical reasoning or, as we shall see, in the principles on which Descartes relies in his first proof of the existence of a god. We cannot, therefore, derive from the conclusiveness of the *cogito* the general authority of clear and distinct perceptions or conceptions in the sense in which Descartes requires it and appeals to it. Nor does the fact that what I can initially establish with certainty is my existence only as a thinking thing, not my material existence, prove that my mind or consciousness is a distinct thing or substance from my body: what is known only as thinking need not therefore exist only as thinking. The arguments by which Descartes advances from the *cogito* are, therefore, not secure against the radical doubt which he adopted in his approach to the *cogito*. Thus his programme of rebuilding human knowledge on absolutely unshakable foundations fails. But, having realized this, we can still consider whether any of his arguments can contribute to a project with more modest, less exacting, standards of certainty.

I shall trace the Third Meditation argument for the existence of a god, putting its theses, as Descartes puts them, in the first person. I have various ideas, including ideas of material things and their qualities, also of animals, of other men, and of angels, and also the idea of a god. This is an empirical premiss, but along with it Descartes uses one which, he claims, is 'manifest by the natural light', namely that 'there must be at least as much reality in the efficient and total cause as in its effect'. From where could an effect get its reality if not from its total cause? And how could the total cause give to its effect more reality than it possesses itself? This principle does not hold only for external real things; it applies also to ideas in a peculiar way. Using scholastic terminology, Descartes distinguishes the 'formal reality' of an extra-mental thing from the 'objective reality' of an idea—that is, its reality as a mental object, as something 'before the mind'. (It is unfortunate and confusing that 'objective' existence in this sense is what later philosophers would rather call 'subjective', using 'objective' to mean 'mind-independent', which is close to what Descartes means by 'formal'.) From what does an idea derive its objective (in this sense) reality? The objective reality of one idea may come from that of others, in that new ideas may be formed by combining old ones, but such a regress within ideas must come to an end: there must be ideas which do not derive their objective reality from other ideas. Such an idea, Descartes concludes, must derive its objective reality from the formal reality of some extra-mental thing, and this thing must have at least as much formal reality as the idea to which it gives rise has objective reality. This means, when we translate out of the scholastic terminology, that there must really be such a thing as the idea is an idea of, which gives rise to this mental representation of itself. Applying this principle to the full range of the ideas that I have—of myself, of other men, of animals, of inanimate objects, of angels, and of God—I have no difficulty in suggesting possible sources for all of these except the last. Ideas that represent other men, or animals, or angels may be formed by combining ideas taken from those of myself, of material, inanimate, things, and of God. Ideas of material, inanimate, things combine ideas of substance—that is, of an independent, self-existent, reality—of number and duration, and of such primary qualities as size and shape, with ideas of such secondary qualities as colours, sounds, heat, and cold. The ideas of secondary qualities, Descartes thinks, contain so much obscurity and confusion and so little reality that they may arise from no source other than myself. Ideas of substance, number, and duration may be borrowed from my idea of myself—I am a (thinking) substance, I persist through time, and I can count some of my ideas—and transferred to supposed non-thinking things. Qualities like shape and size are not, indeed, in me 'formally'—as a thing whose essence is thinking, a mind, I do not have shape, size, and so on—but they might be in me 'eminently'. (This seems to allow an exception to the above-stated principle that the objective reality of an idea must be derived (ultimately) from the formal reality of that of which it is an idea; to say that shape is in me not formally but eminently is just to say that I have some higher kind of reality which is able to generate, from its own resources, the idea of shape. However, we should remember that Descartes is not *asserting* that this is the origin of our ideas of primary qualities, and indeed he does not think it is: he argues later that there really are material substances which have the primary qualities formally. He is merely *allowing* that our ideas of primary qualities might originate from our own minds, in order to contrast with them our idea of God which, he thinks, contains objectively a degree of reality which we do not possess either formally or eminently.)

'By the name God', Descartes continues, 'I understand a substance infinite, independent, all-knowing, all-powerful, and by which I my-self, and every other thing that exists, if any such there be, were created. But these properties are so great and excellent, that the more attentively I consider them the less I feel persuaded that the idea I have of them owes its origin to myself alone.' Hence there must be such a God as I conceive, for the idea I have of him, being that of an infinite substance, could not have come from anything else, and could not originate from my own mind; for I do not have, either formally or eminently, the infinity that belongs to my idea of God.

This argument is open to several possible objections, to which Descartes replies. Perhaps my idea of an infinite being is merely negative, derived by negating the idea of the finiteness or the imper-fections which I find in myself. But Descartes says that I could not recognize these as imperfections except by comparison with a pre-existing idea of perfection. Also, infinity is not merely a negative conception: I have an idea of more reality in the infinite being than in any finite one. Or it may be said that the idea of God might have arisen in me from no source other than myself, as (Descartes thinks) the ideas of secondary qualities like heat and cold do. But this is ruled out on the ground that the idea of God is not, like those of such secondary qualities, obscure and confused, but very clear and distinct, with more objective reality than any other. In saying this Descartes does not pretend to have an adequate idea of God as an infinitely perfect being; a finite mind cannot comprehend the infinite; but even in thinking of God as having in the highest degree (formally or eminently) whatever perfections I know about, as well as others of which I am ignorant, I have a clearer and more distinct idea of God than of anything else. Or it may be suggested that my own mind is potentially infinite, since I am conscious of gradual increases in my knowledge, and may in that way be the source of the idea of an infinite being. But these gradual advances come nowhere near the actual infinity that belongs to God in my conception; what was merely potentially infinite could not produce from itself even the idea of what is actually infinite, but rather the objective reality of that idea must come from something that has a similar degree of reality either formally or eminently.

We may find much of this obscure and unconvincing: not only the scholastic terminology of features existing 'objectively', 'formally', or 'eminently', but also the notion of degrees or quantities of reality, and of one thing's degree or quantity of reality being derived from that of something else. Again, Descartes's principle as he states it does not have the intuitive plausibility which is the very least that is implied by his appeal to the 'natural light'. But the argument may be made both clearer and more persuasive if we express its main ideas in more familiar terms.

The general principle on which Descartes is relying here is that things do not spring into existence from nowhere: *ex nihilo nihil fit*. What exists must have some cause, and it must be an adequate cause. Though we ordinarily admit that great effects can be brought about by very small causes, these can be only partial causes, not the whole cause of the great effects. Large trees can grow from small seeds, but only by taking in a lot of nourishment as they grow. Trivial accidents may precipitate revolutions, but only where there are great repressed forces waiting to be triggered or released. And so on. We commonly assume that there are conservation principles—the conservation of mass, or of energy, or of the sum of the two, or of momentum— which operate as constraints on possible processes of causation or production or growth. Descartes's dictum that there must be at least as much reality in the total cause as in the effect can be understood as an attempt to capture the general form of which such specific conservation principles are instantiations.

Of course, this is not known or knowable *a priori*. We have no rational guarantee, apart from experience, and apart from scientific theories developed from and confirmed by such experience, that it will hold. Yet there is an expectation systematically built into our thinking, no doubt as a result of its general success, which we constantly use in a relatively *a priori* way. We automatically use it to guide both our interpretation of what we observe and our anticipations of what will or will not happen. It cannot do the work that

Descartes intends it to do in an absolutely secure rebuilding of human knowledge, since it is itself supported only by a wide range of interpreted observation, and its precise scope and implications are uncertain. But if we are now looking only for an argument that can build upon what we ordinarily and reasonably take to be knowledge, or well-founded belief, there is no reason why we should not place some reliance on this general principle.

Further, as Descartes sees, this general principle applies in two distinct ways to an idea or a mental state. We can ask about this mental item as an *occurrence* what produced it or how it came about, and we can ask from whence its *content* is derived. A satisfactory explanation will have to cover both these aspects. It is in explaining the content of an idea that Descartes uses the notion of the 'objective' reality of the idea being derived from the 'formal' reality of something of which it is the idea. This merely generalizes an assumption that is implicit in all our ordinary perceptions: we commonly take it for granted, automatically, that there are, in the external world, things that are at least approximately as our perceivings represent them, and that these things are causally responsible for our perceivings being as they are. Of course we also allow, as Descartes does, that an idea can be derived from other ideas: we can in thought rearrange the materials of perception. But still this regress must terminate somewhere, with 'objective' items for which we are entitled to seek a corresponding 'formal' source. Yet we would also allow, as Descartes does, that it is not certain, or even reasonable to assume, that all features in our mental contents are thus derived from corresponding external realities: our ideas of secondary qualities, for example of colours as we see them, may well arise somehow within us, stimulated perhaps by quite different external states of affairs, but without there being external real qualities which they even approximately reproduce. The source of these content elements must lie in some power that our minds themselves have; that is, these qualities are in us 'eminently', and nowhere 'formally'. Descartes's intended order of argument prevents him from explicitly basing the assumptions that he uses in his proof of God's existence on our understanding of our perception of material things; but we are subject to no such constraint in our search for a reasonable reconstruction of his proof.

I suggest, then, that we can understand as follows the essential line of thought that underlies Descartes's formulation. I have this remarkable concept of God, of an infinitely powerful and infinitely perfect being, creator and sustainer of the whole universe. The content of this concept cannot have been built up out of other mental contents, nor can it have been derived in any ordinary way from the perception of material things, or from my awareness of myself and of the operations of my mind. It is also quite different from the ideas of the various secondary qualities for which it is plausible to suppose that my own mind, in conjunction with my senses, is somehow responsible. From what source, then, can the content of this concept be derived? This must be an extra-mental entity which actually possesses the features of which this content includes representations, that is to say, an actually existing infinitely perfect being. In answer to the question *how* this content is derived from that object, Descartes does not suggest that it is by any process resembling sense perception. Rather, the idea of God must be innate in me, implanted in mind by God, so that I apprehend this likeness of him by the same faculty by which I apprehend myself, that is, by rational reflection. I have the idea of God as something with which I necessarily contrast myself. I am implicitly aware of God as a perfect being in being aware of myself as an imperfect one.

Descartes explains elsewhere the sense in which he holds that we have innate ideas: they are constituted by our inborn faculty or power of thinking, though they need some observation as a proximate cause or stimulus to make them explicit.[3] Thus he is not committed to the absurd claim that we are born already thinking explicitly about an infinitely perfect being, or even that such a thought will develop in us by maturation alone. Rather he means that we have divinely implanted in us a power of thinking which enables us to see what are in fact imperfections as imperfections, and he believes that this power can be understood only as having been generated by a real entity which combines all perfections in itself.

(b) *The Argument of the Third Meditation—Discussion*

This argument, then, is not absurd, and its assumptions connect with very familiar and widely used principles of interpretation and explanation. Nevertheless, it is open to criticism. The most serious objection is one of which Descartes himself is aware, and to which, as we saw, he attempts to reply. The idea of perfection or infinity that I have is not an adequate one. I cannot comprehend the infinite.

---

[3] *Notes on a Certain Programme*, Reply to Regius' Article 12, printed in *Descartes: Philosophical Writings*, edited by G. E. M. Anscombe and P. T. Geach (Nelson, London, 1969), pp. 302-3.

I do not have in my mind a genuine picture of perfection. My grasp of this notion resides only in my ability to recognize other things, including myself, as finite and imperfect. But we can find a natural source for this merely relative idea of perfection. As Descartes's own discussion indicates, I am aware of my own knowledge, for example, as progressively increasing, and of my having to correct and revise what I previously thought I knew. Given such a series of past corrections and amplifications, I can easily project it into the future, so as to see my present state of knowledge, and indeed any likely future state, as still defective, as partly mistaken and certainly incomplete. In this way I have a *positive* grasp of my own imperfection, out of which I can construct the merely negative notion of a state of perfect knowledge, that is, one free from *all* such defects, not open to or requiring any further correction or amplification. And this negative notion is really the only representation of omniscience that I possess. Similar accounts can be given of the ideas that I have of the various other divine perfections. Descartes is simply wrong, then, in asserting that 'in some way I possess the perception [or 'notion'] of the infinite before that of the finite'. It is not even necessary to postulate a *special* divinely implanted power of recognizing the imperfect as such; this recognition results, as we have just seen, from the exercise of quite ordinary powers of thinking.

Similarly Descartes asks 'how could I know that I doubt, desire, or that something is wanting to me, and that I am not wholly perfect, if I possessed no idea of being more perfect than myself...?' But it is easy to answer this question. The concept of desire admittedly develops along with that of satisfaction or fulfilment, but of ordinary satisfactions and fulfilments, not of some infinite or perfect counterpart of these. Similarly the concept of doubt develops along with that of knowledge, but again of ordinary incomplete knowledge, not of omniscience. The contrasts required for the awareness of such imperfections need not be supplied by any prior concept of perfection.

This objection corresponds to one which is fatal to one of Plato's arguments. Plato suggests that we have ideas of certain mathematical entities—a perfectly straight line, a perfect circle, exact equality, and so on—which could not have been derived from sensory perception, since no lines perceived by sense are perfectly straight, etc., and must therefore be derived from the mind's direct non-sensory acquaintance with the corresponding ideal entities or 'Forms', perhaps in an existence before the mind entered the body and its intellectual apprehensions were corrupted by becoming mixed up with sensation.[4] The objection to this is that we can easily acquire, through sense perception, the idea of a line's being curved or bent, and of sharper or flatter bends or curves. Hence we can think of one line's being less bent or less curved than another, and so we can form some notion of the limiting case of a line in which all bends and curves have been reduced to a point where there is no room for further reduction. Or, given that we can understand simple negation, we can construct the negative description of a line which is not bent and not curved at all anywhere. To understand such descriptions is to have a negative or limiting notion of a perfectly straight line. In this case, indeed, there is a further factor to which there is no counterpart in Descartes's problem about the idea of infinity or perfection. I can have a sensory perception of a line which is not, indeed, itself perfectly straight, and yet I can see it as being perfectly straight, in that I fail to detect any bends or curves in it. In this way the very defects of sensory perception can add a positive (though illusory) component to my idea of straightness; but in any case the idea of a perfectly straight line can be explained, with respect to its content, wholly in terms of materials drawn from sensory perception, along with the grasp of negation. There is no need to postulate, as Plato does, a direct acquaintance with the Forms to explain either this or any of the other ideas of mathematical perfections.

The main argument of the Third Meditation fails, therefore, and we can show that it fails independently of any doubts that we might have about the scholastic framework within which Descartes develops it, or about the general principles to which he appeals. We can agree that there is a genuine question to be answered about the source of the content of the idea of God as an infinitely perfect being, but undertake to answer it by reference only to natural materials and ordinary ways of thinking. We can also agree that there is another genuine question to be answered about the causes of the idea of God, and of the belief in God, as an occurrence, that is, the question of what brings about this mental state, as distinct from the question of the source of its content. But this was not Descartes's question; we shall be taking it up in Chapter 10.

Towards the end of the Third Meditation Descartes adds a further argument, asking 'whether I, who possess this idea of God, could exist supposing there were no God'. This discussion combines with the question we have been considering, of the source of my idea of

[4] Plato, *Phaedo*, 65–6, 74–5; *Meno*, 82–6.

God, the question of my own origin as a thinking being. Descartes's treatment of it is affected by his view, the argument for which we have already criticized, that he, as a thinking being, is a mental substance, existing independently of his body. It also invokes considerations about the origin of consciousness and about the need to terminate a regress of causes which we shall be discussing in Chapters 7 and 5 respectively.

3

Ontological Arguments

ONTOLOGICAL proofs of the existence of a god resemble the argument discussed in Chapter 2 in that they purport to show that once we even entertain the relevant notion of a god we cannot deny his real existence. But they maintain that it is mere logical coherence that requires this, so that we need no causal or quasi-causal inference to reach this conclusion. They make, therefore, very strong claims to rational cogency, which it should be possible to settle definitely one way or the other.

These proofs have gone in and out of favour. The earliest, and in some ways the subtlest and most interesting, version was put forward by St. Anselm in the eleventh century; it was vigorously debated both then and in the thirteenth century, but it was rejected by St. Thomas Aquinas, and then received little attention until it was rediscovered by Descartes, who gave a very clear and simple version in his Fifth Meditation. Kant criticized the Cartesian form of the proof very forcefully, and most philosophers then thought little of it until it was revived in new forms by Charles Hartshorne, Norman Malcolm, and Alvin Plantinga; it is now once again being taken very seriously. I shall discuss three variants, those of Descartes, Anselm, and Plantinga, and also Kant's criticism.[1]

(a) Descartes's Proof and Kant's Criticism

Having in my mind the idea of a supremely perfect being, I know, Descartes says, with at least as much clearness and distinctness as I

[1] Descartes, *Meditations*; Anselm, *Proslogion*—e.g. in *St Anselm: Basic Writings*, translated by S. N. Deane (Open Court, La Salle, Illinois, 1962), which includes also Gaunilo's *Pro Insipiente* and Anselm's Reply; A. Plantinga, *The Nature of Necessity* (Oxford University Press, 1974), especially Chapter 10; I. Kant *Critique of Pure Reason*, translated by N. Kemp Smith (Macmillan, London, 1933), Transcendental Dialectic, Book II, Chapter III, Section 4.

grasp any mathematical proof, that such a being must actually, and eternally, exist. For existence is a perfection, so that a being that ever failed to exist would be less than perfect. Although with all other things we can distinguish essence from existence, that is, can distinguish the question of what nature an actual or possible thing is from the question whether such a thing actually exists, 'existence can no more be separated from the essence of God than the idea of a mountain from that of a valley'. It is therefore impossible to conceive a god, that is, a supremely perfect being, as lacking existence, just as it is impossible to conceive a mountain without a valley.

Even a would-be theist will feel that this is just too good to be true. It cannot be as easy as this to prove the reality of a god. However, such an instinctive distrust is not criticism. A reasoned objection is stated by Descartes himself: even if it is impossible for me to conceive a god except as existing, this is a restriction only on my thought, and 'my thought imposes no necessity upon things'. But he replies to this objection. He agrees that from the fact that I cannot conceive a mountain without a valley, it does not follow that there is a mountain or a valley anywhere; all that follows is that *if* there is a mountain there is also a valley. But the inseparability of existence from a supremely perfect being is not conditional in this way. In effect, Descartes is arguing that in neither case is my thought imposing any necessity upon things. My inability to conceive a mountain without a valley reveals the fact that there is a real and (in the modern sense) objective necessity connecting being a mountain with having a valley alongside. Analogously, my inability to conceive a god except as existing reveals the fact that there is a real, objective, necessity connecting existence with the essence of a god, and thereby ensuring that there really is one.

We need not quarrel with Descartes's illustration, pointing out that a mountain might rise straight from a plain or from the sea, and so without a valley; let us look rather at the logic of his view. It seems that his argument can be spelled out as follows. The term 'God' by definition includes existing as part of its meaning, so that 'God does not exist' would mean 'The existing such and such does not exist'; since the latter is plainly self-contradictory, so is the former; we must, then, reject them both, and therefore deny 'God does not exist'; that is, we must affirm 'God exists'. But if this were all there was to it, the argument would have to be fallacious; for otherwise it would be all too easy to prove the existence of anything one cares to imagine. We already have, for instance, the term 'Martian', defined as 'an intelligent creature native to the planet Mars', but we have good reasons for doubting whether there are any such creatures. However, to dispel such doubts, let us define the term 'Remartian' (short for 'real Martian') so that it includes existence as part of its meaning, the other part being the meaning we already have for 'Martian'. Then 'The Remartian does not exist' will be self-contradictory; so we must reject it and affirm 'The Remartian exists', and so conclude that there is at least one intelligent creature native to Mars.

In this form, then, the argument must be unsound, though we have not yet found exactly where its weakness lies. However, Descartes would try to distinguish his argument from this patently fallacious one. The term 'Remartian' is artificial, its meaning components are arbitrarily stuck together: there is no necessary connection between the existing and the description implicit in 'Martian'. But with God there is such a connection. All the infinite perfections form a unity: no one of them, and no subset of them, could be fully realized without the rest or even adequately conceived in isolation from the others; hence we cannot coherently think of the rest of God's infinite perfections apart from existence.

Resistance to this objection has thus forced Descartes to take on a heavier load of assumptions. It is not enough for him now light-heartedly to report that his idea of God includes the feature of existence. No doubt it does, but that is not to the point: that would lead only to the fallacious argument of which the Remartian proof is an analogue. Rather he has to assert that in having this concept he is aware of an objective necessity which binds all the divine perfections, including existence, into an indissoluble unity, and we may well wonder how he could be aware of this, especially since he admits that he has only 'some slight conception' of those perfections themselves.

Kant argues that this ontological proof is open to even more radical objections. He makes what seem to be a number of separate criticisms. He says first that 'If, in an identical proposition, I reject the predicate while retaining the subject, contradiction exists ... But if we reject subject and predicate alike, there is no contradiction; for nothing is then left that can be contradicted'. It would be self-contradictory to 'posit a triangle, and yet reject its three angles'; but 'there is no contradiction in rejecting the triangle together with its three angles'. The same applies to the concept of an absolutely necessary being. 'God is omnipotent' is a necessary judgement: we cannot 'posit' God and reject the omnipotence. But if we say 'There is no god', the omnipotence and any other predicates are rejected along with the subject, so that there can be no contradiction here.

This is a picturesque but slightly obscure way of putting the issue. Kant is suggesting that although 'God is non-existent' may be self-contradictory, 'There is no god' is not and cannot be so. And we can see why. 'God is non-existent' would be like our 'The Remartian does not exist'; but there must be something wrong in taking its self-contradictoriness to show that there is a Remartian. It must therefore be distinct from 'There is no Remartian'. But, granting this, we may still ask how Kant can be so sure that no negative existential statement, no judgement of the form 'There is no X', can be self-contradictory, and that no affirmative existential statement, of the form 'There is an X', can be analytic. Admittedly the thesis that there is an 'absolutely necessary subject' is the very thing that the ontological argument was meant to prove, so that it cannot without circularity merely assume this. But to point this out is only to put the onus of making some more positive move on anyone who proposes to use an ontological proof. But this is not to show that an ontological proof is impossible, which Kant undertakes to do by entitling this Section 'The Impossibility of an Ontological Proof of the Existence of God'.

Kant's second claim is that 'There is already a contradiction in introducing the concept of existence—no matter under what title it may be disguised—into the concept of a thing which we profess to be thinking solely in reference to its possibility'. The alleged contradiction is between professing that one is still inquiring open-mindedly whether there is a god or not and putting the concept of existence, disguised within the phrase 'infinitely perfect', into the description of what would count as God. But this criticism is unfair. Someone who, like Descartes, uses this proof is indeed asserting that the description of what will count as a god guarantees the existence of one; but he is not pretending to be open-minded about the issue. He is saying quite firmly that the very concept of a god guarantees that a god exists. But to be thus non-open-minded is not to beg the question: he is giving his opponent an *argument* to show why he cannot be open-minded, the ontological proof itself. Perhaps Kant would say that since the use of this concept implicitly presupposes that a god exists, one should not introduce this concept without first establishing independently that there is a god. But, as we have seen, Descartes would reply that this concept as a unified whole is forced upon him: when the discussion starts he already has this concept of a supremely perfect being, it is not artificially constructed like our term 'Remartian'.

Kant's third criticism is much more radical, and rests upon his own clear distinction between analytic and synthetic judgements: 'But if ... we admit, as every reasonable person must, that all existential propositions are synthetic, how can we profess to maintain that the predicate of existence cannot be rejected without contradiction? This is a feature which is found only in analytic propositions, and is indeed precisely what constitutes their analytic character'. But now Kant is begging the question, for anyone who uses the ontological proof is claiming precisely that there is at least one analytically true existential proposition, that there is a god. Besides, there are true existential arithmetical propositions—for example, that there is a prime number between 90 and 100—and many philosophers who would have at least the appearance of being reasonable persons have thought that all such truths of simple arithmetic are analytic. Such examples would not worry Kant himself, since he has argued that such arithmetical truths are synthetic, though *a priori*; but they are sufficient to show that it is not simply obvious and indisputable that there cannot be analytic existential truths.

However, what I have called Kant's second and third points are in fact put forward as the two horns of a dilemma. If 'God exists' is synthetic, then the supposed purely logical proof of it is impossible; but if it is analytic, then the conclusion has been assumed in the mere use of the term 'God', or of the concept which it expresses. It is this second horn of the dilemma that Descartes must accept; but he could accept it and still maintain that his use of this term and of this concept is legitimate.

Kant's fourth, and most influential, contribution to the debate attacks this part of Descartes's position. ' "Being" is obviously not a real predicate; that is, it is not the concept of something which could be added to the concept of a thing. It is merely the positing of a thing, or of certain determinations, as existing in themselves. Logically, it is merely the copula of a judgement ... In "God is omnipotent" the small word "is" adds no new predicate, but serves only to posit the predicate *in its relation* to the subject. If, now, we take the subject (God) with all its predicates (among which is omnipotence), and say "God is", or "There is a God", we attach no new predicate to the concept of God, but only posit the subject in itself with all its predicates, and indeed posit it as being an *object* that stands in relation to my *concept*.'

Kant has been led by the puzzling features of the ontological proof to look more deeply into the meaning and logic of assertions of existence. But his formulation, as it stands, is not satisfactory. He is interestingly suggesting a connection between the 'is' of predication and the 'is' of existence; but it is far from clear why a word which in one use served to 'posit' a predicate in relation to a subject would, when we deleted the predicate, serve instead to 'posit' the subject. However, this is merely a linguistic matter. The important thought that underlies this suggestion is that although 'exists' in 'This tree exists' or 'God exists' or 'Disembodied spirits exist' is grammatically a predicate, like 'is green' or 'is omnipotent' in 'This tree is green' or 'God is omnipotent', it plays a different role from these other predicates. Whereas 'is green' describes the tree, and 'is omnipotent' either describes a supposed person to whom the name 'God' purports to refer, or perhaps, like 'has one horn' in 'a unicorn has one horn', states a description which a being would have to satisfy in order to count as God, 'exists' offers no description but merely as it were puts the item mentioned into the picture.

But do we need to go further? If, as Kant says, 'exists' is not really a predicate, what is it? Since Frege, a clear answer is available and has been widely accepted: it is really the existential quantifier. What is said by 'Disembodied spirits exist' is more lucidly expressed as 'There are disembodied spirits' and symbolized as Ex (Sx & Dx). To yield a well-formed sentence, this quantifier 'Ex'—or 'There are ...' or 'There is a ...'—must be attached to a predicate expression, a general description; what the sentence as a whole then says is that the collection of features indicated by the predicate expression is realized or instantiated.[2]

This analysis would indeed be fatal to Descartes's ontological proof. If existence is simply what the existential quantifier captures, it is not something that belongs, strictly speaking, to an individual at all. It cannot then be a kind of perfection that an individual may possess, or part of an essence, part of what constitutes the kind of thing that something may be. This analysis would exclude the reply which Descartes gives to the objection that his thought can impose no necessity upon things, and which we have supposed that he would repeat in response to the attempted *reductio ad absurdum* of his proof which uses the term 'Remartian'. That reply was that his thought

[2] See, e.g., W. C. Kneale, 'Is Existence a Predicate?', in *Aristotelian Society Supplementary Volume* 15 (1936), reprinted in H. Feigl and W. Sellars, *Readings in Philosophical Analysis* (Appleton–Century–Crofts, New York, 1949).

reveals an objective necessity which unifies all the perfections, including existence, in the indivisible essence of God, that his concept is not, therefore, an artificial conjunction of features like our proposed concept of a Remartian. The existential quantifier analysis entails that existence is not in the right category to be unified necessarily with perfections, or even to be artificially conjoined with them, since it is not a feature that can belong to an individual thing or subject at all. (This analysis does not, however, in itself entail that all existential propositions are, as Kant says, synthetic. It guarantees that an existential proposition cannot be made analytic in the way Descartes suggests, by the explicit or implicit inclusion of existence in an essence or a subject concept, but it leaves open the possibility that there should be existential propositions which are analytic for some other reason, as those in arithmetic have been thought to be.)

However, this quantifier analysis is controversial. It implies that there are no well formed propositions expressed directly by such sentences as 'This tree exists' or 'God exists' or 'I exist', as opposed to 'A tree exists', 'A god exists', or 'A thinking being exists', each of which translates easily into the quantifier-plus-predicate-expression form. Yet each of the first three sentences not only is thoroughly grammatical but also seems directly to express something: in thought as well as in the surface forms of language 'exists' seems to be handled as a predicate of individuals. Existing, it appears, is something that individuals do, and thereby ensure the realization of whatever descriptions apply to them, or the instantiation of whatever general features they possess.[3] Thus although Kant's dictum that ' "Being" is ... not a real predicate', expanded and elucidated into the thesis that existence does not properly belong to individuals at all, but dissolves into the existential quantification of predicate expressions, would dispose once and for all of Descartes's ontological argument, further careful discussion is still needed before we can decide whether it is itself to be accepted. For our present purpose we may be able to leave this aside and make do with something less thoroughgoing.

Descartes, as we noted, admits that in all things other than God essence and existence are distinct, but maintains that God is the one exception to this rule. The quantifier analysis of existence would show, on the contrary, that there can be no exceptions to it. But, if we are not to rely on that analysis, we must provisionally allow this as a possibility. Although to say that something exists is not to

---

[3] Cf. my 'The Riddle of Existence', in *Aristotelian Society Supplementary Volume* 50 (1976).

describe it, so that existence does not help to determine of what sort a thing is, it is conceivable that there might be a sort of thing that requires existence. No doubt there is a heavy onus on anyone who uses an ontological proof of showing explicitly how this could be so, and Descartes, at least, has not done this. He has merely asserted, without explanation, that the other perfections require existence. Still, if we are pursuing Kant's project of showing that an ontological proof is impossible, we cannot rely on this *ad hominem* criticism. Let us suppose, then, that there is some general term 'X' such that Xness explicitly or implicitly requires existence, and, to avoid the 'Remartian' type of *reductio ad absurdum*, let us allow Descartes's claim that there is some objectively necessary unity that holds together existence with the other components of Xness. Now consider the sentence 'The X does not exist'. Read in the most natural way, this is doubly self-contradictory. For the phrase 'The X' at least presupposes that there is one and only one X, and the predicate 'does not exist' denies this; and again, on our present presupposition, calling something an X implicitly asserts that it exists. However, the rejection of this statement on these grounds does not compel us to reject the statement 'It is not the case that there is an X', or the neater formulation 'There are no Xs'. What either of these two sentences expresses is, in itself, perfectly coherent, though it cannot be coherently expressed by saying 'The X does not exist'. In saying this we are indeed relying on the fact that we have the existential quantifier or its ordinary language equivalents, 'There is a ...' and 'There are ...'; but we can rely on this without taking the controversial step of denying that 'exists' can *also* be a genuine predicate of individuals. We can allow that it is such a predicate. Whatever description the term 'X' represents, it is an open question whether or not there is an X; but if there is, say, just one X, then this individual, the X, exists: *it* is there. Again, we can consider the sentence 'An X necessarily exists'. This has at least three possible readings. As a statement about what is involved in the concept of an X—as analogous to 'A dragon necessarily breathes fire'—it is, by hypothesis, true. If it means that a certain X has the feature of necessarily-existing, it is doubtful whether it will be true even if there is an X, but it will certainly be false if there are no Xs. But the crucial reading is that which makes it say 'It is necessarily true that there is an X'. And this is simply false: no such necessity results even from our assumption that Xness includes existence.

What this amounts to is that just as the self-contradictoriness of

'The Remartian does not exist' does not entail the falsity of 'There are no Remartians' or the truth of 'There is a Remartian', so the self-contradictoriness of 'The X does not exist' does not entail the falsity of 'There are no Xs' or the truth of 'There is an X'. This non-entailment holds even if, as we have provisionally allowed, existence is necessarily united with the other aspects of Xness, no less than where existence is artificially tacked on to Martianity to yield the concept of a Remartian.

Kant sums up his argument by saying 'Whatever, therefore, and however much, our concept of an object may contain, we must go outside it, if we are to ascribe existence to the object'. This is exactly right. It is a clear restatement of his first, initially obscure, thesis that there can be no contradiction if we reject subject and predicate alike. Our argument has vindicated his thesis, showing that, even if, contrary to what Kant would allow, our concept of an object does contain existence, and involves it inextricably, as Descartes demands, we must still go outside that concept in order to ascribe existence to the object. Even if Xness includes existence in just the way that Descartes postulates, it is still a further question whether there is an X or not, since the judgement that there are no Xs would, even on this supposition, involve no contradiction. It is this that establishes the impossibility of an ontological proof. In showing this, we have relied on the availability of existentially quantified statements; but this is non-controversial. We have not relied on the still controversial thesis that 'exists' is never, when properly understood, a predicate of individuals, that existence can always be made to disappear completely into the existential quantifier.

(b) *Anselm's Ontological Proof and Gaunilo's Reply*

Contrary to what is sometimes said, Anselm's argument was put forward explicitly as a *proof* of the existence of a god. Anselm's own belief did not, of course, depend on the proof, but preceded it; equally his first critic, the monk Gaunilo, presumably believed in God though he rejected the proof. None the less, the argument is not at home only in the thoughts of those who believe on other grounds, but is designed to convince someone who is initially uncertain or who does not believe that there is a god, by showing that such disbelief cannot be coherently maintained. Anselm concludes his first statement of the argument by saying: 'I thank thee, gracious Lord, I thank thee; because what I formerly believed by thy bounty, I now so understand by thy illumination, that if I were unwilling to believe that thou dost exist, I should not be able not to understand this to be true'.[4]

The argument has the form of a *reductio ad absurdum*. Anselm's supposed atheistic opponent is identified with 'the fool' who, according to Psalm 14, 'hath said in his heart "There is no God" '. Anselm first lays it down that God is, by definition, a being than which nothing greater can be conceived. It would make no difference if we took this, more accurately, as a definition of 'a god' rather than of 'God'. That is, what he is initially setting out to prove is just that there *is* a being than which nothing greater can be conceived. It would be a further question whether, if there is at least one such being, there is only one; and if that question is answered in the affirmative, it will be a yet further question whether this one being than which nothing greater can be conceived must have the various features which theism traditionally ascribes to God, and so can be called 'God' and identified with the traditional object of worship. But these further questions are also minor ones. It is not a serious criticism of Anselm that he tends to take the affirmative answers to these further questions for granted. The crucial issue is whether he has devised a conclusive proof that there is a being than which nothing greater can be conceived.

Anselm first insists that the fool can understand the phrase 'a being than which nothing greater can be conceived'. If so, such a being exists at least in the fool's mind or understanding, as a mental object. The fool, Anselm thinks, will admit this, but will say that such a being exists only in his mind (and the minds of others), as a painting that an artist has conceived but not yet executed exists only in his mind. But then, Anselm argues, such a being can be conceived to exist not only in someone's mind, but also in reality; and such a being, existing in reality, would be greater than one existing only in someone's mind. Therefore the fool is contradicting himself. On the one hand he is claiming to conceive a being than which nothing greater can be conceived, and yet, since he says that this exists only in his mind, he must admit that something greater than it can be conceived, namely a corresponding being existing in reality. Hence the fool cannot coherently maintain that such a being exists only in his mind and not in reality; but since he cannot deny that it exists at least in his mind (since he understands the phrase) he must admit that a being than which nothing greater can be conceived exists in reality and not only in his mind. Thus Anselm's identification of the

[4] *Proslogion*, Chapter 4.

atheist with the fool is not gratuitous abuse borrowed from the psalmist: someone must indeed be a fool if he is too stupid to follow this argument, so that he goes on asserting what cannot even be coherently conceived. But is this fair? Is Anselm's own argument sound?

In his own presentation of the argument, Anselm shifts from the indefinite description 'something than which nothing greater can be conceived' to the definite description 'that than which nothing greater can be conceived'. This shift has been marked (by Jonathan Barnes) as an error.[5] But I do not think it plays any important part in the argument, and I have eliminated it from my paraphrase, showing that Anselm could still construct his *reductio* even if he used the indefinite description throughout. Once the fool grants that *a* being than which nothing greater can be conceived exists in his mind, but says that it exists only there, Anselm can, of course, refer to *that* mental existent, and argue that something greater than *it* can be conceived.

There seems to be a more serious shift from 'The fool understands the phrase "a being than which nothing greater can be conceived"' to 'The fool conceives (or 'imagines') a being than which nothing greater can be conceived', and thence to 'There is in the fool's mind, as a mental object, a being than which nothing greater can be conceived'. This transition presupposes and uses a particular account of what it is to understand a linguistic expression and what it is to conceive something. But let us, provisionally, allow this transition. Anselm is now saying that the fool is committed to a contradiction, since he says that he has in his mind a being than which nothing greater can be conceived, while at the same time he must admit that a greater being than this can be conceived, namely something like this existing in reality. But is not Anselm himself also committed to this contradiction, if it is indeed a contradiction? For he too is saying that a being than which nothing greater can be conceived exists in the fool's mind, and yet that something greater than this can be conceived, and this is just as much a contradiction whether one says that that greater being actually exists or not.

If Anselm is to avoid being thus hoist with his own petard, he must either abandon the talk about this being existing in the fool's mind or else recognize it for what it evidently is, a mere manner of speaking whose literal equivalent is given by saying 'The fool conceives (or 'imagines') a being than which nothing greater can be conceived'.

[5] J. Barnes, *The Ontological Argument* (Macmillan, London, 1972), pp. 4–5.

Anselm should therefore accept this amendment and restate his argument as follows: 'The fool conceives a being than which nothing greater can be conceived, but conceives this only as a mental object, only as the content of his own conceiving; but this is incoherent; for to conceive it only as such a mental object is to conceive it as a being than which something greater can be conceived, namely such a being existing in reality'. The contradiction is now firmly placed wholly within the fool's conceiving, and Anselm himself is not committed to it.

Now if the fool were conceiving *a not-really-existing being than which nothing greater can be conceived*—where this whole italicized phrase represents the content of his conception—then, provided that the fool accepted Anselm's assumption that existence contributes to greatness, this conception would be incoherent: the fool would be conceiving something as being at once maximally great and yet lacking something that he saw as a constituent of greatness, as a requirement for maximal greatness. But the fool can avoid being caught in this trap. His conceiving of a being than which nothing greater can be conceived is just that: it is no more than is involved in his understanding of the key phrase, an understanding which he shares with Anselm and with any other reasonably intelligent person. He does not need to, and presumably does not, include non-existence within this concept. But, separately, he thinks and says that there is no such being, that this concept is not realized or instantiated, whereas Anselm, for example, thinks and says that it is realized and instantiated. The fool's judgement that this concept is not realized does not commit him to reading non-existence back into the content of that concept, which is what would be needed to involve him in incoherence.

This, I suggest, is the real reason why Anselm's argument fails. This criticism does not attempt to catch Anselm out on any fine points of logic, like the move from an indefinite to a definite description, nor does it query his assumption that existence helps to constitute greatness and is required for maximal greatness, which is, of course, similar to Descartes's assumption that existence is a perfection. Rather it comes to grips with what must be the crucial weakness of any ontological proof, the impossibility of establishing some concrete reality on the basis of a mere definition or concept, even with the help of the minor empirical fact that someone, such as the fool, actually has that concept. In Humean terms, the real existence of a being than which nothing greater can be conceived would be a distinct occurrence from the fool's having any state of mind what-ever, and the former could not therefore be logically required by the latter. In fact, despite the surface differences, there is a close under-lying analogy between Anselm's argument and Descartes's, and cor-respondingly between the vital criticism of each of these. As we saw, if there were a general term 'an X', such that Xness explicitly or implicitly included existence (whether in some inseparable way or by the artificial conjoining that yields our term 'a Remartian') we could not coherently say 'The X does not exist'. Anselm's term 'a being than which nothing greater can be conceived' is, given his assumption that existence helps to constitute greatness, just such a term as our 'an X'. Just as we cannot coherently say 'The X does not exist', so the fool cannot coherently conceive a not-really-existing being than which nothing greater can be conceived. But, equally, just as we can coherently say 'It is not the case that there is an X', so the fool, having conceived a being than which nothing greater can be con-ceived, can still coherently conceive that there is no such being.

We can, indeed, pursue this analogy further. As soon as Anselm's proof became known, it was criticized by Gaunilo, writing 'On behalf of the fool'. Some of his criticisms are obscure and perhaps confused, but one clear point that he makes is this: if Anselm's proof were valid, we could equally validly prove the existence somewhere in the ocean of the imaginary 'lost island' that surpasses in its attractions all inhabited countries; for actually existing is an essential element in such superiority. This is a damaging objection, for, of course, Anselm would not admit that we can prove the existence of the lost island in this way. But it shows only that there must be something wrong with Anselm's original argument, and does not in itself identify the error. Nor do Gaunilo's other remarks succeed in identifying it: some of them merely stress what Anselm has all along admitted, that in general something can be conceived and yet not exist in reality, and others stress that we do not really conceive—that is, comprehend, or have an adequate idea of—God. This, too, Anselm grants, but it does not undermine his proof.[6]

Faced with this objection, Anselm maintained that there is a sig-nificant difference between his proof and Gaunilo's proof of the lost island, that the 'sequence of [his] reasoning' cannot be adapted to this case. This is like the reply which Descartes made to a similar objection, and which we applied on his behalf to the Remartian suggestion; but Anselm's explanation of it is clearer and better than

[6] Gaunilo, *Pro Insipiente*, and Anselm, *Reply to Gaunilo*.

Descartes's. His view of this significant difference seems to depend
on an addendum which was included in his original argument,[7] but
which we have not yet considered.

It is, Anselm says, possible to conceive a being which cannot be
conceived not to exist—as we may put it, a being whose existence is
conceptually necessary—and such a being is greater than one which
can be conceived not to exist. It follows that a being than which
nothing greater can be conceived *cannot* be conceived not to exist;
for, if it could, it would be less great than something else that is
conceivable. Anselm reiterates this argument in his reply to Gaunilo,
immediately after referring to the lost island; so that although he does
not say this explicitly, I think we can infer that his reply to the lost
island argument is that whereas that island can be conceived not to
exist, God, or a being than which *nothing* greater can be conceived,
cannot. And this would be a good reply, pointing to a real distinction,
if Anselm were right in saying that it is possible to conceive a being
which cannot be conceived not to exist.

But is it not precisely of this thesis that our previous criticism has
deprived him? We have shown that the main part of the original
argument has *not* demonstrated that the concept of a being than
which nothing greater can be conceived is a concept of a being which
cannot be conceived not to exist. But perhaps Anselm could start
again, saying 'Of course it is possible to conceive a being which
cannot be conceived not to exist: I do so now conceive. Moreover,
you (the fool, or Gaunilo, or the modern reader) can also conceive
this, since you have plainly understood the phrase "a being which
cannot be conceived not to exist"'.

Let us then concede this. Let us grant that there is a concept of *a
being than which nothing greater can be conceived and which cannot be
conceived not to exist.* But then the discussion merely repeats itself at
a higher level. It is still a further question whether *this* concept is
realized or instantiated. If we say that it is not realized we are not
contradicting ourselves. We are not saying that a being which cannot
be conceived not to exist can be conceived not to exist; we are not
putting 'can be conceived not to exist' into the concept, where it
would clash with the other part of that concept. We are merely saying
that *there is not* a being which cannot be conceived not to exist.
Equally Gaunilo, without *asserting* this, can coherently entertain the
possibility: he can conceive there not being a being which cannot be
conceived not to exist. This has the appearance of a verbal tangle,

[7] *Proslogion*, Chapter 3.

but careful attention to the construction will show that there is no incoherence. In effect, we are still, justifiably, appealing to and illustrating Kant's final dictum that 'Whatever, and however much, our concept of an object may contain, we must go outside it, if we are to ascribe existence to the object'.

(c) *Plantinga's Ontological Proof*

What I have called the addendum to Anselm's argument introduced a modal notion: that of a being whose existence is, as I put it, conceptually necessary. Interesting modern versions put forward by Charles Hartshorne, Norman Malcolm, and Alvin Plantinga have also used modal terms, but with reference to metaphysical rather than merely conceptual possibility and necessity.[8] Plantinga's in particular makes use of elaborate recent developments in modal logic, whereby a system of possible but non-actual worlds is taken to give the appropriate semantics for statements about possibility and necessity, the truth-value of any such statement being determined by what holds in various possible worlds.

Some knowledge of Plantinga's argument, and of the general suggestion that modal logic may rescue philosophical theology from the criticisms of Hume and Kant and their empiricist or positivist successors, has begun to leak out from purely philosophical discussions and to receive wider publicity.[9] So perhaps St. Alvin will eventually take his place beside St. Anselm; at least he should have no difficulty in meeting the miracle-working requirement for canonization, after the success that he has achieved in subverting (as Hume would say) all the principles of the understanding of so many intelligent readers.

A crucial feature of Plantinga's system of modality and possible worlds is the recognition of 'world-indexed' properties. For example, if 'α' is the name used for the actual world, and if Socrates was actually snub-nosed, then not only does Socrates have, in α, the property of being snub-nosed, but also, if he exists in some other possible but non-actual worlds, Socrates has, in every world in which he exists, the world-indexed property of being snub-nosed-in-α. (pp. 62–3) This may seem to be a harmless and merely pedantic elaboration; but in fact it plays a vital part in his argument.

---

[8] C. Hartshorne, *The Logic of Perfection* (Open Court, La Salle, Illinois, 1962); N. Malcolm, 'Anselm's Ontological Arguments', in *Philosophical Review* 69 (1960); references in the text to Plantinga are to pages in the work named in n. 1 (p. 41) above.

[9] E.g. *Time* 7 Apr. 1980, p. 66.

Plantinga also introduces two special terms, 'maximal excellence' and 'maximal greatness'. '*Maximal excellence*', he lays down, 'entails *omniscience, omnipotence*, and *moral perfection*'—in effect, it includes all the perfections which Descartes took to be definitive of God's essence—while 'The property *has maximal greatness* entails the property *has maximal excellence in every possible world*'. (p. 214) What these defining rules amount to is this. Something might be maximally excellent in some one possible world W_1, but might exist in some other world W_2 and yet not be maximally excellent in W_2, and it might not exist at all in some third possible world W_3. If so, it would be, although maximally excellent, not maximally great in W_1. But if it was maximally great in W_1, it would follow that it existed in every possible world and was maximally excellent in each of them, and in fact maximally great in each of them.

Once we have these terms with their entailments, the actual argument is essentially quite simple. But Plantinga gives first a more elaborate version of it, reserving the simpler and more straightforward version until later. '*Maximal greatness*', he says, 'is possibly exemplified'. From this it follows that 'There is a world W^* and an essence E^* such that E^* is exemplified in W^* and E^* entails *has maximal greatness in W^**'. Now if W^* had been actual, E^* would have entailed, for every world W, the property *has maximal excellence in W*; that is, 'it would have entailed the property *has maximal excellence in every possible world*'. In other words, if W^* had been actual, the proposition 'For any object x, if x exemplifies E^*, then x exemplifies the property *has maximal excellence in every possible world*' would have been necessarily true. But, Plantinga argues, 'what is necessarily true does not vary from world to world', so this proposition *is* necessary. Hence 'E^* entails the property *has maximal excellence in every possible world*'. It follows that if W^* had been actual, E^* would have been exemplified by something which existed and exemplified it in every possible world. Hence, 'if W^* had been actual, it would have been impossible that E^* fail to be exemplified'. Now comes the crucial step: 'what is impossible does not vary from world to world; hence it is *in fact* impossible that E^* fail to be exemplified; so E^* is exemplified; so ... there exists a being that has maximal excellence in every world'. This means both that there actually is a being who combines the traditional theistic perfections, and that this being both exists necessarily and is necessarily perfect, since it has maximal excellence in every possible world. (pp. 214-16)

We might well be suspicious of what I have called the crucial step.

Is it obvious that what *would have been* impossible if W^* had been actual *is in fact* impossible? Clearly we could construct a system of possible worlds such that this would not hold. We could think of each possible world as carrying with it its own set of possibly possible worlds, and so on: we could have 'nested' sets of possible worlds. Then we should say that if W^* had been actual, E^* would have been exemplified in all actually possible worlds, but that if W^* is only possible and not actual, E^* is exemplified in all the possibly possible worlds attached to or 'accessible from' W^*, but perhaps not in other possible worlds or in the actual one. In other words, all that would follow from the fact that maximal greatness is *possibly* exemplified is that it is *possible* that there should be something with maximal excellence in every possible world. The existence of something having the essence E^* would be not necessary, but only possibly necessary.

However, this conceivable system of possible worlds is not Plantinga's. It allows for iterated modalities—statements of such forms as 'It is possible that it is necessary that it is possible that *p*' which retain their complexity. But in Plantinga's system all such iterations collapse so as to leave single modal statements. If we write 'L' for 'it is necessary that' and 'M' for 'it is possible that', '$MLMp$' is equivalent simply to 'Mp', and '$MMMLp$' to 'Lp', and so on. All the earlier 'L's and 'M's drop off, leaving only the final modal operator and the non-modal statement on which it operates. Now the choice between such systems is not obvious or inevitable.[10] There are perfectly respectable systems of modal logic that go with such different structures of possible worlds. It is true that S5, the modal logic in which all iterated modalities collapse into the final modal operator, seems to be the appropriate system for what we understand as *logical* possibility and necessity. But, as we shall see, there is a feature of Plantinga's system which makes it impossible to carry over into it everything that holds for logical possibilities, so that we cannot argue on these grounds that S5 is the right form of modal logic for the kind of possibilities with which he is dealing.

This crucial step, then, could be queried. But since there is a more obvious and more elementary objection to Plantinga's argument let us leave this one aside. Let us grant that, *with the structure of possible worlds which he has adopted*, if there is even one *possible* world in which maximal greatness is exemplified, there is something that has maximal excellence in every possible world, including the actual world.

[10] A. N. Prior, *Formal Logic* (Oxford University Press, 1962), Part III, Chapter 1.

As I said, Plantinga also offers a simpler version of his argument, which brings out its essential character more plainly. He defines 'unsurpassable greatness' as equivalent to 'maximal excellence in every possible world'. Then, he says, there is a possible world in which unsurpassable greatness is exemplified. The property of having unsurpassable greatness, that is, of having maximal excellence in every possible world, is one which is either instantiated in every possible world or not instantiated at all. So it *is* instantiated in every possible world, including the actual one. Once again the crucial step rests on the principle that what is necessary or impossible does not vary from world to world, and this amounts to the rejection of significant, non-collapsing, iterated modalities and the system of nested sets of worlds that would go with this, and hence to the adoption of S5. But, as I have said, having noted this as a possible point of dispute, let us provisionally concede it.

Thus, given Plantinga's chosen system of possible worlds, his argument, in either the simpler or the more complicated form, is valid. And its conclusion asserts the actual and necessary existence of a maximally excellent being, that is, a god with the traditional or Cartesian perfections. But these truths only raise, all the more acutely, two questions about the key non-definitional premiss, the statement that maximal greatness, or unsurpassable greatness, is possibly exemplified. Is it true? And has anyone who is not already independently persuaded of the truth of traditional theism any reason to accept it?

Plantinga's answer to the second of these questions is equivocal. On the one hand he says that his argument 'is not a successful piece of natural theology', since natural theology 'typically draws its premisses from the stock of propositions accepted by nearly every sane man, or perhaps nearly every rational man', whereas the key premiss of his proof is not of this sort: 'a sane and rational man who thought it through and understood it might none the less reject it'. On the other hand he suggests that this key premiss is rather like Leibniz's Law: if we carefully ponder it, considering objections and its connections with other propositions, 'we are within our rights in accepting it'. Thus although these new versions of the ontological argument 'cannot, perhaps, be said to *prove* or *establish* their conclusion ... it is rational to accept their central premiss, [so] they do show that it is rational to *accept* that conclusion'. (pp. 220–1) We must look more carefully into the reasons for this equivocation before deciding what final comment is justified upon the argument itself.

What reasons, then, might one have for either accepting or rejecting that key premiss? As far as I can see, the only reason for accepting
it, for supposing that maximal greatness is possibly exemplified, is
that there is no contradiction, either open or latent, in the notion of
maximal or unsurpassable greatness. Whatever is not internally
self-contradictory is logically possible. Does it not follow that it is
possible in such a sense that we can infer that there is a possible
world in which there is something maximally or unsurpassably great?
Why should this not follow? Why should not the set of all possible
worlds cover the full range of (complex) logical possibilities? But
unfortunately there is a good reason why it cannot do so, which is
brought out by some of Plantinga's own discussion.

He defines another term, 'no-maximality'. This is the property of
being such that there is no maximally great being. Then someone
might argue as follows: no-maximality is possibly exemplified; that
is, there is a possible world in which no-maximality is exemplified,
and therefore in which maximal greatness is not exemplified; but if
maximal greatness is not exemplified in every possible world, it is not
exemplified in any; therefore there cannot be any possible world in
which maximal greatness is exemplified, that is, maximal greatness is
not possible. Since we could argue before from the premiss that
maximal greatness is exemplified in some possible world to the conclusion that no-maximality is not exemplified in any, we can argue
equally validly from the premiss that no-maximality is exemplified in
some possible world to the conclusion that maximal greatness is not
exemplified in any. (pp. 218-19)

Thus the two premisses, 'No-maximality is possibly exemplified',
in the sense that there is a possible world in which it *is* exemplified,
and 'Maximal greatness is possibly exemplified', in a corresponding
sense, cannot both be true. Yet the reason that was suggested above
for accepting the key premiss of Plantinga's ontological argument,
that there is no logical contradiction in the notion of maximal or
unsurpassable greatness, is an equally good reason for accepting the
premiss of the counter-argument: there is equally no logical contradiction, either open or latent, in the notion of no-maximality. If we
could argue from the absence of logical contradiction to possibility,
and thence to the existence of a possible world in which that possibility is realized, in the one case, we could do so with equal cogency
in the other. Since we cannot, without contradicting ourselves, argue
thus in both cases, it follows that we cannot reasonably do so in
either. And, as I have said, there seems to be no other reason why

anyone who is not antecedently persuaded of the truth of theism should accept the premiss that maximal or unsurpassable greatness is possibly exemplified. That is why, as Plantinga admits, his argument is not a successful piece of natural theology.

But what has gone wrong here? If we choose to play with possible worlds at all, whether we adopt a realist view about them or not,[11] we ordinarily assume that for any logically possible statement or conjunction of statements there is at least one possible world that realizes it. That is, we do ordinarily expect to be able to argue from non-contradiction to possibility and thence to a possible world. What has ruled out this pattern of inference, in Plantinga's system, is the introduction of world-indexed properties. For the admission of these makes features of one world dependent in part on features of all other possible worlds. If each possible world were independent of every other, then we could allow the existence of a possible world for every maximal set of consistent sentences, and hence could say that every logical possibility is realized in at least one possible world. But if possible worlds are made dependent upon one another, the existence of even a possible world in which one non-contradiction is realized may be incompatible with the existence of a possible world in which some other non-contradiction is realized. We cannot retain *both* the principle that we can always argue from non-contradiction to a possible world *and* the principle that world-indexed properties can be introduced without restriction.

Since Plantinga has freely introduced world-indexed properties, making one possible world dependent upon another, his system of possible worlds does not and cannot correspond to the full range of logical possibilities. This is the reason why we cannot argue from the fact that S5 is the appropriate modal logic for logical possibilities and necessities to the conclusion that it is appropriate for possible worlds with world-indexed properties. This casts doubt on the collapsing of iterations of modalities into their last members in the way required for the crucial step in his ontological proof, which, as we saw, relies on the principle that whatever is possibly necessary is necessary *tout court*.

We can, therefore, press our earlier doubt about that crucial step. But the more important point that has now emerged is that we have simply no reason for accepting the key premiss of Plantinga's argument, rather than the premiss of the no-maximality counter-argu-

---

[11] For a defence of such realism, see D. Lewis, *Counterfactuals* (Basil Blackwell, Oxford, 1973), pp. 84-91.

ment. The admission of world-indexed properties, which is *also* essential for his version of the ontological proof, undermines *both* what I have called the crucial step *and* the key premiss.

But he might reply that, given his system of possible worlds, *one* of the two arguments, his ontological one and the no-maximality one, must be sound: each is valid, and the key premisses of both, while they cannot both be true, equally cannot both be false. Is it then a toss-up which we accept? This is all that Plantinga can properly mean when he says, at the very end of this chapter, that it is 'rational' to accept the central premiss of his argument, and therefore 'rational' also to accept its conclusion. (p. 221) It is rational in the sense in which it is rational to do either of two things when one must do one or other of them, but has no reason for preferring either to the other. If this is all that he does mean, he has chosen a most misleading way of expressing it. His words would certainly tempt the unwary or theistically hopeful reader to take him as saying that he has shown that it is *more* rational to accept theism than to reject it, particularly since he has entitled this section 'A Victorious Modal Version'.

However, he would not be justified in claiming even that it is a toss-up. For one thing, suspense of judgement, not accepting the premiss either of the ontological argument or of the counter-argument, is another option. For another, if we are to choose between these premisses, in default of any other reason, we must ask which is the more modest and which the more extravagant, which can be accused of multiplying entities beyond what is necessary. And surely the more extravagant is that which asserts that maximal greatness is realized in some possible world. For this one carries with it the requirement that a maximally excellent being—and, indeed, a maximally great one—should exist in every possible world, whereas the rival premiss that no-maximality is realized in some possible world, still allows maximal excellence to be realized in some possible worlds though not in others. The latter, then, is less restrictive, less extravagant, and so on very general grounds the more acceptable.

It is to Plantinga's credit that he draws attention to the no-maximality counter-argument, for if we failed to consider this his ontological argument would be insidiously attractive. The premiss that it is just *possible* that there should be something unsurpassably great looks innocent. We are usually ready enough to concede that something, however extravagant, is possible, and to confine our critical scrutiny to the question whether it is not merely possible but actual. But unsurpassable greatness, given both the world-indexing that is involved in its definition and the S5-style insistence that whatever is even possibly necessary *is* necessary, is a Trojan horse, not an innocent little possibility. It is a gift of a sort that we should be very wary of accepting. Anyone who is not already and independently persuaded that traditional theism is true has good reason to reject rather than to accept the key premiss of Plantinga's argument: it is not even just a toss-up.

This argument, then, is not only 'not a successful piece of natural theology', but is not even in any sense 'victorious': there is no rival view over which it is victorious, or which it can be plausibly said to defeat. In fact a plausible system of modal logic and possible worlds would either reject the world-indexing of properties or else adopt nested sets of possible worlds and so resist the collapsing of iterated modalities into their final members. With either of these amendments, Plantinga's argument would not get off the ground. But even if we accept the rather arbitrary modal system which makes it valid, we have good reason to reject rather than to accept its key premiss. Altogether, then, the argument is worthless as a support for theism, and is interesting mainly as a logical peculiarity. It is a much less serious challenge to the theological sceptic than Anselm's version. The view which is now being popularly disseminated, that recent advances in modal logic permit the construction of arguments which should disturb atheistic or agnostic philosophers, and give some long-awaited comfort to theistic ones, is simply false and quite without foundation.

But Plantinga's treatment throws some light on Leibniz's defence of the ontological proof. Leibniz said that Descartes's version (and he referred also to Anselm's) is not fallacious but merely incomplete. It shows, he thought, that if God, as a being of supreme grandeur and perfection, is possible, then he exists; to complete the proof one must show that such a being is possible, which he did by arguing that there can be no incompatibility between different perfections.[12] Leibniz may be right in saying that there is no logical impossibility concealed in the proposed definition; but he is wrong, for reasons we have already seen, in thinking that once this is granted the Cartesian version goes through. On the other hand, Plantinga has found a definition of a god, as a being with maximal greatness as he explains this, and an account of possibility, which together make it true that if such a being is possible then it actually and indeed necessarily exists. But at the same time his account of possibility brings it about that a demonstration that there is no logical impossibility in the proposed definition of a god is no longer sufficient to show that such a being is possible in the required sense. What is gained at one point is lost at another.

We have not examined all the versions of the ontological argument that have been put forward, and no doubt still more will be devised. But I think we have seen enough to be reasonably confident that nothing of this sort will prove in the end to be 'a successful piece of natural theology', that is, will show, using only premisses and principles which nearly every rational person must accept, that there is a god in the traditional sense.

4

Berkeley's God and Immaterial Realism

(a) *Berkeley's Theism—Exposition*

BERKELEY'S immaterialist philosophy is even less likely than any form of the ontological argument to figure among widely accepted supporting reasons for religious belief. Yet as a philosophical view it deserves to be taken seriously, and as a form of theism it has the merit of giving a very clear meaning to the traditional doctrine that God has not only created the world but also continuously sustains it, and that our finite minds depend, for most of their knowledge, directly upon the infinite mind of God. We should not lightly dismiss it merely because it goes against common sense—which it does, though Berkeley strenuously denied this—but rather examine his arguments, and reject his conclusions only if we find his arguments less than cogent.

The outlines of his theory are well known. All that exists, he holds, is minds and ideas, and ideas are entities whose *esse* is *percipi*, which exist in and by being perceived. What we ordinarily take to be material things are really only collections of ideas. Ideas are wholly passive: there are regularities in the ways in which they accompany or follow one another, but one idea does not really bring about another—or produce anything else. All genuine activity and causation belong only to minds and wills. Both human minds and the divine mind are active, but God's mind is much more powerful than ours. In reply to the objection that his theory reduces the whole realm of ordinary, material, things to an illusion, Berkeley insists that there is still a distinction between illusion and reality, to be drawn on two grounds. From the perceiver's point of view, what we call real things are a sub-class of ideas, distinguished from another sub-class which includes various sorts of illusory or imaginary items, 'chimeras', by features of three kinds: the former ('ideas of sense') are independent of the perceiver's will, whereas the latter are not; the former are more 'strong, lively, and distinct' than the latter; and they display 'steadiness, order, and coherence', that is, they appear in accordance with the regularities which we call the laws of nature. But these immediately evident differences reflect, and are evidence for, the fact that the ideas of sense are excited in our minds by the will of a more powerful spirit, namely God. Also, these ideas which constitute 'reality' need not pass in and out of existence as a human mind comes to perceive them or ceases to perceive them, but may continue in existence as being constantly perceived by the mind of God, whether any human mind perceives them or not.[1]

Within this general position, however, there is one point on which Berkeley's view is obscure, and on which he seems to say different things at different places. If an idea exists only in and by being perceived, it would appear to be simply a mental content or intentional object, and then it will be impossible for more than one mind to perceive what is literally the same idea. Each mind has its own ideas, which are constituted by that mind's being in a certain perceptual or imaginative state. Different minds might have systematically similar, perhaps exactly similar, contents, but one mind's having such a content or being in a certain condition of awareness is a numerically distinct state of affairs from any other mind's having even a content exactly like that of the first mind. But then it follows that the tree which I see, being an idea of mine only, *does* cease to exist when I stop seeing it, even if a very similar tree-idea continues to exist as perceived by someone else or by God. This is one possible interpretation. An alternative account would be that although ideas are *causally* dependent on minds for their existence, they are not *constituted* by being perceived, and are something more than mental contents or intentional objects. On this interpretation, 'real things' would be ideas produced directly by God's will; the very tree that I see would have an existence wholly independent of *my* mind, and its *esse* would certainly not be *percipi* by me: it would not be something *excited* in my mind by God, but would be brought into being and maintained in being, independently of my mind, by God, and perceived by me as a real object distinct from the perceiving. Some things that Berkeley says in his *Principles of Human Knowledge* suggest one of these readings, some the other, so we shall have to allow for both interpretations. On the whole, however, the former

[1] G. Berkeley, *Principles of Human Knowledge* (many editions), Sections 1–33. References in the text are to the numbered sections in this work.

would give him the more consistent and more interesting position. (This interpretation is clearly spelled out by Samuel Johnson in his first and second letters to Berkeley, and it seems to be accepted by Berkeley in his second reply.[2])

Whichever of the two interpretations is adopted, Berkeley's view can be described as immaterial realism. 'Immaterial', because he not only denies the existence of 'matter' as a substratum, but also denies that there are material things existing in space and time independently of minds. But 'realism' because from the point of view of any individual perceiver, there is, according to Berkeley, a world not constituted by his perceptions, consisting of other minds and of ideas other than his own, in particular of the divine ideas which constitute the 'reality' which we contrast with illusions and with what we merely imagine.

For our present purposes, this philosophy is interesting because it includes theses which resemble the doctrines of traditional theism, though they go beyond them in some respects and fall short of them in others. Berkeley's general philosophy gives us a god who is very powerful but not necessarily omnipotent, in that although 'real things' are wholly dependent on his will, human minds might have some measure of independence, and although his 'wisdom and benevolence' are testified by the admirable orderliness of the 'real world', this does not require that he should be *wholly* good. But Berkeley argues, against those who raise the problem of evil, that if we had a sufficiently comprehensive view of the whole 'real world' we should see it to be wholly good, and could therefore ascribe perfect goodness also to its author. Theism usually asserts that the physical world somehow depends upon God, and not only was created but also is constantly maintained in existence by him; but it leaves this as an obscure and unexplained relationship. Berkeley's theory, by contrast, yields a clear and intelligible account of how the 'physical world' depends upon God, since it simply consists of ideas that exist primarily in the divine mind, and perhaps of other but like ideas in our minds, excited there by his will. Berkeley wrote his *Principles* and his *Three Dialogues* in explicit opposition to 'scepticism, atheism, and irreligion', which he saw, perhaps rightly, to be the ultimate consequences of the Lockean philosophy and the scientific approach which it formulates and reflects. His main arguments

---

[2] See the Philosophical Correspondence between Berkeley and Samuel Johnson, printed, e.g., in *Berkeley: Philosophical Works* (Dent, London, and Rowman & Littlefield, Totowa, NJ, 1975), pp. 337–55.

can properly be taken as an unusual method of attempting to prove the existence of the god of traditional theism.

Berkeley's philosophy was provoked by that of Locke and developed through criticisms of Locke. Later thinkers have often treated it—and welcomed it—simply as a *reductio ad absurdum* of some of Locke's doctrines. But whether this use of it has any force or not, it is irrelevant to our present purpose. If we are to consider Berkeley's views as giving an argument for the existence of a god, we must see whether they can be defended as direct arguments, not as *reductiones ad absurdum*. If he is to be able to reach the conclusions he wants as positive doctrines, his Lockean starting-points will have to be vindicated, not discredited.

His first step is to say that not only thoughts and passions and 'ideas formed by the imagination' exist only in the mind, but also 'ideas imprinted on the sense', which he identifies with 'sensible things'. What we perceive, even in what we call sense perception, is always our own ideas, which exist in and by being perceived. Since Locke also says this about direct perception, if we wanted only an *ad hominem* argument against Locke this premiss would be secure enough. But can it be defended in itself? Can it resist what, as Berkeley admits, is the ordinary view that houses, mountains, and rivers have an existence distinct from their being perceived? Berkeley argues that this ordinary view involves an impossible sort of abstraction: 'it is impossible for me to conceive in my thoughts any sensible thing or object distinct from the sensation or perception of it'. (§5)

His argument, I suggest, runs together two different lines of thought, one sound and one fallacious. The fallacious one (on which Berkeley twice says, imprudently, that he is willing to rest his whole case) is that there is a 'repugnance' (that is, a contradiction) in the conceiving of a tree or a house existing by itself, independently of and not perceived by any mind. Since anyone who claims to do this is himself conceiving the house, it cannot be unconceived by or independent of all minds. (§23) However, while it would be self-contradictory to say 'I am conceiving a house which is unconceived', there is no contradiction if I say 'I conceive that there is a house which is not perceived or conceived by anyone': to conceive that there is a house (somewhere) is not to have a house which one is conceiving—that is, imagining. This is enough for the realist about houses, and the argument of Section 23 is powerless against it. This argument is also faulty in two other ways. First, if it were sound, it would show only that we cannot coherently suppose that there are houses (etc.) which are not, *as well as* existing, *also* perceived or conceived. It would not even begin to show that houses (etc.) exist *in and by* being perceived or conceived, which is what Berkeley wants to show. Secondly, if the argument were sound, it would prove too much. Although he states it with regard to sensible objects like houses and books, their nature as sensible objects plays no part in the argument; so, if it held at all, it would hold equally against the suggestion that I can conceive that there are minds that are not conceived by me; thus it would establish solipsism, in which I would reject as not even conceivable the existence not only of material things but also of other minds and spirits, including God, except in so far as they are conceived by me. This line of argument is, therefore, not only fallacious but also, in these two ways, misdirected.

The other line of argument is directed specifically to sensible things, meaning 'the things we see and feel', or whatever we are immediately aware of in sensory experience. Our sensory states have, as I would prefer to say, a content, and this content cannot, even in thought, be separated from the perceiving of it. The same point can be made in other terms, that we must recognize ideas as intentional objects. Yet another way to put it is to give an 'adverbial' analysis of perception: when I say that I see something red, the seen redness belongs not to any object either outside me or inside me, but to *how I perceive*: as we may put it, I perceive redly. But, however it is to be described, this aspect of perceptual experience is undeniable. It is of ideas in this sense that many of Berkeley's dicta hold: their *esse* is *percipi*, and it is impossible to abstract them, even in thought, from their being perceived or conceived. Some philosophers seem to deny that there are ideas in this sense, but it would be more charitable to take them as saying that their importance has been exaggerated or misunderstood, or that it is misleading to speak of such contents as 'direct' or 'immediate' objects of perception, and to say, by contrast, that independently existing material things are perceived only 'indirectly', and also misleading to call an account of perception that explicitly takes note of these contents a 'representative' theory, rather than as attempting to deny what is undeniable. The crucial question is this: having recognized these contents or intentional objects, what must we then say about the commonsense belief that we perceive and thereby know about houses, mountains, and in general a material world, as existing distinguishably from and independently of their being perceived?

The first and vital point is that this recognition opens up a gap which leaves room for scepticism with regard to the material world as we ordinarily conceive it. It is, as Descartes said, coherently supposable that I should be, intrinsically, with regard to my experiential state in itself, just as I am, and yet that there should be no material world. Our ordinary ways of speaking mask this truth. We describe someone's experiential state by saying 'He is seeing a river with a mountain behind it', in a sense in which this would not be true unless there really were a river and a mountain there, as well as this person in an appropriate perceptual state, and indeed unless there were a suitable causal connection between the river-mountain complex and his perceptual state. But the aspects that are all wrapped up together in this ordinary description can be distinguished. Although this person couldn't be *seeing a river* (in the ordinary sense) if there were no river, yet he could be in just the same intrinsic state as he is in now even if there were no river, though we should then have to say 'It is with him as if he were seeing a river', and so on. It is no argument against this possibility of scepticism that this last description is verbally parasitic upon the ordinary language which is meant to describe an independently existing material world. Indeed, any adequate description of the experiential state of an ordinary perceiver would have to incorporate the beliefs and interpretations that are bound up with his purely sensory condition—he sees that *as* a river etc.—but this in no way commits *us*, in describing that state, to adopting these beliefs and interpretations, or even the general categories within which they are framed.

Berkeley's purpose, however, is not to propound or defend scepticism but to eliminate it. His method is to argue that the view of an independently existing material world, about which the distinction of contents or intentional objects of perception from independent objects allows us to be sceptical, is not even coherently formulable. For this he gives a number of arguments, but they can be summarized briefly.

First, since it is agreed that ideas (or contents, or intentional objects) exist only in the mind, the question is whether there might be external entities which are like them, of which they are copies. But Berkeley asserts that an idea can be like nothing but an idea. (§8)

Secondly, he has an *argumentum ad hominem* against Locke and his followers: they concede that nothing resembling our ideas of secondary qualities, such as colours and sounds and heat and cold and so on as we perceive them, can exist independently; but they give no reason for supposing that it is otherwise with the primary qualities like shape and size and motion; also, we cannot even frame a coherent idea of bodies with primary qualities alone, without any secondary qualities. (§§9-10)

Thirdly, specific or determinate values of such primary qualities as distance and velocity are only relative; this, Berkeley thinks, shows them not to exist apart from minds. And the corresponding determinables or general features—distance in general, motion in general, and so on—would be abstractions, ruled out by his criticism (in the Introduction to the *Principles*) of abstract general ideas. (§11)

Fourthly, matter, or material substance, as a substratum which is supposed to support the primary qualities in the external world, would be an 'unknown somewhat'; even Locke admits that he can give no account of it except the relative one that it supports qualities. But this word 'support' is here an unexplained metaphor; no real account has been or can be given of either the substratum itself or its relation to primary qualities. (§§16-17)

Fifthly, even if we could make sense of the *supposition* that there is a material world, we can have no reason for *asserting* that it exists: the Lockeans themselves admit that material things are not perceived directly, and there are no necessary connections between them and our ideas, and hence no *a priori* principles by which we could infer them from our ideas. As we have seen, scepticism about such a material world would always be possible. (§18)

Sixthly, even if we did postulate a material world, this would in no way help to explain the ideas that we have, since it is admittedly inexplicable how material bodies could act on minds to produce ideas. (§19)

Seventhly, ideas are inert, lacking any causal power; so if there were qualities like extension and motion, resembling (as the Lockeans suppose) our ideas, they too would be inert, and could not be the causes of our ideas or of anything else. (§25)

It might be expected that someone who was persuaded by these arguments would adopt phenomenalism or even solipsism, concluding that we have no good reason for going beyond our minds and their intentional objects. Alternatively, someone who found this conclusion unacceptable might take the whole argument as a *reductio ad absurdum*, and reject, after all, the recognition of intentional objects from which it starts. But Berkeley does neither of these. He argues that although we do not have what he would call *ideas* of minds or of their operations, yet we do have some awareness of our own minds and of their power to call up ideas at will. We can, therefore, coherently postulate a more powerful mind as the cause of those of our ideas which are not subject to our own wills, whereas we could not coherently postulate material, or in general non-mental, causes of them. The order that we find in the ideas of sense justifies us in supposing there to be *something* systematic behind them, and hence in adopting *some* kind of realism as opposed to a pure phenomenalism. But what we can be thus realist about must be a supreme mind or spirit, not, for the reaons already given, a material world. Thus the rejection of materialism leads not to phenomenalism or solipsism or scepticism, nor to any second thoughts about the doctrine of ideas or intentional objects from which Berkeley's argument set out, but to theism. The only defensible account of the world and of our experience displays it as the immediate product of a supreme mind. This, then, is Berkeley's argument for the existence of a god. (§§26–30)

(b) *Berkeley's Theism—Discussion*

A possible objection to Berkeley's argument will occur at once to the reader: even if we reject material causes and seek mental causes for the ideas of sense, why should we arrive at a single divine mind rather than many minds? Why theism rather than panpsychism? I do not think that Berkeley has any good answer to this objection; rather, he took it for granted that a single all-powerful divine mind was the only rival candidate to the material world. If pressed, he would certainly have appealed to the order that we can find in the ideas of sense as evidence for a unitary cause. But since the materialist can explain the data by reference to many interacting bodies, it must be equally possible to explain them by reference to many interacting minds.

But even more important questions are whether, as Berkeley held, immaterialism of some sort can defeat materialism, and whether realism of some sort—materialist or immaterialist—can defeat phenomenalism.

I have argued that Berkeley's starting-point, the recognition of 'ideas' as intentional objects, is correct. I would also argue that a pure phenomenalism is not acceptable. But the reason is not merely that the ideas of sense are independent of the perceiver's will. After all, dreams, visions, and hallucinations are also independent of our wills, as are the stray ideas that float into our minds by association or for no apparent reason; yet we are ready enough to say that all these are caused by something in the mind that has them, and we

often have some ground for saying this. Nor is the reason quite, as
Berkeley suggests, that we find a degree of order in the ideas of sense
themselves, as actually experienced, which calls strongly for explanation. Rather it is, as Hume explained, that there is a certain amount
of order within the ideas of sense as actually experienced, but that
these seem to be or to represent fragments of a much more thoroughly
ordered system of things: they invite us to supplement them by
postulating further items, and only with that supplementation do we
arrive at a really orderly world.[3] That this *is* the reason will have a
bearing upon the ultimate choice between rival explanations. Still,
alternative explanations are available. We can do the necessary supplementing either by supposing that there are material things which
our mental contents represent more or less accurately, and which are
picked out in perception from a much larger world of fairly persistent
but also regularly changing and interacting things, or by supposing
that our mental contents have archetypes in the divine mind which
they represent more or less accurately, and that their particular
archetypes are only a sprinkling out of an equally large and coherent
system of divine ideas. Which of these alternatives should we prefer?
Do Berkeley's arguments, as summarized above, really tell in favour
of immaterialism?

The first of these arguments, that an idea can be like nothing but
an idea, collapses when we see what sort of likeness or resemblance
the materialist view requires. This is just, for example, that when I am
in a perceptual state whose content is describable by saying that I
seem to be seeing something square, there should be something that
is (approximately) square. Or again, that when it is with me as if I
were seeing two objects of similar shape and size, say two billiard
balls, there should really be two similarly shaped and sized objects in
the neighbourhood. The likeness or resemblance required is just that
where the content is as of an X; the reality should be (roughly) an X.
There simply is no *a priori* impossibility or even implausibility about
something other than an idea being like an idea in this sense.

The second argument, that what Lockeans say about secondary
qualities must hold for primary qualities too, is rebutted by the
realization that the case for the Lockean view about secondary
qualities is not just that they are subject to illusions—admittedly this
applies to the primary ones too—but that a plausible explanatory
hypothesis about vision, touch, hearing, etc., uses as starting-points
objects located and extended in space, persisting and moving as time

[3] D. Hume, *A Treatise of Human Nature*, Book I, Part iv, Section 2.

passes—that is, objects with primary qualities that at least roughly resemble (in the sense just explained) our ideas of them—but has no corresponding need, or even room, for corresponding likenesses of our ideas of secondary qualities. It is true that such an explanatory hypothesis needs to postulate at least one space-occupying property, that solidity will not fill this bill, and that none of the other primary qualities on Locke's list is a space-occupier; but since such a hypothesis need not confine itself to qualities which correspond to ordinary sense-contents it is not forced to call upon secondary qualities to play this role, and therefore is not forced, as Berkeley thinks, to give the primary qualities the same status as the secondary ones.[4]

The third argument has no force. Even if we accepted Berkeley's relativism about length, size, motion, and so on, there is no reason why such relative spatial features should not be objective: relativity does not entail mind-dependence. In any case—though this is another story, too long to follow out here—there are strong arguments for a more absolutist view of spatio-temporal features of some kinds, though perhaps not the Lockean or Newtonian ones.[5]

The possibility of postulating space-occupying properties which have no mental contents that resemble them, noted as a reply to Berkeley's second argument, also rebuts his fourth: at least one way of taking the 'substratum' is to see it as whatever occupies space, and then the sense in which it 'supports' primary qualities becomes clear: by occupying space through time in a certain way a bit of this stuff, whatever it is, has a certain (possibly changing) shape, size, motion, and so on.

Berkeley's fifth argument raises what is called the veil-of-perception problem, and has been widely believed to be fatal to any sort of representative view. It is not so, because, provided that a hypothesis about a reality distinct from our mental states can be meaningfully and coherently formulated, it may be confirmed by being a better explanation than any rival one of the data that we have, namely those mental states.[6] But for our present purpose it is enough to note that if this argument had any force it would tell equally against any kind of representative realism, and hence (among others) against Berkeley's own view that our ideas have ideas in God's mind as their

---

[4] Cf. my *Problems from Locke* (Oxford University Press, 1976) pp. 24–6.

[5] Cf. my 'Three Steps towards Absolutism', in the forthcoming report of a Royal Institute of Philosophy conference on Space, Time, and Causality.

[6] *Problems from Locke*, Chapter 2.

archetypes. This argument is of no use to Berkeley because it does not bear differentially against materialism as opposed to immaterialist realism. If it had any force, it would support either phenomenalism or some kind of direct realism which avoided the veil-of-perception problem by refusing to distinguish the contents of perceptual states from independently existing objects. But neither of these is defensible, for other reasons, nor is either of them what Berkeley wants.

The sixth argument, about the incomprehensibility of the action of material things on minds to produce ideas, is, I concede, a real difficulty for the materialist view. But it is only a difficulty: it does not show that view to be untenable.

The seventh argument, about the inertness of ideas, fails in view of the reply we have given to the first argument. That reply explained *how* material things can be 'like ideas', namely by realizing, at least roughly and in part, the features of the contents of our perceptual states. Mental contents are inert because they are not really things at all, or even qualities; to talk of them is only to describe our mental condition 'adverbially', to say how we are appeared to. But it does not follow from this that things or qualities which are 'like ideas' in the sense that they realize those contents, that they *are* (roughly and in some respects) as it appears to us that things are, must also be inert or lack causal properties or powers.

None of Berkeley's arguments against materialism, therefore, is at all conclusive. Materialism, then, is at least a rival hypothesis to Berkeley's theism, an alternative explanation of our basic situation of having experiences with a certain content. The question is, which of these rival hypotheses provides the better explanation?

In answering this question, we must take account of some of the details of the material world hypothesis. Of course, a considerable part of that hypothesis is incorporated in the perceptual experiences of almost everyone: these experiences are as of seeing physical objects which we now automatically take in general to persist when no longer perceived and to occupy places in a three-dimensional space; they are as of touching and moving some of the very same things that we see; and of hearing sounds and noticing tastes and smells as coming from some of these same things. But although this interpretation is now, in these ways, part of the content of our experience, we want, for our present purpose, to consider it *as an interpretation* which has been imposed upon and combined with some more elementary data. We do not ordinarily separate these out and identify them as data; but we can reconstruct them by considering our sensory input without the ordinary automatic interpretation.

Once we look at it in this way, we see it as a striking fact, first, that our various visual presentations, in themselves two-dimensional—or strictly, as Thomas Reid saw, having the geometry of part of the inside of a sphere at whose centre our eyes are located[7]—fit together so well as views of a three-dimensional roughly Euclidean world of fairly persistent and on the whole relatively stationary objects. Secondly, it is a remarkable fact that the combination of tactual and kinaesthetic data, which (Berkeley insists) are in themselves of totally different kinds from visual data, can nevertheless be correlated with visual data in such a way that we can take ourselves to be moving among and touching the very same things that we see. Thirdly, the data of hearing and taste and smell can be interpreted as belonging to this same system—a sound comes from a bell which we can see and touch and move so as to make it ring; it is a visible and touchable cherry that tastes sweet when I put it in my mouth, and we are often fairly successful in tracing smells to flowers, pieces of cheese, or dead rats. Fourthly, it has been found possible, particularly with the growth of science over the last 400 years, to give further explanations of the behaviour of the supposed physical objects in this three-dimensional world, particularly by postulating that they have micro-structures and various further features which are never directly perceived by our senses. And, fifthly, the processes leading to sensory perceptions themselves have been traced, and the sensations therefore partly explained, by the identification of sense-organs and nerves leading from them to the brain—most notably the parts of the eye, the formation of images on the retina, and the connection between it and the optic nerve. All of this forms a remarkably successful system of detailed explanation of our sensory input, of the data of sense as distinguished from their interpretation. We are liable not to notice how remarkable this is, just because we take it all for granted, having read this interpretation back into the data themselves. It is true that parts of the explanatory system have changed: for example, pre-scientific common sense takes the three-dimensional objects literally to have colours as we see colours, but science since the seventeenth century has taken a roughly Lockean view of all the secondary qualities, while twentieth-century science has replaced the Euclidean view of space with an account of a four-dimensional space-time, of which an only approximately Euclidean three-dimensional space is

[7] T. Reid, *An Inquiry into the Human Mind*, Chapter VI, Section 9.

a somewhat arbitrary cross-section. But these are minor changes within a substantially constant outline hypothesis to which further detail is added in a mainly cumulative way.

This at least sets a problem for the rival theistic hypothesis. How is it to account for the fact that our sensory data—that is, on this view, the ideas put into our minds by God—lend themselves so thoroughly to these sorts of interpretation and explanation?

The theistic hypothesis is itself open to two different interpretations, which yield different answers to. this question. According to one of these, there is no literal truth in the above-specified details of our ordinary and scientific pictures of the world—a three-dimensional world of persisting objects with unperceived insides, with micro-structure, and with features like electric charge that are not directly perceived by us. Not only does this picture not hold for a material world; it does not hold for God's ideas either. The truth is just that God feeds into our minds ideas which happen to lend themselves to an interpretation of this sort: the sensory data which, for us, constitute reality as opposed to illusion and imagination occur in combinations and sequences which are *as if* they arose from such a world of very complex objects. What further ideas God himself may have we simply cannot say. According to the other interpretation, God's ideas are in themselves as rich and systematic as the physical world is on the materialist view, and in the same sort of way. That is, God perceives a three-dimensional Euclidean world or, more probably, a four-dimensional Einsteinian one, with micro-structure, with electric charges which figure somehow as perceptual objects for him, and so on. Everything that we take to be a correct description of the physical world, and every scientific advance, if it really is an advance, is either a correct description of some of God's ideas or at least a closer approximation to a correct description of them.

Provided that there is some workable and consistent physical world hypothesis, the first of these two interpretations of the theistic view is utterly implausible. It is hard to see how God could feed us data which are as if they represented a physical world in such detail unless he had at least a pretty complete conception of the world which they appear to represent. The one thing that might give support to this interpretation would be bodies of data which resisted any *consistent* physical theory. For example, if we really were faced with a situation where some of the behaviour of light was explained by a wave theory and some by a particle theory, and no coherent theory could be found which covered both aspects of its behaviour, then we would have some reason for thinking that there is no reality of light itself even as a set of divine ideas, that the truth is only that God intends our sensations to succeed one another in some respects *as if* there were light waves and in other respects *as if* there were light particles. God would then be behaving rather like a typical dishonest witness, who, having abandoned the guaranteed coherence of truth, tells two different stories which he cannot reconcile with one another. God would similarly be conjoining two incompatible *as if* accounts, not having even the reality of a system of his own ideas to ensure compatibility, though of course he would not really be any more dishonest with this than with any other development of Berkeley's hypothesis.

The general point here is that if there were a serious difficulty in constructing any consistent account of a physical world, this would lend support to any radically different metaphysical view—perhaps to phenomenalism, perhaps to the first interpretation of the theistic hypothesis. But it is not clear that we are faced with such a serious difficulty, and on the other hand there is an enormous body of material that fits in surprisingly well with the physical world hypo- thesis, and whose coherence would be left unexplained by this first interpretation of theism.

The second interpretation is more plausible. By making God's ideas mirror so closely the world that seems to be revealed to common sense and to science, it shares some of the advantages of the material- ist view. Yet there are at least four serious difficulties even for this version of Berkeley's theism. One of these concerns the fifth of the kinds of detail listed above: a well-established part of the physical world, and therefore, on this view, also of the system of divine ideas that replaces it, is the anatomy and physiology of sense perception itself. For example, there is the sequence from an object via light rays, the lens of the eye, the retina, the optic nerve, and the visual cortex, which leads to our having a visual sensation that is in some respects a fairly correct representation of that object. But on the theistic hypothesis all the earlier steps in this sequence are utterly irrelevant to the final stage, for the sensation is now an idea put directly into our minds by God, and the apparent causal connections between the sensation and the various changes earlier in the sequence are illusory. This makes the occurrence of all these anatomical and physiological details very odd. As Berkeley's correspondent Samuel Johnson said, 'It is ... still something shocking to many to think that there should be nothing but a mere show in all the art and contrivance appearing in the structure (for instance) of a human body, particularly of the organs of sense. The curious structure of the eye, what can it be more than merely a fine show, if there be no connection more than you admit of, between that and vision?'[8] And Berkeley gave no direct reply to this objection, as related specifically to sense-organs and sensation, either in his letters or in the text of the *Principles* to which he referred his correspondent. The process of perception, therefore, raises problems not only for the materialist hypothesis but also for the theistic one. Berkeley's sixth argument against materialism, that we cannot understand the apparent causal connection between brain states and experiences, is, as I have conceded, a difficulty for materialism; but there is a greater difficulty for the theistic hypothesis in denying that there is any causal connection here at all. The final transition in the apparent sequence of sensation is indeed obscure, but the details of the earlier steps and their correlations with that final stage would be quite mysterious on the rival theistic view.

A second serious difficulty concerns the voluntary actions of human beings. Since we seem able to bring about changes in the physical world, we must, on the present view, be allowed analogously to bring about changes in God's ideas, since these are now a near-perfect counterpart of the supposed physical world. Though God, on this view, puts into my mind all the ideas of sense that I have, some of these are ones that I have first, or simultaneously, put into his. If I move my hand I am thereby altering a few of God's ideas, and altering them directly, by mind-to-mind contact, not merely by moving a neutral physical object of which he has knowledge. Berkeley could accept this, but he might be reluctant to do so. If, instead, he maintained that my mind does not thus directly control God's, his theory would have much the same unpalatable consequences as some versions of extreme materialism, according to which such mental occurrences as our decisions are epiphenomenal, and do not really bring about changes in the material world.

A third difficulty is more subtle. When I was discussing the first interpretation of the theistic hypothesis, I said that what might tell in its favour would be an apparent impossibility of constructing a consistent physical theory: if the reality is merely that God intends us to have sensations *as if* this and that, the various items governed by the 'as if' need not be mutually compatible. On the second interpretation of the theistic hypothesis, part of the reality is a system

[8] *Berkeley: Philosophical Works*, p. 341.

of God's ideas, and one might expect these to be all mutually compatible. But though what we wrongly take to be a physical world should,
therefore, on this view, be *consistent*, there is no need for it to be
complete or fully *determinate*. God's ideas would have the status of
intentional objects, and presumably, therefore, also the logic that is
characteristic of intentional objects. Just as I can think of an object,
say a book, being on a certain shelf, without thinking of it as being
at a particular place on that shelf, so too, presumably, God could
have somewhat indeterminate ideas. If we think, for simplicity, of
the whole of space-time as being divided into numbered cells, there
might be some cells with regard to which God did not have ideas as
of their containing objects of certain sorts, nor yet ideas as of their
being empty. In this respect we might expect some discrepancy
between a genuinely objective physical world and a divine-idea
counterpart of one. But on the whole—perhaps with some reserva-
tions arising from current versions of the quantum theory—our
sensory data seem to reflect a fully determinate (though not necessarily deterministic) physical world, as we should expect if there were
an objective physical world, rather than an indeterminate or incomplete one, which would be at least possible if the corresponding
reality consisted in God's having such and such ideas as intentional
objects. However, this does not quite provide a crucial experiment to
decide between materialism and the second interpretation of Berkeley's theism, because the theist could hold that it is a characteristic
perfection of God that *his* system of intentional objects is complete
as well as consistent, though the logic of intentional objects as such
does not require this, just as a more conventional form of theism
holds that God's knowledge of the world that is to some extent
independent of his is complete down to the last detail.[9]

There is also a vaguer but still significant objection to this version
of Berkeley's theism. The kinds of detail and complexity that we are
led to ascribe to the material world are natural enough if it is indeed
an objective material world, but they seem alien to the intentional
objects of a divine mind. Some of Berkeley's own comments reflect
this. 'We are miserably bantered, they [that is, the Lockeans] say, by
our senses, and amused [that is, deluded] only with the outside and
show of things. The real essence, the internal qualities, and consti-

[9] E.g. Samuel Clarke says that 'this divine Knowledge ... is a *perfect* comprehension
of every thing, in all possible respects *at a time*, and in all possible circumstances
together ... a clear, distinct, and particular knowledge of every even the minutest thing
or circumstance. (*Works of Samuel Clarke*, London, 1738, Vol. I, p. 71.)

tution of every the meanest object, is hid from our view; something there is in every drop of water, every grain of sand, which it is beyond the power of human understanding to fathom or comprehend.' (§101) By contrast, he thinks that his own theory avoids such complications: 'I need not say, how many hypotheses and speculations are left out, and how much the study of nature is abridged by this doctrine'. (§102) That is indeed what one might hope for from the theistic hypothesis, and our first interpretation, which Berkeley is here favouring, would have this result. But, as we have seen, that first interpretation would make the hypothesis extremely implausible for other reasons. On the present, second, interpretation we do not get this result; instead, all the detail which a post-Lockean physicist is led to ascribe to the physical world will now have to be ascribed to God's ideas, but with less intrinsic plausibility, just because such detail is not at home in an essentially mental world.

A further curious consequence of this interpretation, which Berkeley would certainly not have wanted, is that God's ideas might well not include secondary qualities as we perceive them. God's ideas, at least as far as we can tell, would include only counterparts of the features that the best physical theory ascribes to material things, though, as I have said, he might also have further ideas of which we know nothing. Perhaps, then, God does not himself see things as coloured, or hear sounds as we hear them, whereas we do precisely because we are capable of suffering from illusions. We might then misquote Francis Thompson, saying

> 'Tis ye, 'tis your estranged faces
> That find the many-splendoured thing.[10]

But since God would know how we see and hear things, he could as it were see colours through our eyes and hear music through our ears, though he could not see or hear them in his own right. An ingenious theist might offer this as a reason for God's otherwise puzzling decision to create the human race.

Altogether, therefore, when we consider the successful detailed development of the materialist hypothesis, and the difficulty that the rival theistic hypothesis, on either of the two possible interpretations, has in coping with those features of the sensory data to which that success is due, we must conclude that, even if we give Berkeley's theistic hypothesis a fair run and discount any initial prejudice against it, the materialist hypothesis is to be preferred to it.

[10] Francis Thompson, 'In No Strange Land', in H. Gardner, *The New Oxford Book of English Verse* 1250–1950 (Oxford University Press, 1972), p. 802.

5

Cosmological Arguments

THE rejection of Berkeley's form of theism entails that if a god is to be introduced at all, it must be as a supplement to the material world, not as a substitute for it. The rejection of all forms of ontological argument then entails that the theist must argue from the world (or from some part or aspect of our experience) to a god. This brings us to the cosmological argument, which is *par excellence* the philosophers' argument for theism. It has been presented in many forms, but in one version or another it has been used by Greek, Arabic, Jewish, and Christian philosophers and theologians, including Plato, Aristotle, al Farabi, al Ghazali, ibn Rushd (Averroes), Maimonides, Aquinas, Spinoza, and Leibniz.[1] What is common to the many versions of this argument is that they start from the very fact that there is a world or from such general features of it as change or motion or causation—not, like the argument from consciousness or the argument for design, from specific details of what the world includes or how it is ordered—and argue to God as the uncaused cause of the world or of those general features, or as its creator, or as the reason for its existence. I cannot examine all the variants of this argument that have been advanced, but I shall discuss three intendedly demonstrative approaches and an inductive, probabilistic, approach. And although arguments to a first cause or a creator are more immediately attractive, and appeared earlier in history, than those which argue from the contingency of the world to a necessary being, the latter are in some respects simpler and perhaps more fundamental, so I shall begin with one of these.

[1] W. L. Craig, *The Cosmological Argument from Plato to Leibniz* (Macmillan, London, 1980). Quotations from al Farabi and al Ghazali are taken from this work.

(a) *Contingency and Sufficient Reason*

Leibniz gives what is essentially the same proof in slightly different forms in different works; we can sum up his line of thought as follows.[2] He assumes the *principle of sufficient reason*, that nothing occurs without a sufficient reason why it is so and not otherwise. There must, then, be a sufficient reason for the world as a whole, a reason why something exists rather than nothing. Each thing in the world is contingent, being causally determined by other things: it would not occur if other things were otherwise. The world as a whole, being a collection of such things, is therefore itself contingent. The series of things and events, with their causes, with causes of those causes, and so on, may stretch back infinitely in time; but, if so, then however far back we go, or if we consider the series as a whole, what we have is still contingent and therefore requires a sufficient reason outside this series. That is, there must be a sufficient reason *for* the world which is *other than* the world. This will have to be a necessary being, which contains its own sufficient reason for existence. Briefly, things must have a sufficient reason for their existence, and this must be found ultimately in a necessary being. There must be something free from the disease of contingency, a disease which affects everything in the world and the world as a whole, even if it is infinite in past time.

This argument, however, is open to criticisms of two sorts, summed up in the questions 'How do we know that everything must have a sufficient reason?' and 'How can there be a necessary being, one that contains its own sufficient reason?'. These challenges are related: if the second question cannot be answered satisfactorily, it will follow that things as a whole cannot have a sufficient reason, not merely that we do not know that they must have one.

Kant's criticism of the Leibnizian argument turns upon this second objection; he claims that the cosmological proof depends upon the already criticized ontological proof.[3] The latter starts from the concept of an absolutely necessary being, an *ens realissimum*, something whose essence includes existence, and tries to derive from that concept itself alone the fact that there is such a being. The cosmological proof 'retains the connection of absolute necessity with the highest reality, but instead of reasoning ... from the highest reality to

[2] The clearest account is in 'On the Ultimate Origination of Things', printed, e.g., in G. W. Leibniz, *Philosophical Writings* (Dent, London, 1934), pp. 32-41.

[3] *Critique of Pure Reason*, Transcendental Dialectic, Book II, Chapter III, Section 5 (see n. 1 to Chapter 3 above).

necessity of existence, it reasons from the previously given uncondi-
tioned necessity of some being to the unlimited reality of that being'.
However, Kant's claim that the cosmological proof 'rests' or 'depends' on the ontological one, that 'the so-called cosmological proof
really owes any cogency which it may have to the ontological proof
from mere concepts' is at least misleading. The truth is rather this.
The cosmological argument purports to show, from the contingency
of the world, in conjunction with the principle of sufficient reason,
that there must be something else which is not contingent, which
exists necessarily, which is or contains its own sufficient reason.
When we ask how there could be such a thing, we are offered the
notion of an *ens realissimum* whose essence includes existence. This
is the notion which served as the starting-point of (in particular)
Descartes's ontological proof. But the notion is being used quite
differently in the two cases. Does this connection imply that successful criticism of the ontological proof undermines the cosmological
one also? That depends on the nature of the successful criticism. If
its outcome is that the very concept of something's essence including
existence is illegitimate—which would perhaps have been shown by
Kant's thesis that existence is not a predicate, or by the quantifier
analysis of existence in general, if either of these had been correct
and uncontroversial—then at least the final step in the cosmological
proof is blocked, and Leibniz must either find some different explanation of how something might exist necessarily and contain its own
sufficient reason, or else give up even the first step in his proof,
abandoning the search for a sufficient reason of the world as a whole.
But if the outcome of the successful criticism of the ontological proof
were merely that we cannot validly start from a mere concept and
thence derive actual existence—if we allowed that there was nothing
illegitimate about the concept of a being whose essence includes
existence, and insisted only that whatever a concept contains, it is
always a further question whether there is something that instantiates
it—then the cosmological proof would be unaffected by this criticism.
For it does offer something that purports independently to answer
this further question, namely the first step, the claim that the contingency of the world shows that a necessary being is required. Now
our final criticisms, not only of Descartes's version of the ontological
proof, but also of Anselm's and Plantinga's, were of this second sort.
I said that the view that existence disappears wholly into the existential quantifier is controversial, and therefore did not press the first sort
of criticism. Consequently the cosmological proof is not undermined

by the so far established weakness of the ontological, though, since Kant thought he had carried through a criticism of the first sort, it would have been consistent for him to say that the cosmological proof was at least seriously threatened by it, that Leibniz would need to find some other account of how there could be a necessary being.

But perhaps we can still make something like Kant's point, even if we are relying only on a criticism of the second sort. Since it is always a further question whether a concept is instantiated or not, no matter how much it contains, the existence even of a being whose essence included existence would not be self-explanatory: there might have failed to be any such thing. This 'might' expresses at least a conceptual possibility; if it is alleged that this being none the less exists by a metaphysical necessity, we are still waiting for an explanation of this kind of necessity. The existence of this being is not logically necessary; it does not exist in all logically possible worlds; in what way, then, does it necessarily exist in this world and satisfy the demand for a sufficient reason?

It might be replied that we understand what it is for something to exist contingently, in that it would not have existed if something else had been otherwise: to exist necessarily is to exist but not contingently in this sense. But then the premiss that the natural world as a whole is contingent is not available: though we have some ground for thinking that each part, or each finite temporal stretch, of the world is contingent in this sense upon something else, we have initially no ground for thinking that the world as a whole would not have existed if something else had been otherwise; inference from the contingency of every part to the contingency *in this sense* of the whole is invalid. Alternatively, we might say that something exists contingently if and only if it might not have existed, and by contrast that something exists necessarily if and only if it exists, but it is not the case that it might not have existed. In this sense we could infer the contingency of the whole from the contingency of every part. But once it is conceded, for reasons just given, that it is not logically impossible that the alleged necessary being might not have existed, we have no understanding of how it could be true of this being that it is not the case that it might not have existed. We have as yet no ground for believing that it is even possible that something should exist necessarily in the sense required.

This criticism is reinforced by the other objection, 'How do we know that everything must have a sufficient reason?'. I see no plausibility in the claim that the principle of sufficient reason is known *a priori* to be true. Leibniz thought that reliance on this principle is implicit in our reasoning both about physics and about human behaviour: for example, Archimedes argued that if, in a symmetrical balance, equal weights are placed on either side, neither will go down, because there is no reason why one side should go down rather than the other; and equally a rational being cannot act without a motive.[4] But what is being used by Archimedes is just the rule that like causes produce like effects. This, and in general the search for, and expectation of, causes and regularities and reasons, do indeed guide inquiry in many fields. But the principles used are not known *a priori*, and Samuel Clarke pointed out a difficulty in applying them even to human behaviour: someone who has a good reason for doing either A or B, but no reason for doing one of these rather than the other, will surely choose one arbitrarily rather than do neither.[5] Even if, as is possible, we have some innate tendency to look for and expect such symmetries and continuities and regularities, this does not give us an *a priori* guarantee that such can always be found. In so far as our reliance on such principles is epistemically justified, it is so *a posteriori*, by the degree of success we have had in interpreting the world with their help. And in any case these principles of causation, symmetry, and so on refer to how the world works; we are extrapolating far beyond their so far fruitful use when we postulate a principle of sufficient reason and apply it to the world as a whole. Even if, within the world, everything seemed to have a sufficient reason, that is, a cause in accordance with some regularity, with like causes producing like effects, this would give us little ground for expecting the world as a whole, or its basic causal laws themselves, to have a sufficient reason of some different sort.

The principle of sufficient reason expresses a demand that things should be intelligible *through and through*. The simple reply to the argument which relies on it is that there is nothing that justifies this demand, and nothing that supports the belief that it is satisfiable even in principle. As we have seen in considering the other main objection to Leibniz's argument, it is difficult to see how there even could be anything that would satisfy it. If we reject this demand, we are not thereby committed to saying that things are utterly unintelligible. The sort of intelligibility that is achieved by successful causal inquiry and scientific explanation is not undermined by its inability

[4] *The Leibniz–Clarke Correspondence*, edited by H. G. Alexander (Manchester University Press, 1956 and 1976), Leibniz's Second Paper.

[5] *The Leibniz–Clarke Correspondence*, Clarke's Third and Fifth Replies.

to make things intelligible through and through. Any particular explanation starts with premises which state 'brute facts', and although the brutally factual starting-points of one explanation may themselves be further explained by another, the latter in turn will have to start with something that it does not explain, *and so on however far we go*. But there is no need to see this as unsatisfactory.

A sufficient reason is also sometimes thought of as a final cause or purpose. Indeed, if we think of each event in the history of the world as having (in principle) been explained by its antecedent causes, but still want a further explanation of the whole sequence of events, we must turn to some other sort of explanation. The two candidates that then come to mind are two kinds of purposive or teleological explanation. Things are as they are, Plato suggested, because it is *better* that they should be so.[6] This can be construed either as implying that (objective) value is in itself creative—an idea which we shall be taking up in Chapter 13—or as meaning that some intelligent being sees what would be better, chooses it, and brings it about. But why must we look for a sufficient reason of either of these sorts? The principle of sufficient reason, thus understood, expresses a demand for some kind of absolute purposiveness. But if we reject this demand, we are not thereby saying that 'man and the universe are ultimately meaningless'.[7] People will still have the purposes that they have, some of which they can fulfil, even if the question 'What is the purpose of the world as a whole?' has no positive answer.

The principle of sufficient reason, then, is more far-reaching than the principle that every occurrence has a preceding sufficient cause: the latter, but not the former, would be satisfied by a series of things or events running back infinitely in time, each determined by earlier ones, but with no further explanation of the series as a whole. Such a series would give us only what Leibniz called 'physical' or 'hypothetical' necessity, whereas the demand for a sufficient reason for the whole body of contingent things and events and laws calls for something with 'absolute' or 'metaphysical' necessity. But even the weaker, deterministic, principle is not an *a priori* truth, and indeed it may not be a truth at all; much less can this be claimed for the principle of sufficient reason. Perhaps it just expresses an arbitrary demand; it may be intellectually satisfying to believe that there is, objectively, an explanation for everything together, even if we can only guess at what the explanation might be. But we have no right to

[6] Plato, *Phaedo*, 97–9.
[7] Craig, op. cit., p. 287.

assume that the universe will comply with our intellectual prefer-
ences. Alternatively, the supposed principle may be an unwarranted
extension of the determinist one, which, in so far as it is supported,
is supported only empirically, by our success in actually finding
causes, and can at most be accepted provisionally, not as an *a priori*
truth. The form of the cosmological argument which relies on the
principle of sufficient reason therefore fails completely as a demonstrative proof.

(b) *The Regress of Causes*

There is a popular line of thought, which we may call the first cause
argument, and which runs as follows: things must be caused, and
their causes will be other things that must have causes, and so on;
but this series of causes cannot go back indefinitely; it must terminate
in a first cause, and this first cause will be God. This argument
envisages a regress of causes in time, but says (as Leibniz, for one,
did not) that this regress must stop somewhere. Though it has some
initial plausibility, it also has obvious difficulties. Why must the
regress terminate at all? Why, if it terminates, must it lead to a single
termination, to one first cause, rather than to a number—perhaps an
indefinitely large number—of distinct uncaused causes? And even if
there is just one first cause, why should we identify this with God? I
shall come back to this argument and to possible replies to these
objections; but first I want to look at a more elaborate philosophical
argument that has some, though not much, resemblance to it.

Of Aquinas's 'five ways', the first three are recognizably variants
of the cosmological proof, and all three involve some kind of terminated regress of causes.[8] But all of them are quite different from our
first cause argument. The first way argues to a first mover, using
the illustration of something's being moved by a stick only when
the stick is moved by a hand; here the various movings are
simultaneous, we do not have a regress of causes in time. Similarly
the 'efficient causes' in the second way are contemporary agents.
Both these arguments, as Kenny has shown, depend too much on
antiquated physical theory to be of much interest now. The third
way is much more significant. This argument is in two stages, and
can be freely translated, with some condensation, as follows:

First stage: If everything were able-not-to-be, then at some time
there would have been nothing (because what is able-not-to-be,

---

[8] A. Kenny, *The Five Ways* (Routledge & Kegan Paul, London, 1969).

at some time is not); and then (since what does not exist cannot begin to be except through something which is) even now there would be nothing. It is plainly not true that there is nothing now; so it cannot be true that everything is able-not-to-be. That is, there must be at least one thing which is necessary.

Second stage: Everything that is necessary either has a cause of its necessity outside itself, or it does not. But it is not possible to go to infinity in a series of necessary things each of which has a cause of its necessity outside itself; this is like what has been proved about efficient causes. Therefore we must assume something which is necessary through itself, which does not have a cause of its necessity outside itself, but which is the cause of the necessity of the other things; and this men all call God.

This argument is quite different from our first cause argument and also from Leibniz's argument from contingency. Although it uses the contrast between things which are able-not-to-be (and therefore contingent) and those which are necessary, it is not satisfied with the conclusion that there is something necessary; it allows that there may be many necessary things, and reaches God only at the end of the second stage, as what has its necessity 'through itself' (*per se*). Clearly 'necessary' does not mean the same for Aquinas as for Leibniz. What it does mean will become clearer as we examine the reasoning.

In the first stage, the premiss 'what is able-not-to-be, at some time is not' seems dubious: why should not something which is *able* not to be nevertheless just happen to exist always? But perhaps Aquinas means by 'things that are able-not-to-be' (*possibilia non esse*) something like 'impermanent things', so that this premiss is analytic. Even so, the statement that if everything were such, at some time there would have been nothing, does not follow: some impermanent things might have lasted through all past time, and be going to display their impermanence by perishing only at some time in the future. But we may be able to understand Aquinas's thought by seeing what is said more explicitly by Maimonides, by whom Aquinas appears to have been influenced here.[9] His corresponding proof seems to assume that past time has been finite—and reasonably so, for if past time has been finite there would seem to be an easier argument for a divine creator, such as we shall consider below. The suggestion is that it would not have been possible for

[9] Craig, op. cit., Chapter 4.

impermanent things to have lasted throughout an infinite time, and hence they would have perished already.

However, another objection is that there might be a series of things, each of which was impermanent and perished after a finite period, but whose periods of existence overlapped so that there never was a time when there was nothing. It would be a clear logical fallacy (of which some commentators have accused Aquinas) to infer 'at some time everything is not' from 'each thing at some time is not'. But we might defend Aquinas in either of two ways. First, if each thing were impermanent, it would be the most improbable good luck if the overlapping sequence kept up through infinite time. Secondly, even if this improbable luck holds, we might regard the series of overlapping things as itself a thing which had already lasted through infinite time, and so could not be impermanent. Indeed, if there were such a series which never failed, this might well indicate that there was some *permanent* stock of material of which the perishable things were composed and into which they disintegrated, thereby contributing to the composition of other things.

A third objection concerns the premiss that 'what does not exist cannot begin to be except through something that is'. This is, of course, a form of the principle that nothing can come from nothing; the idea then is that if our series of impermanent things had broken off, it could never have started again after a gap. But is this an *a priori* truth? As Hume pointed out, we can certainly conceive an uncaused beginning-to-be of an object; if what we can thus conceive is nevertheless in some way impossible, this still requires to be shown.[10] Still, this principle has some plausibility, in that it is constantly confirmed in our experience (and also used, reasonably, in interpreting our experience).

Altogether, then, the first stage of Aquinas's argument falls short of watertight demonstration, but it gives some lower degree of support to the conclusion that there is at least one thing that is necessary in the sense, which has now become clear, that it is permanent, that *for some reason* it is not able-not-to-be.

The second stage takes this conclusion as its starting-point. One permanent thing, it allows, may be caused to be permanent, sustained always in existence, by another. But, it holds, there cannot be an infinite regress of such things. Why not? Aquinas refers us to his earlier proof about efficient causes, in the second way. This runs:

[10] *Treatise*, Book I, Part iii, Section 3; contrast Kenny, op. cit., p. 67.

It is not possible to go to infinity in a series of efficient causes. For in all ordered efficient causes the first item is the cause of the intermediate one and the intermediate is the cause of the last (whether there is only one intermediate or more than one); now if the cause is removed, so is the effect. Therefore if there has not been a first item among efficient causes there will not be a last or an intermediate. But if one goes to infinity in a series of efficient causes, there will not be a first efficient cause, and so there will not be a last effect or intermediate efficient causes . . .

Unfortunately this argument is unsound. Although in a *finite* ordered series of causes the intermediate (or the earliest intermediate) is caused by the first item, this would not be so if there were an infinite series. In an infinite series, every item is caused by an earlier item. The way in which the first item is 'removed' if we go from a finite to an infinite series does not entail the removal of the later items. In fact, Aquinas (both here and in the first way) has simply begged the question against an infinite regress of causes. But is this a sheer mistake, or is there some coherent thought behind it? Some examples (some of which would not themselves have been available to Aquinas, though analogues of them would have been) may suggest that there is. If we were told that there was a watch without a mainspring, we would hardly be reassured by the further information that it had, however, an infinite train of gear-wheels. Nor would we expect a railway train consisting of an infinite number of carriages, the last pulled along by the second last, the second last by the third last, and so on, to get along without an engine. Again, we see a chain, consisting of a series of links, hanging from a hook; we should be surprised to learn that there was a similar but infinite chain, with no hook, but links supported by links above them for ever. The point is that in these examples, and in the series of efficient causes or of necessary things, it is assumed that there is a relation of *dependence*— or, equivalently, one in the reverse direction of *support*—and, if the series were infinite, there would in the end be nothing for the effects to depend on, nothing to support them. And the same would be true if the regress were not infinite but circular.

There is here an implicit appeal to the following general principle: Where items are ordered by a relation of dependence, the regress must end somewhere; it cannot be either infinite or circular. Perhaps this principle was intended by al Farabi in the dictum that is translated 'But a series of contingent beings which would produce one another cannot proceed to infinity or move in a circle' (p. 83). As our examples show, this principle is at least highly plausible;

the problem will be to decide when we have such a relation of dependence.

In the second stage of Aquinas's argument, therefore, the key notion is that any necessary—that is, permanent—thing either depends for its permanence on something else or is *per se necessarium* in a sense which can apply only to God. The actual text of the third way does not reveal Aquinas's thinking about this. But comparison of it with other passages in his writings and with Maimonides's proof suggests that the implicit assumption is that anything whose essence does not involve existence must, even if it is permanent, depend for its existence on something else.[11] This assumption would give the dependence which would call for an end to the regress and also ensure that nothing could end it but a being whose essence involved existence—which would explain the assertion that what is *per se necessarium* is what men all call God.

But the final objection to the argument is that we have no reason for accepting this implicit assumption. Why, for example, might there not be a permanent stock of matter whose essence did not involve existence but which did not derive its existence from anything else?

It is obvious that, as I said earlier, Aquinas's third way is very different from Leibniz's cosmological proof. Yet there has been a tendency to assimilate the former to the latter.[12] This is understandable, in that Aquinas would need something like the principle of sufficient reason to support what I have called the implicit assumption against our final objection: for example, there being a permanent stock of matter would be just a brute fact that had no sufficient reason, whereas something whose essence involved existence would seem to have, in itself, *per se*, a sufficient reason for its permanence. But in view of our criticisms of Leibniz's argument, no borrowing from it can rescue that of Aquinas.

But what about the popular first cause argument? Can we not now answer our earlier queries? Why must the regress of causes in time terminate? Because things, states of affairs, and occurrences *depend* on their antecedent causes. Why must the regress lead to one first cause rather than to many uncaused causes, and why must that one cause be God? Because anything other than God would need something else causally to depend upon. Moreover, the assumption needed for this argument is more plausible than that needed for

[11] Craig, op. cit., pp. 142–3, 146–8.
[12] Craig, op. cit., p. 283.

Leibniz's proof, or for Aquinas's. The notion that everything must have a sufficient reason is a metaphysician's demand, as is the notion that anything permanent must depend for its permanence on something else unless its essence involves existence. But the notion that an effect *depends* on a temporally earlier cause is part of our ordinary understanding of causation: we all have some grasp of this asymmetry between cause and effect, however hard it may be to give an exact analysis of it.[13]

Nevertheless, this argument is not demonstratively cogent. Though we understand that where something has a temporally antecedent cause, it depends somehow upon it, it does not follow that everything (other than God) *needs* something else to depend on in this way. Also, what we can call al Farabi's principle, that where items are ordered by a relation of dependence, the regress must terminate somewhere, and cannot be either infinite or circular, though plausible, may not be really sound. But the greatest weakness of this otherwise attractive argument is that some reason is required for making God the one exception to the supposed need for something else to depend on: why should God, rather than anything else, be taken as the only satisfactory termination of the regress? If we do not simply accept this as a sheer mystery (which would be to abandon rational theology and take refuge in faith), we shall have to defend it in something like the ways that the metaphysicians have suggested. But then this popular argument takes on board the burdens that have sunk its more elaborate philosophical counterparts.

(c) *Finite Past Time and Creation*

There is, as Craig explains, a distinctive kind of cosmological argument which, unlike those of Aquinas, Leibniz, and many others, assumes or argues that the past history of the world is finite.[14] This, which Craig calls, by its Arabic name, the *kalam* type of argument, was favoured by Islamic thinkers who were suspicious of the subtleties of the philosophers and relied more on revelation than on reason. Nevertheless, they did propound this as a rational proof of God's existence, and some of them used mathematical paradoxes that are descended from Zeno's, or that anticipate Cantor's, to show that there cannot be an actual infinite—in particular, an infinite past time. For example, if time past were infinite, an infinite stretch would have

---

[13] Cf. Chapter 7 of *The Cement of the Universe* (see n. 2 to Chapter 1 above).
[14] Craig, op. cit., Chapter 3.

actually to have been traversed in order to reach the present, and this is thought to be impossible. Then there is an ingenious argument suggested by al Ghazali: the planet Jupiter revolves in its orbit once every twelve years, Saturn once every thirty years; so Jupiter must have completed more than twice as many revolutions as Saturn; yet if past time were infinite they would each have completed the same (infinite) number; which is a contradiction. (pp. 101–2) The first of these (which Kant also uses in the thesis of his First Antinomy) just expresses a prejudice against an actual infinity. It assumes that, even if past time were infinite, there would still have been a starting-point of time, but one infinitely remote, so that an actual infinity would have had to be traversed to reach the present from there. But to take the hypothesis of infinity seriously would be to suppose that there was no starting-point, not even an infinitely remote one, and that from any specific point in past time there is only a finite stretch that needs to be traversed to reach the present. Al Ghazali's argument uses an instance of one of Cantor's paradoxes, that in an infinite class a part can indeed be equal to the whole: for example, there are just as many even numbers (2, 4, 6, etc.) as there are whole numbers (1, 2, 3, etc.), since these classes can be matched one–one with each other. But is this not a contradiction? Is not the class of even numbers both equal to that of the integers (because of this one–one correlation) and smaller than it (because it is a proper part of it, the part that leaves out the odd numbers)? But what this brings out is that we ordinarily have and use a criterion for one group's being smaller than another—that it is, or can be correlated one–one with, a proper part of the other—and a criterion for two groups' being equal in number—that they can be correlated one–one with each other—which together ensure that *smaller than* and *equal to* exclude one another for all pairs of finite groups, but not for pairs of infinite groups. Once we understand the relation between the two criteria, we see that there is no real contradiction.

In short, it seems impossible to disprove, *a priori*, the possibility of an infinite past time. Nevertheless, many people have shared, and many still do share, these doubts about an actual infinite in the real world, even if they are willing to leave mathematicians free to play their Cantorian games—which, of course, not all mathematicians, or all philosophers of mathematics, want to play. Also the view that, whatever we say about *time*, the *universe* has a finite past history, has in recent years received strong empirical support from the cosmology that is a branch of astronomy. So let us consider what the prospects would be for a proof of the existence of a god if we were supplied, from whatever source, with the premiss that the world has only a finite past history, and therefore a beginning in time, whether or not this is also the beginning of time. Here the crucial assumption is stated by al Ghazali: '[We] know by rational necessity that nothing which originates in time originates by itself, and that, therefore, it needs a creator' (p. 102). But *do* we know this by rational necessity? Surely the assumption required here is just the same as that which is used differently in the first cause argument, that anything other than a god needs a cause or a creator to depend on. But there is *a priori* no good reason why a sheer origination of things, not determined by anything, should be unacceptable, whereas the existence of a god with the power to create something out of nothing is acceptable.

When we look hard at the latter notion we find problems within it. Does God's existence have a sheer origination in time? But then this would be as great a puzzle as the sheer origination of a material world. Or has God existed for ever through an infinite time? But this would raise again the problem of the actual infinite. To avoid both of these, we should have to postulate that God's own existence is not in time at all; but this would be a complete mystery.

Alternatively, someone might not share al Ghazali's worries about the actual infinite, and might rely on an empirical argument—such as the modern cosmological evidence for the 'big bang'—to show that the material world had a beginning in time. For him, therefore, God's existence through an infinite time would be unproblematic. But he is still using the crucial assumptions that God's existence and creative power would be self-explanatory whereas the unexplained origination of a material world would be unintelligible and therefore unacceptable. But the first of these leads us back to the criticism stated in section (a), on page 84. The notion, embedded in the ontological argument, of a being whose existence is self-explanatory because it is not the case that it might not have existed, is *not* defensible; so we cannot borrow that notion to complete any form of the cosmological argument. The second assumption is equally questionable. We have no good ground for an *a priori* certainty that there could not have been a sheer unexplained beginning of things. But in so far as we find this improbable, it should cast doubt on the interpretation of the big bang as an absolute beginning of the material universe; rather, we should infer that it must have had *some* physical antecedents, even if the big bang has to be taken as a discontinuity so radical that we cannot explain it, because we can find no laws which we can extrapolate backwards through this discontinuity.

In short, the notion of creation seems more acceptable than any other way out of the cosmological maze only because we do not look hard either at it or at the human experiences of making things on which it is modelled. It is vaguely explanatory, apparently satisfying; but these appearances fade away when we try to formulate the suggestion precisely.

(d) *Swinburne's Inductive Cosmological Argument*

We might well have anticipated, from the beginning, the conclusion that our discussion in this chapter has thus laboriously reached. We have no general grounds for expecting to be able to demonstrate, by deductively valid arguments, using premisses that are known with certainty, conclusions which go far beyond the empirical data on which they are based. And particularly since Hume and Kant philosophers have tended to be very sceptical about such a possibility. On the other hand we do have good general grounds for expecting to be able to confirm, provisionally but sometimes quite strongly, hypotheses that go far beyond the observational data that support them, and to confirm them in a sense that makes it reasonable for us to rely, for practical purposes, on their being either true or at any rate fairly close to the truth. The successful growth of the empirical sciences over the last 400 years justifies such a general expectation, no matter what problems there may still be in developing a satisfactory theory of the confirmation of hypotheses or of the justification of inductive reasoning. Though the theologians of the past wanted much more, many thinkers today would be content if theism were as well confirmed as one of the better-established scientific theories. So we might well consider whether there is a good inductive or hypothesis-confirming variant of the cosmological argument; and this is what Swinburne has tried to present.[15]

Swinburne prefixes to his whole discussion of the existence of a god an account of inductive reasoning in general. The statement that a hypothesis is 'confirmed' by certain evidence is ambiguous: it may mean that the evidence has raised the probability of the hypothesis as compared with what it was, or would have been, apart from that evidence; or it may mean that the evidence makes the hypothesis

[15] In Chapter 7 of *The Existence of God* (Oxford University Press, 1979). References in the text are to pages in this work.

more likely than not to be true. Swinburne speaks of a 'good C-inductive argument', meaning one in which the premises or evidence confirm the conclusion or hypothesis in the former sense, and of a 'good P-inductive argument' where they confirm it in the latter sense. As he says, it is harder to tell when we have a good P-inductive argument than when we have a good C-inductive argument. But in either case it is a question of an *argument*: we are concerned with relations of non-deductive support between certain evidence, in the light of some body of background knowledge or belief, and a hypothesis or conclusion. Any judgment that we reasonably make will be provisional, in that further evidence, or a change in the background knowledge or belief, may alter the degree of confirmation or the balance of probabilities, and one important kind of change in the background is the introduction of further, rival, possible explanatory hypotheses, or a change in the initial probability of such hypotheses.

There is an important principle which serves as a criterion for a good C-inductive argument. A hypothesis is confirmed by certain evidence if and only if (apart from or prior to that evidence's being observed) the addition of the hypothesis to the background knowledge or belief makes it more probable that that evidence would occur than it would be in relation to the background knowledge or belief alone. Symbolically, if 'h' stands for the hypothesis, 'e' for the evidence, 'k' for the background knowledge or belief, and '$P(x/y)$' for the probability of x in relation to y, then h is confirmed—in the sense of having its probability raised—by e if and only if $P(e/h\&k) > P(e/k)$. Or, equivalently, a hypothesis is in this sense confirmed by evidence if and only if that evidence would have been more likely to occur if the hypothesis had been true than if it had been false: h is confirmed by e if and only if $P(e/h\&k) > P(e/\sim h\&k)$. In other words, the evidence raises the probability of the hypothesis if and only if the addition of the hypothesis raises the antecedent probability of the evidence. This holds provided that the initial probability of the hypothesis in relation to the background knowledge or belief is not zero.

This principle may be illustrated by a simple detective story example. The finding, in the dried mud of a path, of footmarks which closely match Fred's shoes in shape, size, and degree of wear, and the distances between which match the ordinary length of his stride, makes it more likely that Fred walked along that path when it was last wet than it would have been without this evidence. Why? Because the hypothesis that Fred walked there then raises the probability that there would now be just such footmarks as compared with what it would be without that hypothesis, or on the supposition that he did not walk there then. If our background information makes it quite likely that there would be such marks even if Fred had not walked there—for example, if Fred has a twin brother who frequently borrows Fred's shoes and who uses that path—the addition of the hypothesis that Fred walked there does not raise the antecedent probability of the footmarks so much (since it was fairly high without that hypothesis, or even in relation to the denial of that hypothesis), and finding the marks is no longer so good a confirmation that Fred was there. Again (even if Fred has no twin brother) if our background knowledge makes it impossible that Fred should have walked on the path when it was last wet—for example, if Fred died before the last heavy rain—then although the addition of the hypothesis would raise the antecedent probability of that evidence, the evidence cannot confirm the hypothesis: its zero initial probability cannot be raised.

This principle concerns C-inductive arguments, the conditions for the raising of the probability of a hypothesis by evidence. When we come to P-inductive arguments, to the question whether the evidence makes the hypothesis on balance more likely than not, the initial probability of the hypothesis is very significant. Even if the evidence *raises* the probability of the hypothesis in comparison with what it was otherwise, it may fail to make it more likely than not, because the initial probability of the hypothesis was low. This was illustrated in our discussion of miracles: because the initial probability of a miracle's occurring is so low, it would need very good evidence indeed to make it more likely than not that one had occurred. Even evidence which the miracle's occurrence would explain and make probable, but which would have been very unlikely to come about without the miracle, may be insufficient to overcome the antecedent improbability of the miracle so as to make it now more likely than not that it occurred.[16]

These can be taken as agreed principles of inductive reasoning; the problem is to apply them to the cosmological argument. Swinburne's first point is an adaptation of one of Leibniz's. Even if the universe has an infinite history in which each event is causally explained by the conjunction of laws and earlier events, that history as a whole is still unexplained. It might have been radically different—either with different laws or with the same laws but different specific situations all the way along—or there might have been nothing at all; no

[16] Cf. Chapter I above.

explanation has been given to show why neither of these possibilities was fulfilled. But, secondly, Swinburne suggests, the hypothesis that there is a god would to some extent explain the existence and the actual history of the universe. He is claiming that there is a kind of explanation, quite different from causal explanation, which is used when we explain something as the intentional action of a rational being; he calls this 'personal explanation'. On the assumption that there is a god such as traditional theism proclaims, it follows that he could make a physical universe if he chose, and that he might have had some reason to do so. Swinburne does not, indeed, say that the hypothesis (h) that there is such a god makes it very probable that (e) there should be such a universe as this:

However I do not claim that $P(e/h.k)$ is especially high. $P(e/h.k)$ measures how likely it is if there is a God that there will be a physical universe. The choice before God among worlds to create includes a world where there is just God; a world where there are one or more finite non-physical objects (e.g. non-embodied spirits); a world consisting of a simple physical universe (e.g. just one round steel ball); and a world which is a complex physical universe. There are good reasons why God should make a complex physical universe. For such a universe can be beautiful, and that is good; and also it can be a theatre for finite agents to develop and make of it what they will ... But I cannot see that God has overriding reason to make such a universe ... Nor can I see that he has overriding reason to make or not to make any alternative world. (pp. 130-1)

Swinburne is not saying, then, that this is obviously the best of all possible worlds; so $P(e/h\&k)$ is not high. On the other hand, he thinks that $P(e/k)$ is still lower: a complex physical universe is 'very unlikely to come about but for God's agency'. Consequently we do have that $P(e/h\&k) > P(e/k)$, and therefore that there is a good C-inductive argument from the existence of a complex physical universe to the existence of the god of traditional theism.

As we have seen, this will hold only if $P(h/k)$, the initial probability of the existence of such a god, is not zero. Let us grant this. Still, all that is being said is that the existence of a complex physical universe *raises* the likelihood of a god, makes it more probable than it would have been otherwise, that is, if there had been no such universe. But it is hard to see how this helps us. How can we even think about the antecedent probability that there should be a god, given that there was no such universe? Presumably we must think of an initial probability of there being a god, relative only to tautological information, and if we have rejected the ontological argument this will be pretty low. But there is very little analogy with Fred's case, where it was, perhaps, apart from the footmarks, not very likely that he had walked along that path, but the discovery of the footmarks makes it much more probable. The trouble is that if the evidence, *e*, is to be that there is a complex physical universe, then the background know-ledge or belief *k* must exclude this, and so will be able to include only logical and mathematical truths. What likelihood could the god-hypothesis have had in relation to these?

We may be asking the wrong question, then, if we ask whether there is a good C-inductive argument from the sheer existence of a complex physical universe to the existence of a god. Swinburne's summary puts the issue differently:

> There is quite a chance that if there is a God he will make something of the finitude and complexity of a universe. It is very unlikely that a universe would exist uncaused, but rather more likely that God would exist uncaused. The existence of the universe is strange and puzzling. It can be made com-prehensible if we suppose that it is brought about by God. This supposition postulates a simpler beginning of explanation than does the supposition of an uncaused universe, and that is grounds for believing the former supposi-tion to be true. (pp. 131-2)

We are now comparing the two rival hypotheses, one that there is no further cause or explanation of the complex physical universe, the other that there is a god who created it. That there is this universe is common ground, shared by the two hypotheses. Swinburne is argu-ing that in relation to our background knowledge—which can now include everything that we ordinarily know about ourselves and the world, though it must exclude any specifically religious beliefs—it is more likely that there should be an uncaused god who created the world than simply an uncaused universe—that is, a universe with internal causal relationships, but no further cause for its basic laws being as they are or for its being there at all. The analogy would be with the reasoning in which we postulate a common ancestor for a group of similar manuscripts, on the ground that their other-wise unexplained and therefore improbable resemblances can be explained as being due to their having been copied, directly or indirectly, from this ancestor; the surviving-manuscripts-plus-common-ancestor hypothesis is more acceptable than a surviving-manuscripts-with-no-common-ancestor hypothesis.

But now the fact that the uncaused universe would, by definition, have no further explanation does not justify the claim that it is 'strange and puzzling' or 'very unlikely'. The mere fact that it is a

complex physical universe does not mean that it includes anything
comparable to the resemblances between our manuscripts that would
be surprising if not further explained. (The suggestion that some
specific features of the universe are surprising in this way will be
considered in our discussion of the argument from consciousness and
the argument for design in Chapters 7 and 8.) On the other side, the
hypothesis of divine creation *is* very unlikely. Although *if* there were
a god with the traditional attributes and powers, he would be able
and perhaps willing to create such a universe as this, we have to
weigh in our scales the likelihood or unlikelihood *that* there is a god
with these attributes and powers. And the key power, involved in
Swinburne's use of 'personal explanation', is that of fulfilling intentions *directly*, without any physical or causal mediation, without
materials or instruments. There is nothing in our background knowledge that makes it comprehensible, let alone likely, that anything
should have such a power. All our knowledge of intention-fulfilment
is of *embodied* intentions being fulfilled *indirectly* by way of bodily
changes and movements which are *causally* related to the intended
result, and where the ability thus to fulfil intentions itself has a *causal
history*, either of evolutionary development or of learning or of both.
Only by ignoring such key features do we get an analogue of the
supposed divine action. But even apart from this I see no plausibility
in the statement that it is 'rather more likely that God would exist
uncaused'. Swinburne's backing for this is that 'the supposition that
there is a God is an extremely simple supposition; the postulation of
a God of infinite power, knowledge, and freedom is the postulation
of the simplest kind of person which there could be', whereas 'There
is a complexity, particularity, and finitude about the universe which
cries out for explanation' (p. 130). (It is somewhat ironic that whereas
God seemed to Anselm and others to be self-explanatory because he
is something than which nothing greater can be conceived, he now
seems to Swinburne to be relatively self-explanatory because he is
simple.) But, first, the 'simplicity' achieved by taking everything to
infinity is bought at the cost of asserting a whole series of real actual
infinites, about which, as I mentioned, many thinkers, like al Ghazali
above, have had doubts. Secondly, the particularity has not been
removed, but only shelved: we should have to postulate particulari-
ties in God, to explain his choice of the particular universe he decided
to create. And the very notion of a non-embodied spirit, let alone an
infinite one, is intrinsically improbable in relation to our background
knowledge, in that our experience reveals nothing of the sort.

Some of the themes we encountered in dealing with the older forms of cosmological argument recur here. Like Leibniz, Swinburne is looking for explanation and intelligibility. He does not, like Leibniz, demand a complete explanation, a sufficient reason for everything, or intelligibility through and through; but he is trying to minimize the unexplained part of our total picture. But without introducing the concept of something that contains its own sufficient reason, or whose essence includes existence—unsatisfactory though, in the end, these notions are—he has nothing to support the claim that by adding a god to the world we *reduce* the unexplained element. Although his starting-point is like Leibniz's, his conclusion is more like that of the *kalam* argument, in taking creation by a person as the one satisfactory beginning of things. But when we look hard at it, such 'personal explanation' is not a satisfactory beginning at all, and certainly not one that is given any initial probability by the ordinary information that we have to take as our background knowledge.

The prospects for an inductive or probabilistic or hypothesis-confirming variant of the cosmological argument are, therefore, no better than those for a demonstrative one. However, our criticisms have been directed particularly against a *cosmological* argument in the sense explained at the beginning of this chapter, that is, one whose empirical datum is either the mere fact that there is a world at all or such very general facts about it as that there is change or motion or causation. These criticisms leave open the possibility that the hypothesis that there is a god may be confirmed by evidence of more detailed and specific kinds, for example by the existence of conscious beings, or the presence of what have been seen as 'marks of design'. This possibility will be examined in Chapters 7 and 8; but we shall turn first, in Chapter 6, to evidence of another sort.

6

Moral Arguments for the Existence of a God

(a) *A Popular Line of Thought*

I T is often suggested that morality requires and presupposes religion, and that moral thinking will therefore support theistic beliefs. A familiar line of popular thought runs somewhat like this. Moral principles tell us what we must do, whether we like it or not. That is, they are commands, and such commands must have a source, a commander. But the requirements of morality go beyond what any human authority demands of us, and they sometimes require us to resist all human authorities. Moral requirements go beyond, and sometimes against, what the law prescribes, or the state, or our friends, or any organized church, or the public opinion of any community, even a world-wide one. They must therefore be the commands of some more than human, and hence supernatural, authority. Also, if these commands are to overrule, as they claim to do, all other considerations, we must have an adequate motive for obeying them no matter what threats or temptations urge us to disobey. Such a motive can be supplied only by our knowing that there is a being who has both the will and the power to give rewards and to impose penalties which outweigh all worldly losses and gains. Morality needs a god, therefore, both as a supreme source of commands and as an all-powerful wielder of sanctions to enforce them. Besides, moral thinking includes a confident demand for justice, an assurance that what is unfair and unjust cannot in the end prevail, and justice requires that there should be some power which will somehow balance happiness with desert.

Such an argument has, perhaps, seldom served as an original ground of religious belief; but it has seemed to many to be a powerful reinforcement for that belief, and, in particular, a strong reason for continuing to adhere to it when it is threatened in some other way. It is felt that if theistic beliefs are given up, moral convictions will lose their point and their force, and also their determinacy. Religious beliefs that we see some ground for doubting are thus buttressed by the feeling that we can neither abandon morality nor leave it without religious support.

I shall come back later to this popular line of thought. But first I want to examine several different and even incompatible philosophical versions of the argument from morality, each of which can be seen as a development or refinement of some elements in the popular line of thought. These versions are ones put forward by Newman and by Kant, and one that is considered, but not endorsed, by Sidgwick.

(b) *Newman: Conscience as the Creative Principle of Religion*

Newman, in *A Grammar of Assent*, starts from the thesis that 'Conscience has a legitimate place among our mental acts'; he compares it in this respect with memory, reasoning, imagination, and the sense of beauty. He claims that 'in this special feeling, which follows on the commission of what we call right or wrong, lie the materials for the real apprehension of a Divine Sovereign and Judge'. Newman distinguishes two aspects of conscience. On the one hand it is a moral sense which supplies us with 'the elements of morals', particular judgements about what we must or must not do, 'such as may be developed by the intellect into an ethical code'. On the other hand it is a sense of duty which enforces these prescriptions. It is on this second aspect, on conscience as 'a sanction of right conduct', that Newman relies. This side of conscience, he suggests, 'does not repose on itself, but vaguely reaches forward to something beyond self, and dimly discovers a sanction higher than self for its decisions, as is evidenced in that keen sense of obligation and responsibility which informs them'. In this respect it is, he says, quite unlike 'taste'—that is, the aesthetic faculty, the sense of beauty—which 'is its own evidence, appealing to nothing beyond its own sense of the beautiful or the ugly, and enjoying the specimens of the beautiful simply for their own sake'. Pursuing this contrast, he says that 'Conscience has an intimate bearing on our affections and emotions'. Someone who recognizes that his conduct has not been beautiful does not feel any fear on that account. But someone who recognizes his own conduct as immoral 'has a lively sense of responsibility and guilt, though the act be no offence against society,—of distress and apprehension, even though it may be of present service to him,—of compunction and regret, though in itself it be most pleasurable,—of confusion of face, though it may have no witnesses'. Such affections, Newman says, 'are correlative with persons'. 'If, as is the case, we feel responsibility, are ashamed, are frightened, at transgressing the voice of conscience, this implies that there is One to whom we are responsible, before whom we are ashamed, whose claims upon us we fear.' And equally the enjoyment of a good conscience implies a person in whose approval we are happy. 'These feelings in us are such as require for their exciting cause an intelligent being.' Yet there is no earthly person who systematically fills this role. Conscience, therefore, must be related to a supernatural and divine person: 'and thus the phenomena of Conscience, as a dictate, avail to impress the imagination with the picture of a Supreme Governor, a Judge, holy, just, powerful, all-seeing, retributive, and [are] the creative principle of religion, as the Moral Sense is the principle of ethics'.[1]

I suggested above that the popular moral argument is seldom an original ground of religious belief. Newman is not here denying this, but making the rather different suggestion that not the argument but the actual experience of conscience is the original ground of such belief, that the sense of duty and responsibility—that is, answerability—gives rise to religion in much the same way that the other aspect of conscience, the moral sense, gives rise to ethical beliefs. However, he is not only making this genetic claim: he is also saying that the phenomena of conscience are a good reason for theistic beliefs. So understood, his argument rests on three premises: that conscience is legitimate or authoritative; that it looks beyond the agent himself to a further imperative and a higher sanction; and that these must stem from a person, an intelligent being, if they are to arouse powerful emotions with exactly the tone of those that moral awareness involves. If we grant all three premises, we must admit that the argument is cogent, though the god that it introduces need not have the infinite attributes of Descartes's god, or Anselm's. But must we grant all three premises? In fact this argument faces a dilemma. If we take conscience at its face value and accept as really valid what it asserts, we must say that there is a rational prescriptivity about certain kinds of action in their own right: that they are of this or that kind is in itself a reason for doing them or for refraining from them. There is a to-be-done-ness or a not-to-be-done-ness involved *in that kind of action in itself*. If so, there is no need to look beyond this to

[1] J. H. Newman, *A Grammar of Assent* (Longmans, London, 1870), Chapter 5.

any supernatural person who commands or forbids such action. Equally the regret, guilt, shame, and fear associated with the consciousness of having done wrong, although normally such feelings arise only in relations with persons, are in this special case natural and appropriate: what conscience, taken at its face value, tells us is that this is how one should feel about a wrong action simply in itself. That is, if we whole-heartedly accept Newman's first premiss, we must reject the second and the third. But if we do not take conscience at its face value, if we seek critically to understand how conscience has come into existence and has come to work as it does, then we do indeed find persons in the background, but human persons, not a divine one. If we stand back from the experience of conscience and try to understand it, it is overwhelmingly plausible to see it as an introjection into each individual of demands that come from other people; in the first place, perhaps, from his parents and immediate associates, but ultimately from the traditions and institutions of the society in which he has grown up, or of some special part of that society which has had the greatest influence upon him. In thus understanding conscience we do, admittedly, look beyond conscience itself and beyond the agent himself, but we look to natural, human, sources, not to a god. We are now in a way accepting Newman's second and third premisses, but modifying the first. It is not easy to accept all three. Newman's argument walks, as it were, a tight-rope, allowing to conscience, as it claims, an authority and an origin independent of all human feelings and demands, and yet not endorsing its claim to complete autonomy. But it is arbitrary to choose just this degree of critical reinterpretation, no more and no less.

Perhaps Newman will rely not on conscience in general, as a mode of thinking almost universal among human beings, but on the particular form of conscience which already ties its moral ideas to belief in a god. If he takes this special form of conscience at its face value, he can indeed assert all three premisses; but then his argument will carry conviction only with those who already accept his conclusion. Addressed to a wider public or to an initially open-minded audience, it becomes the hopelessly weak argument that there must be a god because some people believe that there is a god and have incorporated this belief into their moral thought. Something more would be needed to show that this special form of moral thinking is distinctively valid, and this would have to include an independent argument precisely for the existence of a god of the appropriate sort.

This criticism may be restated in terms of the confirmation of hypotheses by evidence, which is undermined by the availability of better rival explanations. The phenomena of conscience to which Newman draws attention could indeed be explained by the hypothesis that there is a supernatural person with the traditional theistic attributes, or some rough approximation to them, of whose presence and demands and attitudes and powers everyone, in thinking morally, is at least dimly aware. But there are at least two rival hypotheses which would explain these phenomena equally well: these are ethical objectivism or intuitionism on the one hand, and the naturalistic, psychological, account of the origin of conscience on the other.[2] Since there are these alternative explanations, of which at least the second is intrinsically less demanding, less metaphysically improbable, than the theistic one, the latter is not significantly confirmed by the phenomena which, I concede, it would explain.

(c) *Kant: God as a Presupposition of Morality*

In the *Critique of Pure Reason* Kant argues that there is no sound speculative proof of the existence of a god. We have already referred to his criticisms of the ontological and cosmological arguments, and we shall see what he says against the design argument in Chapter 8. But in the *Critique of Practical Reason* he suggests that moral reasoning can achieve what speculative reasoning cannot, and that the existence of a god, and also affirmative solutions to the other great metaphysical questions of the immortality of the soul and the freedom of the will, can be defended as being necessarily presupposed in moral consciousness.[3]

Kant's view is much further than Newman's from the popular line of thought with which we began. He stresses the autonomy of morality, to which I appealed in the first horn of the dilemma used to criticize Newman's argument. What is morally right and obligatory is so, Kant holds, in itself, and can be rationally seen in itself to be so. Each rational being is, as such, competent to determine the moral law, to prescribe moral commands to himself, and therefore does not need God to command him—or even, it would seem, to advise him. 'Moreover, it is not meant by this that it is necessary to suppose the

---

[2] Cf. my *Hume's Moral Theory* (Routledge & Kegan Paul, London, 1980), especially pp. 145–50.

[3] I. Kant, *Critique of Practical Reason*, e.g. in T. K. Abbott, *Kant's Theory of Ethics* (Longmans, London, 1927), especially Part I, Book II, Chapter 2. References in the text to this work and to Kant's *Metaphysic of Morals* are to the pages in the German edition of Rosenkranz and Schubert, given at the top of each page in Abbott.

existence of God *as a basis of all obligation in general* (for this rests
... simply on the autonomy of reason itself).' (267) Moral agents, or
rational beings, are the citizens of an ideal commonwealth, making
universal laws for themselves and one another. Morality is corrupted
if it is derived from prudence and self-interest: divine rewards and
punishments, therefore, far from supplying a necessary motive for
morality, would introduce heteronomy, substituting an alien and
morally worthless motive for the only genuinely valuable one of
respect for the moral law.

However, Kant finds another and more appropriate place for a
god in the moral universe. His positive argument starts from the
notion of the *summum bonum*, the highest good, which, he says, is
not merely moral rectitude but also includes happiness. Virtue and
happiness together constitute the highest good for a person, and the
distribution of happiness in proportion to morality constitutes the
highest good for a possible world. Whereas the Epicureans made the
mistake of reducing morality to the pursuit of happiness, the Stoics
made the opposite mistake of either leaving happiness out of their
conception of the highest good, or—what amounts to the same
thing—identifying happiness simply with the consciousness of virtue.
In contrast with both these mistakes, an adequate conception of the
highest good must include both virtue and happiness, but each in its
own right. Now since these two elements in the highest good are
independent of one another, there is no logical necessity that they
should go together, and hence no *a priori* guarantee that the realization of this highest good is even possible. Equally, there is no natural,
causal, guarantee of this. Happiness (in this life) depends largely on
what happens in the natural world, but the moral choices of rational
beings are not to any great extent in control of this: our moral efforts
cannot causally ensure that those who will and act rightly will be
happy. Nor does nature as such conform to a moral standard. But,
Kant says, moral thought tells us that we must take the highest good
as a supreme end; that is, 'we ought to endeavour to promote the
highest good, which must, therefore, be possible'. He infers that 'the
existence of a cause of all nature, distinct from nature itself, and
containing the principle ... of the exact harmony of happiness with
morality' is *postulated* in moral thought. 'The highest good is possible
in the world only on the supposition of a Supreme Being having a
causality corresponding to moral character'—that is, a god. Since it
is for us a duty to promote the highest good, there is 'a necessity
connected with duty as a requisite, that we should presuppose the

possibility of this *summum bonum*; and as this is possible only on condition of the existence of God . . . it is morally necessary to assume the existence of God'. But since happiness in this life is pretty plainly not proportioned to morality, it is also necessary to assume that individuals survive in a life after death; Kant has also argued separately for such immortality, again as a presupposition of moral thought, as being necessary to allow for an indefinite progress towards perfection which is involved in the first half of the highest good, complete virtue or 'the *perfect accordance* of the mind with the moral law'. (265–7)

It is not easy to decide just how Kant meant these conclusions to be interpreted. On the one hand he argues for 'the primacy of pure practical reason in its union with the speculative reason', saying that when certain propositions 'are *inseparably* attached *to the practical interest* of pure reason', theoretical reason must accept them, and 'must try to compare and connect them with everything that it has in its power as speculative reason' (261), and this is plainly intended to apply to the propositions asserting the immortality of the soul and the existence of a god, as well as the freedom of the will. But on the other hand, asking whether our knowledge is 'actually extended in this way by pure practical reason', and whether that is '*immanent* in practical reason which for the speculative was only *transcendent*', Kant replies 'Certainly, but *only in a practical point of view*'—which seems to take away what it gives. We do not in this way gain knowledge of our souls or of the Supreme Being as they are in themselves. Theoretical reason 'is compelled to admit *that there are such objects*, although it is not able to define them more closely'; knowledge of them has been given 'only for practical use'. In fact speculative reason will work with regard to these objects only 'in a negative manner', to remove '*anthropomorphism*, as the source of *superstition*, or seeming extension of these conceptions by supposed experience; and . . . *fanaticism*, which promises the same by means of supersensible intuition'. (276–9) He seems to be saying that the existence of a god and the immortality of the soul can be established as facts by the arguments from morality, but only in a highly indeterminate form. Yet he hints also at a more sceptical position, that the existence of a god, the freedom of the will, and the immortality of the soul cannot be established as facts, even by reasoning based on the moral consciousness, but can only be shown to be necessarily presupposed in that consciousness, to be, as it were, implicit in its content. In other words, we as rational beings cannot help thinking morally, and if we develop our moral thinking fully and coherently we cannot help supposing that there is a god; but whether in fact there is a god remains an open question. Kant says that 'the righteous man may say: I *will* that there be a God, that my existence in this world be also an existence outside the chain of physical causes, and in a pure world of the understanding, and lastly, that my duration be endless; I firmly abide by this, and will not let this faith be taken from me; for in this instance alone my interest, because I *must* not relax anything of it, inevitably determines my judgement', and he speaks of a *faith of pure practical reason*, which, he admits, is an 'unusual notion'. (289–92)

But in whichever of these ways we interpret his conclusion, Kant's argument is open to criticism. The most glaring weakness is in the step from the proposition that 'we ought to seek the highest good' to the claim that it 'must therefore be possible'. Even if, as Kant argues elsewhere, 'ought' implies 'can', the thesis that we ought to seek to promote the highest good implies only that we can *seek to promote* it, and perhaps, since rational seeking could not be completely fruitless, that we can to some extent actually *promote* it. But this does not require that the full realization of the highest good should be possible. For example, it is thoroughly rational to try to improve the condition of human life, provided that some improvement is possible; there is no need to entertain vain hopes for its perfection. And even for the *possibility* of that full realization the most that would be needed is the possible existence of a wholly good and all-powerful governor of the world; the actual existence of such a governor would ensure not merely the possibility but the actuality of the highest good. Kant might say that we can and should aspire to the ultimate realization of the highest good, and that a *hope* for such ultimate realization is necessarily involved in moral thought. But he cannot claim that even its possible realization is a necessary postulate of moral thought in general; it is not even a necessary postulate of that particular sort of moral theory which Kant himself developed. The willing of universal laws by and for all rational beings as such could be a strictly autonomous activity.

There are, indeed, recurrent tensions between Kant's theism and his stress on the autonomy of morals. In sharp contrast with the popular view, and with Newman's, Kant holds that neither our knowledge of God and of his will, nor that will itself, is the foundation of the moral law. Yet because (as he thinks) we have to postulate a god who *also* wills these laws, as does every other free and rational will, he still calls them 'commands of the Supreme Being', but in a sense which is only a pale shadow of what is intended by most theological moralists. Again, Kant holds that no 'desired results' are 'the proper motive of obedience' to these laws, indeed that fear of punishment or hope of reward 'if taken as principles, would destroy the whole moral worth of actions'. Yet his belief that there is something appropriate about the *proportioning* of happiness to morality—a retributive thesis—again seems to be a pale shadow of the popular reliance on punishments and rewards. Is not this true also of his stress (after all) on happiness, whose conjunction with virtue we are to take not merely as a legitimate hope but as a *postulate* of moral thought? Would not a thoroughgoing recognition of the autonomy of morals lead rather to the Stoic view that morality needs no actual happiness beyond the consciousness of right action itself?

Kant himself seems to have been aware of these difficulties, and a passage in his *Metaphysic of Morals* suggests a quite different proof of God's existence: again a moral proof, but one which anticipates Newman's argument about conscience.

Now this original intellectual and ... moral capacity, called *conscience*, has this peculiarity in it, that although its business is a business of man with himself, yet he finds himself compelled by his reason to transact it as if at the command *of another person* ... in all duties the conscience of the man must regard *another* than himself as the judge of his actions ... Now this other may be an actual or a merely ideal person which reason frames to itself. Such an idealized person .... must be one who knows the heart ... at the same time he must also be *all-obliging*, that is, must be or be conceived as a person in respect of whom all duties are to be regarded as his commands ... Now since such a moral being must at the same time possess all power (in heaven and earth), since otherwise he could not give his commands their proper effect, and since such a moral being possessing power over all is called God, hence conscience must be conceived as the subjective principle of a responsibility for one's deeds before God; nay, this latter concept is contained (though it be only obscurely) in every moral self-consciousness. (293–4)

Here Kant is vacillating between the recognition of the merely psychological phenomenon of the setting up of an ideal spectator (Adam Smith's 'man within the breast'[4]) and the suggestion that moral thought has at least to postulate the real existence of an outside authority—but how weak a reason he offers for the ascription of all power to this moral being! In any case, in so far as this argument anticipates Newman's, it is open to the same criticisms.

[4] A. Smith, *The Theory of Moral Sentiments* (Edinburgh, 1808), Part III, Chapter 2, p. 308.

We need not labour these internal tensions and vacillations. What is important is that even if moral thought is as Kant describes it, it does not follow that such thought has even to postulate the existence of a god, let alone that we can infer the real existence of a god from the character of that thought.

(d) *Sidgwick: the Duality of Practical Reason*

Another variant of the moral argument is clearly stated, but not endorsed, by Sidgwick.[5] This starts from 'the duality of practical reason', the fact that both prudential egoism and the commands of conscience are practically reasonable, each without qualification, and yet that, if there is neither a god nor anything like a god, they will not always coincide. Its premisses are:

1. What I have most reason to do is always what will best secure my own happiness in the long run.
2. What I have most reason to do is always what morality requires.
3. If there is no moral government of the universe, what will best secure my own happiness is not always what morality requires.

The first two of these premisses would indeed entail that prudence and morality always coincide; for if they required different choices in the same situation, it could not be true that each of these different choices was the one that I had most reason to make: that is, these premisses could not both be true. But then, if prudence and morality will always coincide only if there is a moral government of the universe, it follows that there must be such a government, that is, either a god or something like a god.

This argument is plainly valid, though its conclusion is not quite what traditional theism asserts: moral government would not need to include a personal god. But are the premisses true? Sidgwick, for one, regarded the first two as inescapable intuitions about what is reasonable in conduct—taking the second as prescribing social duty in a utilitarian sense. Also, if there is no moral government of the universe, then presumably the present life is all we have to take into account; and it is an easily established empirical truth that in this life the demands of utilitarian morality—the promotion of the general happiness—do not always coincide with what will best promote one's own happiness. This, then, establishes the third premiss.

[5] H. Sidgwick, *The Methods of Ethics* (Macmillan, London, 1874), Book IV, Chapter VI.

But although Sidgwick, for these reasons, accepted all three premisses, he did not accept the conclusion. He preferred to admit that
there is a fundamental and unresolved chaos in our practical reasoning, and that the human intellect cannot frame a fully satisfactory
ideal of rational conduct: 'the mere fact that I cannot act rationally
without assuming a certain proposition, does not appear to me,—as
it does to some minds,—a sufficient ground for believing it to be
true'. Equally he rejects what he calls 'the Kantian resource of thinking myself under a moral necessity to regard all my duties *as if they
were* commandments of God, although not entitled to hold specula-
tively that any such Supreme Being exists "as Real" '. (In this reference to 'the Kantian resource', Sidgwick is clearly favouring the
second of the two interpretations of Kant offered above; but the
previous comment on what appears 'to some minds' would apply to
the first.) Sidgwick adds: 'I am so far from feeling bound to believe
for purposes of practice what I see no ground for holding as a
speculative truth, that I cannot even conceive the state of mind
which these words seem to describe, except as a momentary half-
wilful irrationality, committed in a violent access of philosophic
despair'.

Is Sidgwick perverse in refusing to accept this conclusion? I think
not. It is rather that he has put his finger on the basic weakness of
almost every form of moral argument for the existence of a god. A
set of beliefs, even if they are called 'intuitions', about how one ought
to act cannot be a good reason for settling a factual issue, a way of
determining what is the case, or even for deciding what to 'believe
for practical purposes'. Practical choices must be based on factual
beliefs, not the other way round, though beliefs *alone*, of course, will
not determine choices.

To see this, let us take an analogous case. Most of those who have
discussed imperative logic have assumed that such syllogisms as this
are valid: 'Eat no animal fats; butter is an animal fat; so don't eat
butter'. But if that syllogism is valid, so must this one be: 'Eat no
animal fats; you may eat butter; so butter is not an animal fat'. That
is, there can be a valid syllogism with one imperative and one permissive premiss, and this would still be valid if the permissive premiss
were strengthened to an imperative—in our example, to 'Eat butter'.
But such a pair of imperative premisses (or an imperative along with
a permissive one) could not objectively establish the truth of the
factual conclusion. They show only that anyone who coherently
issues both imperatives (or the imperative and the permission) must

believe the conclusion to be true. Again, what should we say about a general who accepted these three premises:

1. If the enemy are advancing in overwhelming strength, then, if we do not withdraw, our army will be wiped out;
2. We must not allow our army to be wiped out;
3. We must not withdraw, because that would mean letting down our allies;

and concluded, on these grounds alone, that the enemy were not advancing in overwhelming strength?

In all such cases, what it is rational to do depends upon what the facts are; but we cannot take what we are inclined to think that it is rational to do as evidence about those facts. To use a conjunction of practical judgements to try to establish what the facts are would be to put the cart before the horse. We must rely on speculative reasoning first to determine what is the case, and then frame our practical and moral beliefs and attitudes in the light of these facts. There is a direction of supervenience: since what *is* morally and practically rational supervenes upon what is the case, what it is rational to *believe* with a view to practice, or to *choose* to do, must similarly supervene upon what it is rational to believe about what is the case.

But this is what Kant was denying when, as we saw, he maintained the primacy of pure practical reason. He refers, indeed, to Thomas Wizenmann, who had brought what is essentially our objection, or Sidgwick's, against his argument. Kant concedes that we cannot argue from a want founded merely on inclination to the reality of its object or of what is needed to satisfy it, but he thinks it is otherwise when we have 'a want of reason springing from an objective determining principle of the will, namely the moral law'. Since it is a duty to realize the *summum bonum* to the utmost of our power, it must be possible, and 'consequently it is unavoidable for every rational being ... to assume what is necessary for its objective possibility. The assumption is as necessary as the moral law, in connection with which alone it is valid' (289, note). Kant admits that where practical reason 'merely regulat[es] the inclinations under the sensible principle of happiness, we could not require speculative reason to take its principles from such a source'. This, he sees, would lead to absurd fantasies. But he thinks that *pure* practical reason, which determines the moral law, is in a different position. 'But if pure reason of itself can be practical and is actually so, as the consciousness of the moral law proves, then it is still only one and the same reason which, whether in a theoretical or a practical point of view, judges according to *a priori* principles . . .' Propositions established in this way, he holds, 'are not additions to its [i.e. reason's] insight, but yet are extensions of its employment in another, namely a practical, aspect . . .' 'Nor', he says, 'could we reverse the order, and require pure practical reason to be subordinate to the speculative, since all interest is ultimately practical, and even that of speculative reason is conditional, and it is only in the practical employment that it is complete.' (261–2)

However, what this last remark can mean is unclear, and the reply to Wizenmann merely repeats the original argument. Nothing has been done to explain how pure practical reason could escape the constraints which, as Kant admits, apply to practical reason in general. If a certain practical principle presupposes certain factual propositions, then reason, however pure, cannot establish the validity of that practical principle without *independently* showing that those factual propositions are true. We cannot therefore use the practical principle to prove that these are truths of fact. This consideration is fatal to Kant's argument in the *Critique of Practical Reason*, just as it is to the argument which Sidgwick formulated, but rejected precisely on this account.

Whether there are other ways of resolving Sidgwick's paradox is not our present concern. It may be that his first two premises do not hold without qualification as principles of practical rationality. But if all such escape routes were blocked, the right conclusion to draw would be the one that Sidgwick himself drew, that there is no fully coherent ideal of practical reason.

(e) *God and the Objectivity of Value*

There is an element in the popular line of thought which has not, as far as I know, been properly examined by philosophers. This is the suggestion that there are objective moral values and prescriptions, but that they are created by God, and indeed require a god to create them.

Philosophers from Plato onwards have repeatedly criticized the suggestion that moral obligations are created by God's commands. The commands of a legitimate human ruler do not *create* obligations: if such a ruler tells you to do X, this makes it obligatory for you to do X only if it is *already* obligatory for you to do whatever the ruler tells you (within the sphere in which X lies). The same applies to God. He can make it obligatory for us to do Y by so commanding only because there is first a general obligation for us to obey him. His commands, therefore, cannot be the source of moral obligation in general: for any obligation that they introduce, there must be a more fundamental obligation that they presuppose. This criticism decisively excludes one way in which it might be thought that God could create morality.

But there is a further problem. On any plausible objectivist view of ethics, moral values, obligations, and the like are held to supervene upon certain non-moral or 'natural' features of situations or actions. If a state of affairs is good or bad, there must be something about it that makes it good or bad, and similarly there must be something other than its rightness or wrongness that makes an action right or wrong. Now what is the logical character of this *supervenience* or *making*? Swinburne takes it to be analytic: 'Once one has specified fully what it is that makes the action wrong, then it will be (given that it is a truth) an analytic truth that an action of that kind is wrong'.[6] But this cannot be right. Objective wrongness, if there is such a thing, is intrinsically prescriptive or action-guiding, it in itself gives or constitutes a reason for not doing the wrong action, and this holds also for some, if not all, other moral features. To say that they are intrinsically action-guiding is to say that the reasons that they give for doing or for not doing something are independent of that agent's desires or purposes. But the natural features on which the moral ones supervene cannot be *intrinsically* action-guiding or reason-giving in this way. Supervenience, then, must be a synthetic connection. But, if so, then a god whose power was limited only by logical, analytic, constraints—that is, not really limited at all—could presumably make there to be, or not to be, such and such relations of supervenience. This *creation of supervenient value* is, of course, quite different from the creation of obligation by command that has been rejected, with good reason, by Plato and his many followers. In this sense it is not absurd to suppose that a god could create moral values. Besides, we might well argue (borrowing, perhaps, from my own discussion elsewhere[7]) that objective intrinsically prescriptive features, supervening upon natural ones, constitute so odd a cluster of qualities and relations that they are most unlikely to have arisen in the ordinary course of events, without an all-powerful god to create them. If, then, there are such intrinsically prescriptive objective

---

[6] *The Existence of God*, p. 177.

[7] Cf. my *Ethics: Inventing Right and Wrong* (Penguin, Harmondsworth, 1977), Chapter 1.

values, they make the existence of a god more probable than it would have been without them. Thus we have, after all, a defensible inductive argument from morality to the existence of a god. The popular line of thought to which I referred at the beginning of this chapter has regularly included some inkling of this truth.

It might be objected that this argument relies on a perverse and unnecessary formulation of ethical objectivism. Rather than sharply distinguish the 'natural' features from the reason-giving moral ones, and see the supervenience of the latter on the former as a puzzling synthetic connection that invites the postulation of a god to explain it, why should not the objectivist say that certain natural features simply do in themselves constitute reasons for or against the actions that involve them? Objectivism would then be the doctrine that an action's being of a certain naturally identifiable kind may in itself be a reason for doing it or for not doing it: that is, that there may be a fact of a peculiarly moral kind. But this is a mere reformulation, which leaves the substance of the problem unchanged. It will then be this alleged moral fact itself that is the initially puzzling item, which the existence of a god may be postulated to explain.

Some thinkers—R. M. Hare, for example—would reject this argument on the ground that the notion of objective intrinsically prescriptive features, supervening on natural ones and therefore synthetically connected with them, is not merely puzzling but incoherent. However, I have argued elsewhere that it is not incoherent,[8] and the oddity of these features is just what is needed to make their existence count significantly in favour of theism. (Both this objection and this reply can, trivially, be adapted to apply to the reformulation sketched in the last paragraph.)

A third objection: why postulate a god, of all things, to explain this initially puzzling matter? The simple answer to this question is that the more intrinsically puzzling something is, the more it requires, to explain it, something whose power is limited only by logical necessity. But we could add that the way in which intrinsic values are believed to be distributed is, on the whole, in accordance with the supposed purposes of a benevolent god. But a more subtle explanation is this: we can understand a human thinker, either as an agent or as a critic, seeing things as to be done or not to be done, where this is a reflection or projection of his own purposiveness; hence if we are to explain an intrinsic to-be-done-ness or not-to-be-done-ness, which is *not* such a reflection or projection, it is natural to take this as an

[8] *Ethics: Inventing Right and Wrong*, pp. 20–5.

injection into reality made by a universal *spirit*, that is, something that has some analogue of human purposiveness.

There are, nevertheless, some difficulties for the proposed argument. If we put it in terms of truths of supervenience, are these synthetic truths necessary or contingent? Do they hold in all possible worlds or only in some? Are there other worlds in which there are quite different truths of supervenience—so that radically different sorts of actions are right or wrong—or none at all? If the range of possible worlds is to cover all logical possibilities, there must be such variations. So a rational agent has not only to identify the natural situation in which he finds himself and reason about it; he has also to ascertain which of various possible worlds *with regard to moral supervenience* is the actual one—for example, whether the actual world is one in which pain is *prima facie* to be relieved, or one in which, other things being equal, pain is to be perpetuated. However, this problem only brings into the open the intuitionist moral epistemology which is at least implicit in any coherent doctrine of objective prescriptivity. Moral values, on such a view, are not discoverable by any purely general reasoning based on natural facts, but only by some kind of intuition: the moral thinker has, as it were, to respond to a value-laden atmosphere that surrounds him in the actual world.

In any case, there is available an adequate alternative explanation of moral thinking which does not require the assumption of objective prescriptivity.[9] In consequence, although the objectivity of prescriptive moral values would give some inductive support to the hypothesis that there is a god, it would be more reasonable to reject the kind of moral objectivity that is required for this purpose than to accept it and use it as a ground for theism.

When this moral objectivism is replaced by a subjectivist or sentimentalist theory, there can, indeed, be yet another form of moral argument for theism. Hutcheson, who bases both moral action and moral judgement on instincts, on natural human tendencies to act benevolently and to approve of benevolent action, says that 'this very moral sense, implanted in rational agents, to approve and admire whatever actions flow from a study of the good of others, is one of the strongest evidences of goodness in the Author of nature'.[10] This really belongs among the arguments for design that we shall consider in Chapter 8; but it is not a strong one, because it is easy to explain

---

[9] *Hume's Moral Theory* (see n. 2 (p. 106) above), *passim*.

[10] F. Hutcheson, *An Inquiry concerning Moral Good and Evil*, Section VII, in *British Moralists*, edited by L. A. Selby-Bigge (Oxford University Press, 1897), Vol. I, p. 176.

this moral sense as a natural product of biological and social evolution, rather than as having been implanted in us by an Author of nature.

Our survey of specific philosphical forms of the moral argument shows both what is wrong and what is right in the popular line of thought with which we began. Morality does not need a god as a supreme source of commands or as a wielder of decisive sanctions. The phenomena of conscience may help causally to produce and maintain theistic belief, but they do not rationally support it. Nor does moral thinking require that the sort of justice incorporated in Kant's highest good should be realized, so it need not postulate a god, or even, more generally, a moral government of the universe, to realize it. There is no good reason for introducing a god even as an essential part of the content of moral thinking. And even if it turned out that firmly held moral—or, more generally, practical—convictions presupposed the existence of a god, such convictions could not be used to show that there is a god: that would have to be shown independently in order to validate those convictions. But if we take a different point of view, and look at moral thinking from the outside, as a phenomenon to be understood and explained, the position is more complicated. If we adopted moral objectivism, we should have to regard the relations of supervenience which connect values and obligations with their natural grounds as synthetic; they would then be in principle something that a god might conceivably create; and since they would otherwise be a very odd sort of thing, the admitting of them would be an inductive ground for admitting also a god to create them. There would be something here in need of explanation, and a being with the power to create what lies outside the bounds of natural plausibility or even possibility might well be the explanation we require. Moral values, their objectivity and their supervenience, would be a continuing miracle in the sense explained in Chapter 1, a constant intrusion into the natural world. But then our post-Humean scepticism about miracles will tell against this whole view. If we adopted instead a subjectivist or sentimentalist account of morality, this problem would not arise. We can find satisfactory biological, sociological, and psychological explanations of moral thinking which account for the phenomena of the moral sense and conscience in natural terms. This approach dissolves away the premiss of our inductive argument, which given that premiss, would have been the one defensible form of moral argument for the existence of a god.

7

The Argument from Consciousness

How could consciousness arise in a purely material universe? How could minds be made out of matter? This difficulty for materialist and naturalist views has been stressed repeatedly and in various forms. Cicero, for example, argued that there is not enough room inside a man's head for the material recording of everything that someone with a good memory (like Cicero himself, who could learn a whole speech by heart) can store up and recall.[1] Locke gave it a central place in his argument for the existence of a god:

If then there must be something eternal, let us see what sort of being it must be. And to that, it is very obvious to reason, that it must necessarily be a *cogitative* being. For it is as impossible to conceive, that ever bare incogitative matter should produce a thinking intelligent being, as that nothing should of itself produce matter. ... Matter, then, by its own strength, cannot produce in itself so much as motion: the motion it has, must also be from eternity, or else be produced, and added to matter by some other being more powerful than matter ... But let us suppose motion eternal too; yet matter, *incogitative matter* and motion ... *could never produce thought* ... you may as rationally expect to produce sense, thought, and knowledge, by putting together in a certain figure and motion, gross particles of matter, as by those that are the very minutest, that do anywhere exist. They knock, impell, and resist one another, just as the greater do, and that is all they can do. So that if we will suppose nothing first, or eternal: *matter* can never begin to be: if we suppose bare matter, without motion, eternal; *motion* can never begin to be: if we suppose only matter and motion first, or eternal; *thought* can never begin to be.[2]

Locke thus argues that the something that exists from eternity must be a 'cogitative being', an eternal mind, and then appeals to

[1] Cicero, *Tusculan Disputations*, Book I, Chapter XXV, 61.
[2] J. Locke, *Essay concerning Human Understanding*, Book IV, Chapter x, Section 10.

other sorts of evidence to support the ascription to this eternal mind of the traditional attributes of God. It is significant that Locke says only that matter and motion cannot *in themselves* produce thought: he admits that we cannot decide, 'by the contemplation of our own *ideas*, without revelation ... whether omnipotency has not given to some systems of matter fitly disposed, a power to perceive and think'. That is, he leaves it open that a mere material being might think, since it is not impossible for us to conceive that God can 'superadd to matter a faculty of thinking'.[3]

Just before the passage quoted, Locke has argued that '*something must be from eternity*'. He seems here to be guilty of an equivocation, which Leibniz rightly criticized, between saying that at every time there was something, and saying that there is some one thing that has existed at all times. It is only the former that would follow from his claim that 'nonentity cannot produce a real being', but it is the latter that he assumes when he goes on to ask 'what sort of thing it must be' that is eternal. Without this fallacious step, the thesis that thought could not have originated from 'incogitative being', such as matter and motion, would yield only the conclusion that there has always been some mind, not that there is one eternal mind.[4] But perhaps Locke's formulation is merely too condensed, and what he intends is a cosmological argument of one of the types that we considered in Section (b) of Chapter 5: whether the regress of causes, or of beings, terminates or not, we need a necessary—that is, at least permanent—being to explain the series as a whole. If so, his argument is undermined by the criticisms we developed there. Nevertheless, if his argument showed even that thought must always be derived from some pre-existing thinking being, this would significantly weaken the materialist position, and so would be an important step towards theism.

Its plausibility, however, rests on too crude a picture of matter, conveyed by the statement that all that material particles in motion, large or small, can do is to 'knock, impell, and resist one another'. The simplicity of this model has been undermined by later physics, and twentieth-century computer technology should at least make us cautious about laying down *a priori* what material structures could not do—for example, no one today could use Cicero's argument about memory. Locke's position is also weakened by his admission

---

[3] *Essay*, Book III, Chapter iv, Section 6.
[4] *Essay*, Book IV, Chapter x, Section 8; G. W. Leibniz, *New Essays concerning Human Understanding*, Book IV, Chapter x (see n. 12 to Chapter 3, p. 62, above).

that God might have given a power to perceive and think to 'systems of matter fitly disposed'. Since he means this literally, distinguishing it from the possibility that God might have attached an immaterial thinking substance to certain material bodies, he is allowing that, as a result of divine intervention, material structures might think after all. That is, he has abandoned any claim to know *a priori* that material structures simply could not be conscious. But if some material structures could be conscious, how can we know *a priori* that material structures cannot *of themselves give rise to* consciousness? Locke's reason for this admission is also revealing. If, instead of supposing that material structures themselves sometimes think, we assumed that there are immaterial substances, minds, or souls, associated with our bodies, we should have to say that matter somehow acts upon these immaterial things (in perception). This is as hard to understand as how material structures could think; yet we have to accept one or other of these. The problem is one that Berkeley saw very clearly: once we admit that there is a material world at all, we cannot deny that material things causally affect consciousness; but then we have no good reason for saying that material things could not be conscious; nor, finally, for saying that material things could not in themselves give rise to consciousness. It was because he realized this that Berkeley wanted to deny that there is a material world at all; but, as we have seen, that is not in the end a defensible view.

However, Locke might reply to our challenge, 'How can we know *a priori* that material structures cannot of themselves give rise to consciousness?', by saying that if material things did think, it could only be by a very elaborate arrangement and mutual adjustment of their parts, that it is very improbable that they should fall of their own accord into such elaborate patterns, and therefore that conscious material beings would require a divine consciousness to bring them into existence. The argument from consciousness, thus interpreted, would be a special case of the argument for design, which will be examined in Chapter 8.

A similar line of thought has been developed by Swinburne.[5] He does not claim to know that material structures *could not* of themselves give rise to consciousness, but only that we cannot find or

[5] *The Existence of God*, Chapter 9. References in the text are to pages in this work. Locke's argument is interpreted in the way indicated, as a special case of the design argument, in M. R. Ayers, 'Mechanism, Superaddition, and the Proof of God's Existence in Locke's Essay', in *Philosophical Review* 90 (1981), pp. 210–51.

envisage any explanation of how this could happen, and he therefore argues that a 'personal explanation', one in terms of the intentional action of an intelligent agent, is more probable: the latter hypothesis can account better for the phenomena of consciousness, and is therefore confirmed by their undeniable occurrence.

Swinburne's main task, therefore, is to demonstrate 'the scientific inexplicability of consciousness'. He begins by arguing against several versions of the extreme materialist view which denies that there are any distinct mental events, holding that consciousness, phenomenal properties, beliefs, decisions, and so on can either be identified without remainder with neurophysiological states and occurrences or eliminated in favour of these, so that we have a complete and adequate account in purely physical terms of all the things that actually occur. Swinburne maintains that it is just evident and unquestionable that 'there are phenomenal properties, blueness, painfulness, smelling of roses, which are not the same as physical properties'. He says that 'Any world-view which denies the existence of experienced sensations of blueness or loudness or pain does not describe how things are—that this is so stares us in the face'. Consequently 'Some kind of dualism of entities or properties or states is inevitable'. Though some philosophers would disagree, I think that in this he is clearly right. I think, however, that all we have strong grounds for asserting is a dualism of properties, where what counts as the occurrence of an irreducibly mental property is just one's having of such and such an experiential or phenomenal content; distinctively mental events can also be admitted if an event is equated with the instantiation of some property at some time. Swinburne develops his argument in terms of a dualism of mental events as distinct from brain-events, but (as he says) the points he wants to make can be put just as well in terms of a dualism of properties.

To establish a complete scientific explanation of mental events, Swinburne says, the materialist would need to take three distinct steps. He would have first to establish either a one–one or a one–many correlation between each kind of mental event and one or more kinds of brain-events. Secondly, he would have to turn this correlation into a causal account: 'To show that the brain-events are the ultimate determinant of what goes on, the materialist will need to show that the occurrence of all mental events is predictable from knowledge of brain-events alone, and that the occurrence of brain-events is explicable in physiological terms . . . whereas the occurrence of all brain-events is not predictable from knowledge of mental events alone'. (pp. 167-8) Thirdly, he would need to show that the ways in which brain-events cause mental events are natural laws, simple enough to be explanatory.

Each of these three steps, he says, presents difficulties. The lack of public observability of mental events will make the establishment of correlations very dubious. Our experience of freedom of choice—if such freedom is not an illusion—means that 'choices cannot be invariably predicted from prior brain-states'. Also, if, as quantum theory seems to say, the basic physical laws are statistical or probabilistic this would leave a gap for the independent operation of intentions, so that what happens would not be completely predictable from the physical side. But Swinburne rests his case mainly on difficulties about the third step, to which I shall come in a moment.

The alleged difficulties for the first two steps are really not very formidable. Swinburne makes them look greater than they are by misrepresenting the materialist's programme. This is not actually to construct an explanation of all mental events in physical terms, but to defend the thesis that there *is* such an explanation in an objective, realist sense, whether or not we shall ever be able to formulate it— that is, that there are natural laws and relationships by which minds and consciousness could have arisen, and therefore probably did arise, out of physical things which had initially no mental properties. In all this discussion, 'explanations' and 'laws' must be taken to be objective entities, distinct from any knowledge or statement of them. The alleged difficulty for the first step was only a difficulty about discovering and establishing correlations: it casts no doubt on the supposition that there are correlations or laws.

There is, indeed, a well-known argument against the existence of psychophysical laws, developed by Donald Davidson and thinkers influenced by him.[6] Here the main idea is that mental predicates or psychological descriptions are subject to constraints quite different from those to which physical terms are subject: mental and physical schemes of description and explanation have 'disparate commitments'. In particular, the ascription to someone of a desire or belief at one time has to cohere with other ascriptions to him of intentions, hopes, fears, expectations, and so on: 'the content of a propositional attitude derives from its place in the pattern'. Terms which have to be looking over their shoulders, as it were, in these directions are not

[6] D. Davidson, 'Mental Events', in *Essays on Actions and Events* (Oxford University Press, 1980); C. McGinn, 'Mental States, Natural Kinds, and Psychophysical Laws', in *Aristotelian Society Supplementary Volume* 52 (1978).

free to mate with physical description. But I would ask: are these psychological descriptions supposed to be *true*? Is there a mental reality which they can capture and describe, or are they just a manner of speaking? More particularly, are there *occurrent* mental states and events which the psychological terms describe, or is psychological talk both dispositional and general, so that what it describes is a person's whole pattern of behaviour over some longish period of time, or even a long-term pattern of interaction between some numbers of persons? If it is the latter, as the phrase 'the holism of the mental' suggests, then indeed we should not expect there to be psycho-physical correlations, and we could infer *a priori* that (as McGinn says) mental predicates do not denote physically definable natural kinds. But then this style of description has little relevance to our present problem: it does not pick out any occurrent states or events or properties which it might be difficult for natural science to explain. If, on the other hand, we confine ourselves to psychological descriptions which identify occurrent mental states, etc.—and such there must in principle be, since we are introspectively aware of the states, etc., which they would describe—then we cannot rule out correlations between these and physical features as either impossible or even improbable *a priori*. For *these* predicates will have a commitment not so much to a whole scheme of psychological description as to *truth about what is occurrently there*, and this may well pull them into line with physical descriptions.

Another popular argument against psychophysical laws is that there cannot be *necessary biconditional* relationships of this sort.[7] A mental state of desire, belief, and so on surely could be realized in widely different material embodiments. If there were Martians, they might have thoughts which could be equated with some of our thoughts, described in the same 'that'-clauses, but it would not be surprising if these were connected with quite different neurophysiological structures from ours. Certainly; but for our present purpose biconditional relationships are not needed. All that the materialist wants are laws saying that wherever there is such and such a physiological state there is such and such a mental state; the converse is not required, so the possibility even of indefinitely various physical realizations of the same mental state is not a difficulty for him. Nor, indeed, does he need these relationships to be *necessary* in a sense that can be challenged by speculations about Martians and the like: it is enough if in the actual world there are causal laws which ensure

7 McGinn, op. cit.

that certain neurophysiological states give rise to certain mental states.

Thus Swinburne's difficulty for the first step dissolves. The first of his difficulties for the second step is obscure. It seems, he says, to an agent 'that the choice is up to him whether to be influenced by rational considerations or not, his choice not being predetermined for him by his brain, character, or environment; and that it is rational considerations, not brain-states which influence him (though not conclusively)'. But that it is rational considerations which influence him is nothing against the materialist view, which of course assumes that the recognition and weighing of rational considerations are themselves encoded somehow in the neurophysiological basis: 'rational considerations, not brain-states' is a false antithesis in the context of an examination of the materialist view. Equally, that the choice is up to *him* is nothing against the materialist theory, which will accept this, but identify *him* with something which has, we have agreed, distinctively mental properties, but still consists of physical elements interrelated in no doubt very complex ways. The fact that the choice is up to him will seem to tell against the materialist programme only if we have first begged the question against that programme by assuming that there is a not-materially-constituted *he* in the field. But perhaps the point is that some choices are not caused at all, and cannot therefore be physically explicable even in principle. This, however, could not be shown by our experience of freedom of choice: there can be no such thing as an experience of, or even as of, an absence of any cause of one's decision. At most the agent could simply not be aware of any cause; but this is not a positive impression of the decision's not being caused. If it turns out that all choices are caused, there will not be even an illusion of freedom in a contra-causal sense to be explained. Still, it may be that some choices have no antecedent sufficient conditions. This would indeed preclude an explanation of them, even in principle, by physical causes. But it would not preclude their being explained by a coexistent physical basis, provided that that basis itself lacked antecedent sufficient causes. And here what Swinburne puts forward as the second difficulty for this second step, the indeterminism of quantum physics, would be rather a help than a difficulty. If physical processes themselves are to some extent indeterministic, then even if some choices have no antecedent sufficient causes they may well be understandable as necessary correlates of some equally uncaused physical occurrences.

However, it is the third step which Swinburne sees as the main difficulty for the materialist. He says that 'In a scientific theory we demand simple connections between entities of a few kinds in terms of which we can explain diverse phenomena', illustrating this with the way in which the atomic theory explains the empirically discovered laws of fixed proportions in chemical combinations. Nothing like this, he thinks, is available for the explanation of mental events or properties.

Although it is theoretically possible that a scientific theory of this kind should be created, still the creation of such a theory does not look a very likely prospect. Brain-states are such different things qualitatively from experiences, intentions, beliefs, etc. that a *natural* connection between them seems almost impossible. For how could brain-states vary except in their chemical composition and the speed and direction of their electro-chemical interactions, and how could there be a natural connection between variations in these respects and variations in the kind of respects in which intentions differ—say the differences between intending to sign a cheque, intending to square the circle, and intending to lecture for another half an hour? There does not seem the beginning of a prospect of a simple scientific theory of this kind and so of having established laws of mind-body interaction as opposed to lots of diverse correlations; which, just because they are unconnected in an overall theory, are for that reason not necessarily of universal application. If we cannot have scientific laws we cannot have scientific explanation. The materialist's task of giving a full explanation of the occurrence of a man's mental events, and of his intentions, beliefs, and capacities *seems* doomed to failure. For a detailed materialist theory could not be a simple enough theory for us to have reasonable confidence in its truth. (pp. 171–2)

This argument is clearly a remote descendant of Locke's. But too many issues are being run together and hurried over at once. First, as I said, the question is not whether the materialist can *formulate* a theory that would explain the mind–body interaction, but whether he can reasonably believe that *there are* laws that would explain this. Even if he could formulate such a theory, it would be too much to expect that he should be able to explain all a particular man's mental events, simply because he could not ascertain all the relevant initial conditions. Analogously, though no one doubts that there are simple physical laws which account for all meteorological phenomena, no one expects to be able to predict the exact course of the next Caribbean hurricane, or to explain in detail the course of the last one. Secondly, as we saw in connection with the Davidson argument against psychophysical laws, *intending to sign a cheque* is not the sort of item for which we should expect to find a systematic neural correlate, let alone a simple intelligible explanatory law. Rather, we should have to consider what are the constituents of some particular occurrent mental state which falls under the description 'intending to sign a cheque'; these will no doubt include some occurrent believing and some latent striving, the latter being, and being known as, the ground of a disposition to act in certain ways in certain experienced circumstances. Then the question will be whether there could be an explanatory law connecting each of these constituents with some neural counterpart and basis. If there is any problem here, it must be about these *elements*; having seen the variety of things that computers can do—including playing chess, and learning to play it better—and having seen how the circuits used have been repeatedly reduced in physical size, we know (as Cicero could not) that complexity is no problem. Thirdly, when we focus on the elements, the only one that seems hard to explain by a simple law relating it to physical basis is awareness itself, in an occurrent, not a dispositional, sense: the possession of an experiential content. This is the one element in our mental life that we would hesitate to ascribe to a computer, however sophisticated its performances.

Swinburne's argument is, as I said, a descendant of Locke's. His question 'how could brain-states vary except in their chemical composition and the speed and direction of their electro-chemical interactions?' is just a subtler variant of Locke's assertion that all that material particles, big or small, can do is to 'knock, impell, and resist one another'. Now I do not deny that there is a problem here for the materialist or naturalist, but it is important to get the precise problem into focus and cut it down to size. It is just that it is hard to see how there can be an intelligible law connecting material structures, however we describe them, with experiential content. The materialist cannot deny that there are states with such content, and he has to assume that there is a fundamental law of nature which says that such content will arise whenever there is a material structure of a certain complicated sort, and that that content will vary in a certain systematic way with the material basis—a fundamental law, because the basic fact of occurrent awareness seems not to be analysable into any simpler components, so that the law of its emergence could not be derived from a combination of more basic laws.

Granting that this is a difficulty for materialism, we must consider whether any alternative view is better off. Swinburne examines two such possibilities. One is dualism. This is the doctrine that there just are irreducibly different kinds of things in the world, physical things, states, events, and processes on the one hand, and mental entities, states, events, and processes on the other. Physical occurrences will not explain mental ones, nor will mental occurrences explain physical ones. I take it that this means that the items in one category will not *as a whole* be explained by those in the other, since all but the most implausible forms of dualism will allow some interaction between the mental and the physical; and, as we saw with Locke, the recognition of such interaction undermines any *a priori* certainty that the mental cannot *as a whole* arise from the physical. Swinburne assumes that this dualism of kinds of things and occurrences will carry with it a dualism of types of explanation: scientific, causal explanation will hold for physical things, and personal explanation, which explains results as the fulfilments of intentions, will hold for all mental things. It is not at all easy to see how this will work for *all* the phenomena of consciousness, unless we return to the Berkeleian view discussed in Chapter 4; comparatively few of the contents of my conscious states are fulfilments of any intentions of mine. And if we did admit two such radically different kinds of explanation, what sort of explanation could we expect to hold for the interactions between the mental and the physical which, as I said, any plausible dualism must admit? But of course Swinburne is not concerned to defend this sort of dualism, which, as he says, is 'a very messy world-picture'.

'The other alternative', he says, 'is to seek a personal explanation of mind-body correlations and a personal explanation of the operation of the factors cited in scientific explanation. That there are such explanations is a central thesis of theism.' That is, we can avoid a dualism of types of explanation by making all explanation ultimately personal. Scientific explanation is reduced to a special case of personal explanation, because the laws on which it relies are themselves just fulfilments of God's intentions. The fulfilment of God's intentions is the uniform pattern that is exemplified both in the causal laws that govern physical things and in the connections between brain-events and mental events. Whereas the latter connections are not intelligible in themselves, they become so when seen as being intentionally brought about by God. 'The trouble with the materialist's programme', Swinburne says, 'was that there was no natural connection between brain-events and correlated mental events. But the intention of an agent to join them binds them together. There is a very natural connection indeed between an agent's intention to bring about X, and the occurrence of X ... That is why the prospects are so much better for a reduction of all explanation to personal explanation. It can give a natural explanation of all connections in the world in terms of an agent's intention to bring about those connections.' (pp. 172-3)

Swinburne does not question the 'story of the gradual evolution of conscious beings out of inorganic matter', nor does he deny that there is 'a satisfactory scientific explanation ... of the evolution of more and more complex beings'. What he denies is simply that there is a scientific explanation of this complexity's giving rise to conscious life.

It is now a simple matter for Swinburne to put together an argument from consciousness for the existence of a god. He has argued earlier that the god of traditional theism would have some reason for bringing other conscious beings into existence, though not, indeed, an overwhelmingly strong motive for doing so. His recent argument has been meant to show that it is very unlikely that such beings should have come about by normal physical processes. Thus the undeniable existence of conscious beings is, he claims, much more readily explained by the theistic hypothesis than without it, and this yields a good confirmatory inductive argument for that hypothesis.

But how good an argument is it? This depends very much on the alleged naturalness and intelligibility of the connection between an intention and its fulfilment. No doubt this seems, in some central cases, very natural and direct. I decide to raise my arm, and up it goes. But we know that the apparent directness of this connection is illusory. There is in fact a complex causal path joining whatever brain-event is the correlate of my decision through nerves and muscles to the movement of my arm. We form the picture of the *immediate*—that is, not mediated—fulfilment of an intention only by leaving out, and indeed by being normally unaware of, all the intermediate parts of this causal process. Certainly the resulting movement mirrors the content of the decision or intention: that is why it can be said to fulfil it. But the possibility of this apparently simple and satisfactory relationship depends upon a physical mechanism and ultimately on an evolutionary development, and perhaps also on a history of conscious or unconscious learning in one's own early life. I now justifiably expect some such decisions to be fulfilled in a flash: I know that in ordinary circumstances I can raise my arm or even throw a ball. But we have no right to abstract from what is really such a complex process the simple relationship which is all that ordinarily interests us, and to use this as a familiar model for an intelligible immediate efficacy of intentions, to be employed in constructing personal explanations elsewhere, in the supposed creative and governing activity of a god.

Swinburne may reply that it is simply written into the theistic hypothesis that God is capable of such immediate fulfilments of intention. No doubt it is; but that is a fundamentally mysterious element in that hypothesis which makes it antecedently improbable. What I am pointing out is that we cannot reduce its prior improbability by seeing an analogy between this supposed divine ability and any experience we have of the direct fulfilment of an intention.

In fact any personal explanations that we can actually give, as applied to ordinary actions, constitute, when properly spelled out, a sub-class of causal explanations, not a rival mode of explanation to the causal one. We can indeed *describe* an action as the fulfilment of an intention, as the carrying out of a decision, without explicitly making causal claims: we can draw attention to the merely logical relation between some correct description of what is done and the content of the deciding or intending, the 'that'-clause which says what decision or intention it was. But there is no way in which we can explain the *occurrence* or *coming about* of a movement or its result without bringing in some reference, however vague, to ordinary causal explanation. Teleological description may be distinct from anything involving causation; but teleological explanation of anything's coming about is, in all ordinary cases, only a special kind of explanation in terms of efficient causes. For example, to explain an action as purposive is to indicate that it is causally brought about by the agent's desires, beliefs, and decisions. If we say that a plant or an animal has such and such organs, or behaves in a certain way, because this serves some function or tends to produce some result, this is shorthand for a causal account of how these features have been developed by natural selection. And there are causal feedback mechanisms underlying the apparent purposiveness of homing rockets.[8]

These are general difficulties for Swinburne's use of personal explanation as a separate category of explanation in hypotheses about relations between the world and a god: they arise, for example, in his inductive version of the cosmological argument as well as in his argument from consciousness. But there are also special difficulties about his use of it to explain the mind–body connection. Has God somehow brought it about that material structures do now generate

---

[8] The relation between teleological and causal explanation is fully discussed in Chapter 11 of *The Cement of the Universe*—see n. 2 to Chapter 1, p. 20, above.

consciousness? But then is this not almost as hard to understand as that material structures should do this *of themselves*? Or are we to regard each separate body–mind connection, for example the super-vening of each state of perceptual awareness on the appropriate sensory input and neurophysiological disturbance, as the fulfilment of a fresh divine intention, so that sensory perception is, strictly speaking, an indefinitely repeated miracle, so that we have here an endless series of divine interventions in the natural causal order? But further, if, as Locke puts it, omnipotency has given to some systems of matter fitly disposed a power to perceive and think, why is it only to fitly disposed ones? Could not *omnipotency* superadd a faculty of thinking as easily to a block of wood as to a brain? If materialism has difficulty in explaining how even the most elaborate neural struc-tures can give rise to consciousness, theism, with its personal explan-ations and direct intention-fulfilments, has at least as great a diffi-culty in explaining why consciousness is found *only* in them.

I have conceded that having to postulate a fundamental natural law of emergence for awareness is something of a difficulty for the materialist. But when we look at all closely at the rival view we find that the difficulties for theism are at least as great. Of course, the demand that the world and its workings should be completely intel-ligible is an unreasonable one: any theory has to tolerate a certain amount of sheer brute fact. The most we can say is that, among rival hypotheses, relative simplicity (of certain kinds) is an advantage. In fact, once we have rejected, as we must, both the extreme materialism that would deny even distinctively mental properties and the com-plete immaterialism of Berkeley or of phenomenalism, we are stuck with some kind of dualism; and unless this is an absurdly extreme dualism it must admit psychophysical laws or lawlike correlations of some sort. To put it simply, the mind–body gap must be bridged somewhere and somehow. Personal explanation in terms of the un-mediated fulfilment of intentions does not provide an easier bridge than the one that the materialist has to postulate between certain complex electro-chemical systems and awareness. It may seem to do so, but only because we borrow and use as a model for it the merely superficial familiar aspect of what are really complex and mediated causal processes of human action. We ordinarily have an illusion of the literally immediate fulfilment of some of our own intentions. This is even a useful illusion: it is as convenient, for ordinary purposes, to treat action as 'transparent' as it is to treat knowledge and language as being so too. But to develop out of this a theory of a god's bare thought and intention first creating matter out of nothing, then instituting causal laws, and finally annexing animal and human consciousness to certain natural systems, is to build myth upon myth.

8

Arguments for Design

(a) *Hume's* Dialogues—*Exposition*

PERHAPS the most popular way of arguing from the world to a god is what is commonly called 'the argument from design'. However, an argument *from* design to a designer would be trivial: it would not be proper to speak of design unless we were already assuming that there was a designer. The crucial steps are those that lead from certain evidence, from what have been called 'marks of design', to the conclusion that something is indeed the product of design. So let us call it the argument to, or for, design.[1]

This argument flourished particularly in the eighteenth century, when it seemed that (contrary to what Berkeley feared) the progress of natural science was merely revealing richer evidence of the creative activity of God. But the version then current was devastatingly criticized by Hume in his *Dialogues concerning Natural Religion* and (partly following Hume) by Kant. Even more damaging in practice, however, than these philosophical criticisms was the demonstration by Darwin and Wallace in the nineteenth century that one of the most impressive categories of apparent marks of design, the detailed structures of plant and animal bodies and their adaptation to conditions and a way of life, could be explained better by the theory of evolution through natural selection: for example, certain features of the actual geographical distribution of species that were left unexplained by a hypothesis of the special creation of each particular species were readily accounted for by a hypothesis of descent with

---

[1] Cf. A. Flew, *God and Philosophy* (Hutchinson, London, 1966), Chapter 3. Hume's *Dialogues concerning Natural Religion* are edited by N. Kemp Smith (Nelson, Edinburgh, 1947) and by J. V. Price in *David Hume on Religion*, edited by A. W. Colver and J. V. Price (Oxford University Press, 1976). References in the text are to the numbered Parts.

modification. But, despite these setbacks, the argument for design has never died out, and it has been revived from time to time in new forms. Swinburne has put forward a version which sidesteps the evolutionary objection and at least attempts to meet the criticisms of Hume and Kant. Let us begin by examining these criticisms.

The older form of the argument is well summed up in a speech that Hume puts into the mouth of Cleanthes.

> Look round the world: Contemplate the whole and every part of it: You will find it to be nothing but one great machine, subdivided into an infinite number of lesser machines ... All these various machines, and even their most minute parts, are adjusted to one another with an accuracy, which ravishes into administration all men, who have ever contemplated them. The curious adapting of means to ends, throughout all nature, resembles exactly, though it much exceeds, the productions of human contrivance; of human design, thought, wisdom, and intelligence. Since therefore the effects resemble each other, we are led to infer, by all the rules of analogy, that the causes also resemble; and that the Author of nature is somewhat similar to the mind of man; though possessed of much larger faculties, proportional to the grandeur of the work, which he has executed. By this argument *a posteriori*, and by this argument alone, we do prove at once the existence of a Deity, and his similarity to human mind and intelligence. (Part II)

What count, then, as marks of design are those features in which natural objects resemble machines made by men: the fitting together of parts and what can be seen as the adaptation of means to ends. (To call it straight out 'the adapting of means to ends', rather than just noting that it can be seen as such, would be to jump to the conclusion of the argument for design.) Three kinds of these features particularly impressed eighteenth-century thinkers: the world as a whole, especially the solar system as described by Newton's gravitational theory; the bodies of all sorts of plants and animals, especially certain organs like the eye; and the providential arrangement of things on the surface of the earth, enabling all the different plant and animal species to flourish, and especially the provision of things, including plants and the other animals, for the use of men. Hume's *Dialogues* stress examples of the first two kinds, but say little about the third.

The *Dialogues* are a masterpiece of philosophical literature. One of their most striking features is the way in which Hume plays off against one another his three main characters and, through them, the types of view that they represent. Cleanthes represents natural theology. Relying on the argument for design, he stresses its *a posteriori* and probabilistic character. Since he argues by analogy in a commonsense way, his conclusion is that there is a god who closely resembles human minds; and since he is inferring the attributes of this god from the world that he has designed, Cleanthes takes an optimistic view of the ordinary world in order to be able to infer the goodness of God from the goodness and happiness of his creation. Demea is an equally convinced theist, but he is a hardliner of a much grimmer sort. In so far as he engages in natural theology, he relies on *a priori* arguments, claiming that they give a certainty about God's existence that the design argument cannot give. But his real reliance is on faith: 'It is my opinion ... that each man feels, in a manner, the truth of religion within his own breast'. This conviction arises from the miseries and terrors of life, from which we seek relief in religion. Consequently his view of the world is pessimistic in the extreme, but, as we might say, complacently pessimistic. Demea's god is not only infinite but also incomprehensible, and his attributes in no way resemble the human ones from which we borrow terms to describe him. In particular, though we call him good, this does not mean he will act in ways in which men must act to be called good. Philo, the sceptic, allies himself for a while with Demea against Cleanthes, supporting Demea's mysticism only to bring out, in the end, the scepticism latent within it. Similarly he joins with Demea in portraying the utter wretchedness of human (and animal) life in a ceaseless brutal struggle for existence, in preparation for the use of the problem of evil to criticize theism as a whole. But he joins with Cleanthes in criticizing Demea's use of a version of the cosmological argument. He brings many objections against the argument for design, but finally offers Cleanthes a compromise, suggesting that they can agree that there is *some* analogy between the cause of the world and human intelligence, and that any disagreement about the degree of resemblance is merely verbal, because it is indeterminate and so practically meaningless.

Part of Hume's purpose is to bring out the contrasting and inconsistent strains in religious thought which are represented by Cleanthes and Demea. These are often more closely intertwined, so that a single thinker may swing back and forth between them. It is also noteworthy that Cleanthes' views are developed partly by the use of some very characteristically Humean arguments. Nevertheless, there can be no doubt that Hume's own view is represented mainly by Philo, and that the main theme of the *Dialogues* is the criticism of the argument for design. This criticism is stated at considerable length and with a wealth of picturesque detail, but we can perhaps discern five main points. One of these concerns the weakness and remoteness of the analogy between the products of human design and the works of nature, and the resulting vagueness of any conclusion that can be drawn from that analogy. Another consists in the offering of various rival explanatory hypotheses, suggesting that the order (of several sorts) in the natural world, the supposed marks of design, may be due rather to 'generation and vegetation'—even a world as a whole may result from something like biological reproduction—or to random rearrangements of particles which are just naturally in constant motion, or to a multiplicity of supernatural beings, or to a world soul, to which the material world belongs like a body, or even (as, he says, the Brahmins assert) to an 'infinite spider' that spun the world as a spider spins its web: 'Why an orderly system may not be spun from the belly as well as from the brain, it will be difficult for him to give a satisfactory reason'. (Part VII) Philo's third point is that even if it were plausible to explain the order in the material world as the product of design by a divine mind, we should thereby be committed to recognizing in that mind itself a complex order as rich as that in the natural world, and therefore as much in need of further explanation: if it is objected that we know how ideas in a mind 'fall into order of themselves, and without any *known* cause', it can be replied that the same is true, within our experience, of material (and especially living) things. (Part IV) His fourth point concerns the problem of evil and the inference to the moral qualities of a deity: even if—hard as it seems—one could somehow *reconcile* the occurrence of the evils in the world with the existence of an omnipotent and wholly good god, one could still not hope to *infer* a wholly good god from a manifestly imperfect world. Consequently the supposed moral qualities of the deity, God's perfect goodness, are even more problematic than the intellectual ones. (Part V) His fifth point is that whatever one can infer *a posteriori* about the cause of the world from the world itself as we know it, this will be quite useless: we can never argue back to any further conclusions about the ordinary world or our future experience which go beyond the data from which our inference began. (Part XII)[2]

These five points come in a natural order, each later one arising out of a concession with regard to those that precede it, as follows:

1. Is the analogy between natural order and artefacts close enough to make theism a good explanation of the former?

[2] This fifth point was also the main thesis of Section 11 of Hume's earlier *Enquiry concerning Human Understanding*.

2. Even if the answer to 1 is 'Yes', various alternative hypotheses, by their availability, weaken the confirmation of the theistic one.

3. Even if the theistic hypothesis would be confirmed (despite 1 and 2) by its ability to explain the order in the world, its status as a satisfactory explanation is challenged by the fact that the divine mind which it postulates would itself be as much in need of explanation (being another case of order) as the order in the world.

4. Even if the theistic hypothesis were well confirmed (despite 1, 2, and 3) by the order in the world, the moral component in it is disproved or disconfirmed by the occurrence of evil, or is, at the very least, unsupported by a world in which there is evil as well as good.

5. Even if the theistic hypothesis survived 1, 2, 3, and 4, and was well confirmed after all, it would still be useless: we could not use it to argue back to otherwise unknown features of the world or of our own lives—for example, to predictions about the course of nature, to the answering of prayer, to the greater happiness of the pious and virtuous as opposed to the irreligious and wicked, or to a life after death containing appropriate punishments, rewards, and compensations.

(b) *Hume's* Dialogues—*Discussion*

What are we to say about these five points? I shall postpone the fourth until Chapter 9, where I shall be considering the problem of evil as a whole. The first and the fifth depend upon the way in which the design argument and its conclusion are formulated. Hume presents it as an argument from analogy. Houses, watches, and so on are produced by human designers; the world is a bit like a house or a watch or a collection of houses, watches, and the like; therefore it is probably produced by something like a human designer. Thus stated, the initial analogy is indeed pretty remote, and any conclusion to which it points is very vague, so that no new inferences about the world or human life could reasonably be drawn from it. Another approach is to take the argument as introducing a god simply as *that which* causes or explains or is responsible for the natural world. There is then no tentative or probabilistic inference, but rather a sheer assumption that there is something that fills this bill; but again, since this entity is introduced and described only in relation to what it is assumed to produce, no new conclusions will follow from the claim that it exists. However, the argument can be recast as the confirming of a hypothesis, and then this hypothesis can be made as determinate and as fruitful of further conclusions as we please. But the more we put into the hypothesis, the further it goes beyond the evidence; so the less well will it be confirmed by that evidence, and the more exposed will it be to the competition of rival hypotheses.

These, however, are general constraints which apply to explanatory scientific hypotheses and theories of whatever sort. And it is simply not true that such hypotheses and theories are useless in this sense. On the contrary, they do support predictions which both give genuine and fairly reliable information and allow the construction of artefacts of new kinds—notably computers, television sets, nuclear weapons, and the other blessings of civilization. But is there some reason to suppose that these constraints are particularly damaging to the theistic hypothesis as an explanation of the 'marks of design'? I think there is, because the theistic hypothesis does not *differentially* explain specific phenomena in the way that successful scientific theories do: it does not explain why we have these phenomena rather than others. A scientific hypothesis is often confirmed by its success in explaining exactly what is observed, by tying up what on an alternative view remain as loose ends, and perhaps by predicting further, otherwise unexpected, observations which are then made, or possible constructions which are then successfully carried out. This the theistic hypothesis does not do. It may be objected that there are also general scientific theories which do not determine predictions: Darwin's theory of the origin of species by descent and modification through natural selection would be an example. But Darwin's theory still explains details, such as the various *maladjustments* of structure to function, which its rivals leave unexplained—the webbed feet of upland geese and of frigate birds which do not use them for paddling along on the surface of the water, birds and insects that use their wings for swimming, woodpeckers that never go near a tree, and so on. All these can be understood as results of species moving into new ecological niches, but retaining ancestral features that are no longer used or are put to new, not quite appropriate, uses.[3]

Also, what we call 'theories' are sometimes rather general methods of explanation, not propositions which can themselves be true or false, confirmed or disconfirmed. Such a 'theory' only provides a framework within which particular explanations of specific phenomena can be constructed, and the question to ask about it is not 'Is it true?' but rather 'How widely applicable is it?' or 'How many

[3] C. Darwin, *The Origin of Species* (Murray, London, 1900), Chapter VI.

specific phenomena can be successfully explained by detailed hypotheses within this framework?' This is plainly the status of, for example, sociobiology. Indeed the 'theory' of evolution by natural selection can itself operate as such a framework or method. It becomes a theory in the strict sense, a hypothesis that is capable of being true or false, only when it is taken as making the historical claim that all plant and animal species have in fact developed in this way. But the theistic hypothesis does not serve even as such a method for constructing interesting and confirmable specific explanations, which could themselves yield further predictions.

Hume's (or Philo's) second point is developed at great length and with an ingenuity that sometimes lapses into fantasy; this concerns the availability of explanations alternative to that of design. Some of these alternatives are (and are recognized in the *Dialogues* as being) too far-fetched to be taken seriously. But perhaps Hume meant to suggest that the theistic account was no more worthy of being taken seriously than some of its rivals, such as the 'infinite spider'. However, some of the alternative explanations deserve to be taken very seriously indeed. For example, if the order in the world which is supposed to be a mark of design is located in, say, the regular working of the solar system, then we can point out that if Newton's laws represent ways of working which are natural to objects with mass, we need only find some sequence of events—perhaps, as has been suggested, a near-collision between the sun and some other star—which might leave behind a group of bodies with the appropriate relative motions; from there the thing will run on of its own accord. *Given Newton's laws*, it is really quite easy to make a solar system; certainly no great ingenuity is required. If, as modern astronomy might suggest, the order is located not in the solar system but in the multiplicity of galaxies, then what we naturally look for is a cosmological history that will account for the phenomena; but again it seems likely that the solution will lie in laws, not in ingenuity. If the order is located in plant and animal bodies, then plainly the immediate explanation of this order in the organisms that are around now lies in what Hume called 'generation and vegetation', the simple and obvious fact that each individual organism is produced by its parents and then grows. However, this is only an outline explanation; a more adequate immediate explanation would identify and trace the laws and mechanisms and processes of generation and vegetation. If a further explanation is sought, we can now offer the evolutionary one towards which Hume could only make rather fumbling gestures.

Evolution by natural selection mimics purposiveness and so can thoroughly explain what Cleanthes calls 'the curious adapting of means to ends, throughout all nature'. And this is not only *an* alternative hypothesis to that of design, it is clearly the correct one, whereas that of 'special creation' is false. As Darwin so convincingly argued, there are many details which his hypothesis explains while that of special creation does not.[4]

This means that since Darwin wrote anyone who wants to use an argument for design must locate elsewhere the order which the designer is postulated to explain. On the assumption that a full account of the development of life from inorganic materials, and of the gradual evolution of more and more complex organisms, can be given, using as data only the general laws of physics and chemistry and some astronomically understandable initial conditions, this argument for theism will have to take, as the order to be explained, either the atomic and sub-atomic structure of inorganic materials or the basic laws which govern their workings and interactions. Again, after modern developments in cosmology, anyone who wants to use anything like the astronomical variant of the argument must locate the order to be explained in some initial set-up—perhaps somewhere inside the 'big bang'. This shift, however, is sometimes made in a way that attempts, unfairly, to cancel the necessary concession. It may be said that we still have to explain why there should be materials and laws which are *such that* they can give rise to life and the evolution of complex organisms, or again why there should be an initial cosmological set-up which is *such that* it can generate galaxies containing stars and planetary systems. This is misleading in two ways. On the one hand, it invites us to beg the question by supposing that these future developments are not only causally latent within the initial situation—that is, that it will eventually lead to them or bring them about—but are also already *envisaged* at its formation. On the other hand, it suggests that a *potentiality* for the producing of these developments is part of what still needs to be explained. But this suggestion is unfair. If, as we are supposing, the future developments are accounted for by the initial conditions and materials and laws alone, then it is only for those initial conditions and materials and laws as they are in themselves that any further explanation could reasonably be sought. We must not overload the explanandum by adding to it, even as a potentiality, the developments which we can presume it to have accounted for already.

[4] Op. cit., Chapters XII, XIII, XV.

But it may be argued that there is still something that calls for further explanation. With the various basic materials and physical constants as they contingently are, life and evolution and consciousness are naturally possible; but things might so easily have been different. Is it not remarkable and intrinsically surprising that things happen to be just right for the possibility of these developments? Now someone might say in reply to this objection, 'No, we cannot reasonably find it surprising that things should have been such that we could evolve, since if things *had* been otherwise we should not have been here to be surprised'. But this is not a good reply, though something like it would be a good reply to a different objection. If there are many thousands of planetary systems throughout the universe, but the conditions are right for the production of life on just one of them, namely ours, we cannot reasonably find it surprising that things should be just right for life *here*; for *here* has been picked out for attention merely in relation to our presence: from a neutral point of view all that is true is that conditions have been right for life far less often than they have been wrong, so their being right once can well be ascribed to chance, and not seen as calling for any further explanation. But the objection we are considering is different. There is only one actual universe, with a unique set of basic materials and physical constants, and it is therefore surprising that the elements of this unique set-up are just right for life when they might easily have been wrong. This is not made less surprising by the fact that if it had not been so, no one would have been here to be surprised. We can properly envisage and consider alternative possibilities which do not include our being there to experience them.[5]

I suspect, however, that this objection also is being presented in a question-begging way. Though some small variation from the actual initial materials and constants would, perhaps, eliminate the possibility of life's having developed as it did, we really have no idea of what other interesting possibilities might have been latent within others of the endless range of possible initial conditions. We are not in a position, therefore, to regard the actual initial materials and constants as a uniquely fruitful set, and as surprising and as specially calling for further explanation on that account.

Once these matters are cleared up, we can see that the shift of topic due to the work of Darwin and his successors greatly diminishes the plausibility of the argument for design. The reciprocal adjustments of structures and functions in myriads of different organisms are

[5] Cf. Swinburne, *The Existence of God*, pp. 137-8.

indeed so delicate and complicated as to be initially surprising in the extreme, and not merely to invite but to require a search for *some* further explanation; and then the hypothesis of design is at least one to be considered among others. But we find nothing comparable to this in sub-atomic particles or the laws that govern them. Atomic and nuclear physics are, no doubt, intricate enough to be of theoretical as well as practical interest, but we cannot see them as involving reciprocal adjustments which might plausibly be taken as signs of purposiveness.

The shift produced by modern cosmology is less important in this respect, not because any initially surprising reciprocal adjustments have to be postulated in a proposed starting-point of cosmic history, but because none was to be found even in the developed universe. The eighteenth-century thinkers drew quite the wrong conclusion from Newtonian gravitational astronomy. It should, as I have said, have told them not that a solar system is a marvellously coherent machine with mutually assisting and mutually adjusted components (like a watch, only more so), but rather that it is something that, given the gravitational laws, could be botched up with no forethought at all, or that could emerge from a fortuitous concourse of masses. It takes ingenuity to make an orrery, an artificial model of the solar system, precisely because it cannot use the gravitational laws, but no such ingenuity is needed to make a gravitationally governed solar system.

The stock response, however, to the suggestion of alternative, naturalistic, explanations of the supposed marks of design is to say that they only shift the problem further back. If we explain an organism as having arisen by generation and vegetation—and even if we trace these processes in detail—it is said that we still have to explain the parents or ancestors that produced it. If we explain whole species by organic evolution, we still have to explain the primeval organisms from which evolution began. And if we explain these by the action of radiant energy on inorganic mixtures of gases, we still have to explain the atomic structures and the radiation that make this action possible. But, on the one hand, we have seen that in such a shifting back the burden of explanation has grown lighter: there is literally less to explain. And, on the other hand, a similar response is available to the naturalist: if you explain the order in the natural world by a divine plan, you still have to explain the order in the divine mind. As Philo says, 'a mental world or universe of ideas requires a cause as much as does a material world or universe of objects'. This is what I called his third main point. But there are two different ways in which the theist can try to meet this objection, which bring out two radically different interpretations of the design argument itself.

First, he may say, as Cleanthes does, that he is content with one step in explanation. 'Even in common life, if I assign a cause for any event; is it any objection, Philo, that I cannot assign the cause of that cause ...? The order and arrangement of nature, the curious adjustment of final causes, the plain use and intention of every part and organ; all these bespeak in the clearest language an intelligent cause or Author ... You ask me, what is the cause of this cause? I know not; I care not; that concerns not me. I have found a Deity; and here I stop my enquiry.' (Part IV) This sounds like a fair reply, but it plays straight into the hands of the naturalist. For, as we have seen, the phenomena to which Cleanthes refers now bespeak in the clearest language not an Author but an evolutionary process. If one step in explanation is enough, this is where we must stop our inquiry.

Alternatively, the theist may say that the divine mind hypothesis terminates the regress of explanation in a way that no naturalistic explanation can. Any naturalistic explanation uses data for which a further explanation is in principle always needed; but a god is self-explanatory. Consequently, however far alternative explanations can be taken, they must lead back to the theistic account in the end, whereas once God has been introduced as a cause, the search for a cause of this cause is out of order. The theist loses every battle but the last.

This is clearly not Cleanthes' view; but this reply is suggested by Philo in one of his temporary alliances with Demea. 'To say that all this order in animals and vegetables proceeds ultimately from design is begging the question; nor can that great point be ascertained otherwise than by proving *a priori*, both that order is, from its own nature, inseparably attached to thought, and that it can never, of itself, or from original unknown principles, belong to matter.' And Demea himself stresses that what is needed here is an *a priori* argument, offering what seems to be a mixture of Leibniz's argument from contingency with the first cause argument. (Parts VII, IX)

These two replies, as I said, reflect two different interpretations of the design argument. It may be taken as a genuinely empirical, *a posteriori*, argument, strictly analogous to the confirmation of a scientific hypothesis or theory. Or it may be taken with a large admixture of *a priori* principles. As an empirical argument, it needs not only the premiss that certain objects not made by men exhibit a kind of order that is found also in the products of human design; it needs also the premiss that such order is *not* found where there is no designer. But this second premiss is not available as long as we confine ourselves to empirical evidence. As Cleanthes' party constantly reiterates, such order *is* found all over the place where we have as yet no reason to suppose that there is a designer. Paley argued that if we found a watch on the ground we should infer that it had been made by an intelligent being.[6] This is true, because we hardly ever find watches except where the supposition of human manufacture is antecedently plausible—on people's wrists, in their pockets, in jeweller's shops, and so on. But if watches were found as commonly on the seashore as shellfish, or as commonly on dry land as insects, this argument would be undermined. Thus any purely *a posteriori* design argument falls at the first fence: we have no good *empirical* reason for taking the 'marks of design' *as* marks of design. 'We have ... experience', Philo concedes, 'of ideas, which fall into order of themselves, and without any *known* cause: But ... we have a much larger experience of matter, which does the same.' (Part IV) In fact, the position is even worse for the theist. *Within our experience*, mental structures are always based at least partly on perceptual input: 'In all instances which we have ever seen, ideas are copied from real objects, and are ectypal, not archetypal ... You reverse this order, and give thought the precedence'. (Part VIII) The argument for design, therefore, can be sustained only with the help of a supposedly *a priori* double-barrelled principle, that mental order (at least in a god) is self-explanatory, but that all material order not only is not self-explanatory, but is positively improbable and in need of further explanation.

But this double-barrelled principle is recognizable as the core of the cosmological argument, which has already been criticized in Chapter 5 above. There is no reason why mental order as such should be any less in need of further explanation than material order, and the claim that mental order in a god is self-explanatory is just the thesis, central in the cosmological argument, but borrowed there from the ontological one, that God is a necessary being, a being that could not have failed to exist.

Kant, in his criticism of the 'physico-theological proof' (his name for the design argument) makes two points which come close to this.[7]

---

[6] W. Paley, *Natural Theology*, Vol. 6 in *Works* (London, 1805), Chapter I.

[7] *Critique of Pure Reason*, Transcendental Dialectic, Book II, Chapter III, Section 6.

He argues that the most that an argument for design could show is
that there is an architect of the world, working on pre-existing
material; for this is the most that the analogy of human manufacture
could indicate. 'To prove the contingency of matter itself, we should
have to resort to a transcendental argument.' He argues also that we
cannot reach the notions of absolute totality, absolute unity, and so
on by the empirical road. 'Accordingly, we then abandon the argument from empirical grounds of proof, and fall back upon the contingency which, in the first steps of the argument, we had inferred
from the order and purposiveness of the world. With this contingency
as our sole premiss, we then advance, by means of transcendental
concepts alone, to the existence of an absolutely necessary being ...
Those who propound the physico-theological argument ... after
advancing some considerable way on the solid ground of nature and
experience, and finding themselves just as distant as ever from the
object which discloses itself to their reason, they suddenly leave this
ground, and pass over into the realm of mere possibilities.' Kant thus
charges that the design argument has to fall back on the cosmological
one, which, he has already claimed, is only a disguised ontological
proof. His reason is that the design argument could not take us as far
as the theist wants to go. This is a complaint that Hume puts into the
mouth of Demea. Kant allows (with some hints of qualification and
further objection) that the design argument *could* give us an architect
god, though not a creator or a necessary being. But our criticisms
show that the argument will not take us even as far as Kant seems to
allow without borrowing the *a priori* thesis that there is a vicious
metaphysical contingency in all natural things, and, in contrast with
this, the 'transcendental' concept of a god who is self-explanatory
and necessarily existent. It is only with the help of these borrowings
that the design argument can introduce the required asymmetry, that
any natural explanation uses data which call for further explanation,
but that the theistic explanation terminates the regress. Without this
asymmetry, the design argument cannot show that there is any need
to go beyond the sort of alternative hypothesis that Hume fore-
shadowed and that Darwin and Wallace supplied, or that there is
anything satisfactorily explanatory in the postulation of a supernatural designer. The dependence of the argument for design on
ideas that are the core of the cosmological one is greater than Kant
himself realized.

(c) *Swinburne's Restatement*

Can the design argument be restated in a stronger form? This is what Swinburne has attempted.[8] He abandons the eighteenth-century starting-points, and our discussion shows that he is wise to do so. In their place he suggests two possible starting-points, one consisting of spatial order, the other of temporal order.

The suggestion about spatial order—that is, about the existence of things with certain complex structures—takes over and builds upon the results of the evolutionary theory of Darwin and his successors: nature is thereby shown to be a machine-making machine. But the analogy with human products is still maintained, since men in the twentieth century have learned to make not only machines but also machine-making machines. So we can still look for a creator, somewhat analogous to men, who has made the machine-making machine of nature. But Swinburne admits that this is not a strong argument; organisms are relatively rare in the universe, so that nature, he thinks, is not much of a machine-making machine. (pp. 135-6) I do not know how Swinburne can be so sure about the paucity of organisms; but, quite apart from this, the argument is weak for the reasons that told against the older versions. If it is meant to be an empirically based argument, then there is no support for the required premiss that, within our experience, machine-making machines are peculiarly the products of design. Every organism or pair of organisms that is capable of reproduction is a machine-making machine, which, as far as we know, has itself been made by machine-making machines, and is *not* a product of design. But if it is meant to rely on an *a priori* principle, that a divine mind which can make machine-making machines is self-explanatory, whereas any natural object which can do this is in need of further explanation, so that the regress of explanation can be terminated only by the former, then we have in effect gone back to the core of the cosmological argument; but the required principle is not knowable *a priori*.

The form of teleological argument which Swinburne thinks much stronger is based on the temporal order in the world, that is, the sheer fact that there are, pervasively throughout the universe, regularities of succession, what we call laws of nature, whereas 'The universe might so naturally have been chaotic'. He successfully rebuts two objections, that these regularities are ones we invent and impose on the world, and that the regularity we observe is not surprising because

[8] *The Existence of God*, Chapter 8. References in the text are to pages in this work.

if there were no such regularity we should not be here to observe it. He also says, rightly, that although science may explain some regularities by deriving them from others, it cannot explain the highest-level (or most fundamental) laws, since they are what it appeals to in any explanation. Again, since he is aiming only at a confirmatory inductive argument, he need not say that this temporal order could not have occurred without a designer, but only that it is antecedently more probable that there should be such regularities on the hypothesis that there is a god than without this hypothesis, simply because the god of traditional theism might well prefer there to be an orderly world in which, as a bonus, finite intelligent creatures might live and learn. (pp. 136–48)

Swinburne simplifies his task by excluding one of the possibilities which Hume mentioned as an alternative to theism, the activity of a plurality of agents with finite powers. But in the very rarefied atmosphere in which we are now trying to fly, I do not see how he can do as much as this. For even if the same laws hold throughout the universe (which is more of an assumption than an empirical datum), there is, presumably, a plurality of laws, which might be distributed between a plurality of deities. But let us pass over this objection, and assume that the alternatives are 'the first, that the temporal order of the world is where explanation stops, and the second, that the temporal order of the world is due to the agency of God' (p. 142).

At this stage we are forced back into reliance on *a priori* judgements. Although we are using the empirical premiss that there is temporal order, that there are pervasive regularities, the use we are making of it depends on an *a priori* assumption about probabilities: the probability judgements themselves can no longer be based on experience. Since regularities *are* pervasive, we cannot derive a low probability for them from any rarity with which they are found in the world. It is not easy to see what *a priori* judgements we can make about this. It does not follow, for example, from the fact that *fundamental* regularities are necessarily unexplained, on a naturalist approach, that they are, given that approach, highly improbable *a priori*.

This comment can be supported indirectly. Swinburne agrees with all reasonable people that we are justified in arguing inductively, in extrapolating observed regularities to unobserved cases, though we can do so only tentatively, and that it may be more justifiable to be confident about modest extrapolations than about very long-range ones. He relies on the cogency of inductive reasoning in his rebuttal of the second of the above-mentioned objections. But such inductive extrapolation would not be reasonable if there were a strong presumption that the universe is really completely random, that such order as we seem to find in it is just the sort of *local apparent regularity* that we should expect to occur occasionally by pure chance, as in a series of random tosses of a coin we will *sometimes* get a long run of heads, or a simple alternation of heads and tails over a considerable number of throws.[9] Swinburne holds, and his argument requires, that inductive extrapolation is reasonable, prior to and independently of any belief in a god. But, I would argue, this would not be reasonable if there were a strong presumption that the universe is completely random. So he cannot consistently say that, without the theistic hypothesis, it is highly improbable *a priori* that there are any regularities; for the latter assertion of improbability is equivalent to saying that there is a strong presumption of randomness.

Again, whereas Swinburne says that 'the universe might so naturally have been chaotic', it is hard to see how there could be things at all without their having some regular ways of working. No doubt there could have been less regularity and more sheer randomness than there seems to be; but there is no good reason to take one of these to be, in itself and *a priori*, more likely than the other.

Thirdly, we need to maintain here the same distinction that we stressed, in Chapter 5, when discussing Swinburne's inductive variant of the cosmological argument. It is one question whether the addition, to our background knowledge and beliefs, of the theistic hypothesis raises the probability of there being temporal order as compared with what that probability would otherwise have been, so that that hypothesis has its own antecedent likelihood raised somewhat by the fact that there is temporal order; it is quite another question whether the combined hypothesis that there is both temporal order and a god who produces it is more probable than the hypothesis that there is temporal order alone, that this is where explanation stops. If we read enough into the notion of a god, then no doubt we can assert that the postulation of one raises, at least a little, the probability of there being temporal order, just as any suitably *ad hoc* hypothesis would. Anything which is tailor-made to explain such order would, no doubt, raise the antecedent probability of there being order—for this falls short of certainty, and so can be raised. But the resulting

---

[9] Swinburne, op. cit., p. 137; see my 'A Defence of Induction', in *Perception and Identity: Essays Presented to A. J. Ayer*, edited by G. F. Macdonald (Macmillan, London, 1979), pp. 113–30, especially pp. 124–8.

probability of the combined hypothesis will still be low if there are intrinsic improbabilities—either *a priori* or in relation to our background knowledge—in the theistic hypothesis itself. And such there are. Contrary to what Swinburne says, the postulate of a divine mind, if given enough content to raise the probability of there being pervasive regularities, in particular if we assign to this mind the power to create a universe from nothing and to put into it and maintain in it pervasive regularities by unmediated fulfilments of intention, is far from simple. As I said when discussing personal explanation in Chapter 7, the introduction of this category of immediate intention-fulfilment is at variance with what we really know about our own intentional actions, and conforms only to an illusory, over-simplified, naïve understanding of them. For this reason it is unlikely in the extreme in relation to our background knowledge. Or we can look at the issue more generally. If the theistic hypothesis is not the utterly vague postulate that there exists *that which* would account for temporal order, the god that it introduces must be something of a specific sort, with specific ways of working. If these are in time, then the problem of temporal order has merely been re-located. If they are somehow outside time, then we have an even more obscure and antecedently unlikely supposition than that of immediate intention-fulfilment. In comparison with these unlikelihoods, the supposition that there simply is temporal order, as an ultimate, not further explainable, brute fact, is much more probable.

As with the form of the argument based on spatial order, these objections can be avoided only by going back to the supposedly *a priori* principle that a god is self-explanatory, whereas everything else is in need of further explanation. But to make this move is to revert to the core of the intendedly demonstrative forms of the cosmological argument, whose weaknesses have already been exposed in Chapter 5.

I conclude that the argument for design cannot be revived. The advance of science has destroyed the starting-points which made it initially plausible and attractive in the eighteenth century, while the general philosophical objections which were brought against it even then by Kant and, above all, by Hume, remain in force against Swinburne's restatement of it, and, I surmise, against all possible reconstructions.

9

The Problem of Evil

(a) *Survey of the Problem*

We have examined various arguments for theism. We have found none that is conclusive, nor, indeed, any that has much weight, though we have still to consider whether the cumulative effect of a number of arguments, each quite weak in itself, is to constitute some presumption in favour of theism. Those who are sceptical about traditional religious doctrines can resist all the assaults of the believers; but they need not limit themselves to resistance: they can go over to counter-attack. Such a counter-attack will naturally start with the posing of the problem of evil. This problem seems to show not merely that traditional theism lacks rational support, but rather that it is positively irrational, in that some of its central doctrines are, as a set, inconsistent with one another.

According to traditional theism, there is a god who is both omnipotent (and omniscient) and wholly good, and yet there is evil in the world. How can this be? It is true that there is no explicit contradiction between the statements that there is an omnipotent and wholly good god and that there is evil. But if we add the at least initially plausible premises that good is opposed to evil in such a way that a being who is wholly good eliminates evil as far as he can, and that there are no limits to what an omnipotent being can do, then we do have a contradiction. A wholly good omnipotent being would eliminate evil completely; if there really are evils, then there cannot be any such being.

The problem of evil, in the sense in which I am using this phrase, is essentially a logical problem: it sets the theist the task of clarifying and if possible reconciling the several beliefs which he holds. It is not a scientific problem that might be solved by further discoveries, nor a practical problem that might be solved by a decision or an action. And the problem in this sense signally does not arise for those whose views of the world are markedly different from traditional theism.

It is plain, therefore, that this problem can be easily solved if one gives up at least one of the propositions that constitute it. Someone who holds that there is in some sense a god, but one who is not wholly good, or, though powerful, not quite omnipotent, will not be embarrassed by this difficulty.[1] Equally, someone who holds that nothing is really evil in the sense in which evil is opposed to the sort of goodness he ascribes to his god, is not faced with *this* problem, though he may have difficulty in explaining the point of his use of the words 'good' and 'evil', and in saying how it is related to more common uses.

Theists who are not prepared to take any of these drastic steps have, nevertheless, tried to solve the problem. The possibility of a solution lies in the fact that either or both of the additional premisses suggested above may be modified: the opposition between good and evil may be construed in such a way that a wholly good god would not, after all, eliminate evil as far as he could, and (whether this is so or not) it may be argued that there are limits—and limits that matter in this context—to what even an omnipotent being can do.

For example, it would usually be said that God cannot do what is logically impossible; and this, we can agree, would be no real departure from omnipotence. Then it may be suggested that good cannot exist without evil, that evil is necessary as a counterpart to good. If this counterpart relationship is logically necessary, then a wholly good being would presumably not eliminate evil completely, even if he could do so, since this would logically require the disappearance of goodness also, including, presumably, his own. However, the contrast principle that is being invoked here is very dubious. It is plausible enough to say that if some quality or property were strictly universal, that is, if everything whatever had the property and nothing lacked it, then there would be no need in any language for a predicate that picked out that property; it is also fairly plausible, though not fully persuasive, to say that if a property were thus universal no one would notice it. But it is not at all plausible to say that if there were nothing that lacked a property, the property itself would not exist, that by being everywhere it would somehow cease to be anywhere. And even if we granted this implausible principle— and, further, neglected the possibility of things' being neither good

[1] Cf. J. S. Mill, *Three Essays on Religion* (Longmans, London, 1874).

nor evil—and so admitted that a wholly good god, limited only by logical impossibilities, would have a sufficient reason for not eliminating evil completely, this would explain, compatibly with theistic doctrines, the occurrence of only a minute quantum of evil, just enough to satisfy this odd metaphysical principle and so permit the continuance in existence of the otherwise pervasive goodness of creation and its creator. But it is not in this sense that theists traditionally hold that there are evils in the world: they are not content to regard whatever things they take to be wrong or bad as a minute, necessary, and indeed welcome contrast to goodness which would otherwise efface itself.

Popular theodicies, that is, attempts to justify God in the face of the widespread occurrence of what are at the same time held to be evils, make far more use of the notion that evil is often necessary as a means to good. Of course this way of thinking is entirely natural for human agents in the ordinary circumstances of life. It may well be that children can develop into responsible self-governing adults only by being allowed to make mistakes and to learn from them. Parents, teachers, and statesmen, among others, constantly use, or permit, as means to what they see as good, things which, considered on their own, they regret or deplore. Any sensible person may be ready, though he regards pain in itself as an evil, to put up with painful medical treatment if he is convinced that it is necessary as a means to a lasting improvement in his health, or to endure toil that is in itself undesirable for the sake of commensurate rewards. Also, taking a wider view, it is reasonable to say that though pain, as experienced by animals of many kinds, is bad in itself, it performs a useful warning function: it directs the animal away from what would cause greater injury or death. Even pain which does not itself serve this useful purpose is in general causally connected with that which is beneficial: it would be hardly possible for animals to have nervous systems of the sorts that enable them to be guided by pain away from sources of harm without thereby being liable sometimes to suffer pain that, on these particular occasions, brings no good results. Such truths as these are familiar and obvious; but they are also totally irrelevant. For since they all concern causal relationships, in which something counted as evil is seen to be causally necessary as a means to, or as a result or accompaniment of, something that can be seen as a greater, counterbalancing, good, they explain only why agents whose power is limited by independently existing causal laws may reasonably put up with evil for the sake of the associated good. But

God, by hypothesis, is not such an agent. If omnipotence means anything at all, it means power over causal laws. If there is an omnipotent creator, then if there are any causal laws he must have made them, and if he is still omnipotent he must be able to override them. If there is a god, then, he does not need to use means to attain his ends. So it is idle to refer, in a theodicy, to any ordinary, factual, means–end, or in general causal, relationships. One would think that so elementary and obvious a point hardly needs to be made; but it does need to be made, and stressed, because it is constantly ignored or slurred over not only in popular but even in philosophical treatments of the problem of evil.[2]

Much more interesting than this is the suggestion that things that are evil in themselves may contribute to the goodness of an 'organic whole' in which they are found, so that the world as a whole is better as it is, with some evils in it, than it could be if there were no evil. This suggestion may be developed in several ways. It may be supported by an aesthetic analogy, by the fact that contrasts heighten beauty, and that in a musical work, for example, there may occur discords which somehow add to the beauty of the work as a whole. Alternatively, the notion of progress may be used: it may be argued that the best possible organization of the world will be not static but progressive, perhaps with what Kant called an endless progress towards perfection: the gradual overcoming of evil by good is really a finer thing than would be the eternal unchallenged sovereignty of good.

In either case, this solution usually starts from the assumption that the evil whose existence constitutes the problem of evil is primarily what is called physical evil, that is, pain, suffering, and disease. If this is taken as the difficulty, the theist can reply that these things make possible the existence of sympathy, kindness, heroism, and the gradually successful struggle of doctors, reformers, and so on to overcome these evils. Indeed, theists often seize the opportunity to accuse those who raise the problem of taking a low, materialist view of good and evil, equating these with pleasure and pain, and of ignoring the more spiritual goods which arise, and can only arise, in the struggle against evils.

To understand this solution, let us call pain, suffering, disease, and

[2] E.g. J. Hick in *Evil and the God of Love* (Macmillan, London, 1966) seems to combine an instrumental explanation of evil with the more consistent view that 'sin plus redemption is of more value in the sight of God than an innocence that permits neither sin nor redemption'. For other hints of the latter view, see the quotations to which n. 10 to Chapter 14 below (p. 257) refers.

the like 'first-order evil'; what contrasts with these, for example pleasure and happiness, will then count as 'first-order good'. Distinct from this will be 'second-order good' which somehow emerges in an organic whole, a complex situation in which some first-order evil is a necessary component: that is, the first-order evil is logically, not merely causally, necessary for the emergence of the second-order good. Exactly how this emerges will vary from case to case: it may be simply the heightening of happiness by the contrast with misery, or it may include sympathy with suffering, heroism in facing dangers, or the gradual decrease of first-order evil and the gradual increase of first-order good. Then to explain the first-order evils in a theistically satisfactory way it must be held that the second-order good is greater in magnitude or importance than the first-order evil which is logically necessary for it, that the good outweighs the evil it involves.

This is a particularly subtle attempt to solve the problem. It defends God's goodness and omnipotence on the ground that (on a long enough view) this is the best of all possible worlds, because it includes the important second-order goods, and yet it admits that real evils, namely the first-order ones, occur. It reconciles these apparently incompatible theses by, in effect, modifying one of our additional premisses. It denies that a wholly good being would eliminate evil as far as he could, but explains this denial by pointing to a reason why a being who is wholly good, in a sense that is thoroughly intelligible to us and coherent with the ordinary concept of goodness, might not eliminate evils, even though it was logically possible to do so and though he was able to do whatever is logically possible, and was limited only by the logical impossibility of having the second-order good without the first-order evil.

Since this defence is formally possible, and its principle involves no real abandonment of our ordinary view of the opposition between good and evil, we can concede that the problem of evil does not, after all, show that the central doctrines of theism are logically inconsistent with one another. But whether this offers a real solution of the problem is another question. Let us call an evil which is explained and justified in the proposed way an *absorbed* evil. For example, some bit of suffering which is actually the object of kindness or sympathy whose goodness outweighs the badness of that suffering itself will be an absorbed evil, as will be miseries or injustices that are in fact progressively overcome by a struggle whose nobility is a higher good which outweighs the evils without which it could not have occurred. What this defence shows, then, is that the existence of completely absorbed evils is compatible with the existence of an omnipotent and wholly good god. But then the vital question is this: can the theist maintain that the only evils that occur in the world are absorbed evils? When this question is squarely put, it is surely plain that he cannot. On the one hand there are surplus first-order evils, suffering and the like which are not actually used in any good organic whole, and on the other there are second-order evils; these will not be incorporated in second-order goods, but will contrast with them: malevolence, cruelty, callousness, cowardice, and states of affairs in which there is not progress but decline, where things get worse rather than better. The problem, therefore, now recurs as the problem of unabsorbed evils, and we have as yet no way of reconciling their existence with that of a god of the traditional sort.

This brings us to the best known move in theodicy, the free will defence: evils—that is, as we can now say, unabsorbed evils—are due entirely to bad free choices made by human beings and perhaps by other created beings that have free will. But how is this a defence? Why would a wholly good and omnipotent god give to human beings—and also, perhaps, to angels—the freedom which they have misused? The answer must be either that such freedom is itself a higher, third-order, good which outweighs the evils which are either constituted or brought about by its misuse—or, at the very least, which, when the freedom was conferred, outweighed whatever risk of these was even divinely foreseeable—or else that such freedom is logically necessary for some other third-order goods which do the outweighing. Since these (bad) choices are freely made by men or by fallen (or falling) angels, neither they nor their effects can be ascribed to God. All that can be or needs to be ascribed to him is the creation of beings with the freedom to make morally significant choices. But it must also be held that the existence and functioning of such beings either are higher-order goods, or are a logically necessary presupposition of higher-order goods, which outweigh (the risk of) such bad choices and their consequences, so that a god might reasonably choose to create such beings and leave them free.

It is plain that this is the only solution of the problem of evil that has any chance of succeeding. This defence alone allows the theist to admit that there are some real and unabsorbed evils, some items which the world would, from however broad and ultimate a perspective, be better without (so that this is *not* the best of all possible worlds), and yet at the same time to detach their occurrence from

God, to show them as not having been chosen by God, who none the less seems to have been given a reason, compatible with his complete goodness and omnipotence, and perhaps with his omniscience too, for bringing about the state of affairs from which they arise and for allowing them to occur. We shall, therefore, have to examine this solution with some care. But first I want to glance at some other approaches.

(b) *Attempts to Sidestep the Problem*

One of these approaches may be summed up in the phrase 'God's goodness is not ours'. In other words, when the theist says that God is wholly good he does not mean that God has anything like the purposes and tendencies that would count as good in a human being. But then why call him good? Is not this description misleading? Or is 'good' here being used simply as an honorific term, without its usual descriptive meaning? Hume appropriately puts this suggestion into the mouth of his sceptic, Philo, who says that 'we have no more reason to infer, that the rectitude of the supreme Being resembles human rectitude than that his benevolence resembles the human'.[3]

John Stuart Mill, in his *Autobiography*, points out that this approach was implicit in much of the religious teaching of his time. His father, he says, looked upon religion as the greatest enemy of morality, 'above all, by radically vitiating the standard of morals; making it consist in doing the will of a being, on whom it lavishes indeed all the phrases of adulation, but whom in sober truth it depicts as eminently hateful'. In effect God is being *called* good, while at the same time he is being *described* as bad, that is, as having purposes and acting upon motives which in all ordinary circumstances we would recognize as bad; he is depicted as behaving in some respects like a malevolent demon, in others like a petulant tyrant, and in others again like a mischievous and thoughtless child. Now certainly if such motives as these are ascribed to God, there will be no difficulty in reconciling his omnipotence with the occurrence of what would ordinarily be called evils. But to argue in this way is merely to defend a shadow, while abandoning the substance, of the traditional claim that God is wholly good.[4]

Another approach says that it is a mistake to try to minimize

---

[3] *Dialogues concerning Natural Religion*, Part XI.
[4] J. S. Mill, *Autobiography*, edited by Jack Stillinger (Oxford University Press, 1969), Chapter 2.

evil, or even to see it as a problem for religion. Theists, Rolf Gruner says, 'would be wiser still if they not only admitted evil but emphasized it as crucial. For it is no overstatement to say that their faith depends on it. All religious belief is connected with the manner in which men see themselves and the world, and where the "tragic sense" of life is lacking and the consciousness of indigence, deficiency and transitoriness absent, religion will be unknown. Perfect beings in a perfect universe have no need of it, nor apparently have those for whom evils are avoidable defects to be gradually eliminated by man's growing perfection ... the strongest believers have usually been those who have had the firmest conviction of the reality of evil, and many or most of them have never made any attempt at theodicy.'[5]

There is certainly some truth in this, and it is at least a plausible suggestion (which will receive some support in Chapter 10) that men would not have developed religion in a happier or less frustrating world. Of such a world Bishop Heber might have said

> All round, with lavish kindness
> God's gifts like manna fall;
> The heathen, in their blindness,
> Do not bow down at all.

But how does this remove or resolve the problem of evil? Gruner clearly thinks it is paradoxical that 'Christianity depends on the very fact which is said to disprove it'. There is indeed a paradox here, but it lies squarely within orthodox theism. Hume brings this out clearly. While giving the argument for design and the associated task of theodicy to Cleanthes, he puts Gruner's view into the mouth of Demea. What he thus conveys is that both of these represent real and influential, though opposite, trends within orthodox religion. 'It is my opinion', Demea says, 'that each man feels, in a manner, the truth of religion within his own breast; and from a consciousness of his imbecility and misery, rather than from any reasoning, is led to seek protection from that Being, on whom he and all nature is dependent.' And he goes on to stress the miseries of human life. When Cleanthes protests that his experience, at least, does not support this dismal view, Demea replies, 'If you feel not human misery yourself ... I congratulate you on so happy a singularity'. Demea's emphasis on the wretchedness of human life is then used by Philo for

[5] R. Gruner, 'The Elimination of the Argument from Evil', in *Theology* 83 (1980), pp. 416-24.

his presentation of the problem of evil. But Demea, like Gruner, is not disturbed by this problem: 'This world is but a point in comparison of the universe: This life but a moment in comparison of eternity. The present evil phenomena, therefore, are rectified in other regions, and in some future period of existence. And the eyes of men, being then opened to larger views of things, see the whole connection of general laws, and trace, with adoration, the benevolence and rectitude of the Deity, through all the mazes and intricacies of his providence.'[6]

But, as Cleanthes says, these are 'arbitrary suppositions'; we cannot rely on them when the issue whether there is a just, benevolent, and all-powerful deity is still in doubt. And, as Philo says, even if pain and misery in man were *compatible* with infinite power and goodness in the Deity (on the supposition that it will all be put right somehow, somewhere, sometime), this is useless if we are still at the stage of trying to *infer* the existence and the attributes of a god from what we independently know. And even if there were a future life in comparison with which the evils of this one would seem negligible, that still would not explain, compatibly with theism, the occurrence of those evils themselves.

The mere fact, then, that faith often rests upon a tragic sense of the evil in the world does not do away with the need for a theodicy. It means, no doubt, that some of the firmest believers *feel* no need for a theodicy; but one is still needed if their position, and that of theism generally, is to be made rationally defensible. (We shall return, in Chapters 11 and 12, to the question whether religion can simply do without a rational defence.) But can a theodicy be, not dispensed with, but rather supplied by this connection between evil and faith? Does God make this world a wretched place so that men will feel the need for religion? Are not only suffering but also sinfulness necessary for the higher goods of redemption and of man's realization of his utter dependence on God?

Two suggestions need to be distinguished here. The notion that God uses evils as a means to such higher goods is, as we have seen, incompatible with the doctrine that he is omnipotent, and therefore does not need to use deplorable means to achieve his ends. It is, of course, understandable that an all too human deity might decide to make his creatures miserable so that they would be more abject in their devotion: 'I'll make it hot for them, and then they will come crawling back to me'. But this account is inconsistent alike with

[6] *Dialogues*, Part X.

God's goodness and with his power. It would be more coherent to argue that sin, for example, is logically necessary for repentance and redemption, and that 'joy shall be in heaven over one sinner that repenteth, more than over ninety and nine just persons, which need no repentance'.[7] Sin followed by repentance and redemption would then be an absorbed evil. But, however good the authority for it, this is a very strange view. What the parables plausibly say is that a father may rejoice more over the return of a prodigal son than over another's merely constant good behaviour, and that a frugal housewife may be more pleased about recovering a coin she had thought she had lost than about simply not losing several of equal value. But it does not follow that the father prefers on the whole to have a prodigal son who ultimately returns than to have a constantly well-behaved one, or that the housewife would be better pleased on the whole to have lost the coin and found it again than never to have lost it. Perhaps these, odd though they are, would be comprehensible human reactions; even so, it would be hard to transfer them to a supposedly omniscient god, or to endorse the sober evaluation that sin plus repentance is, as an organic whole, better than sinlessness.

Gruner, in fact, does not argue in these ways. He thinks that 'the argument from evil ... cannot be answered at all but only circumvented'. The circumvention consists in attacking as incoherent the demand, supposedly implicit in the sceptic's attack on theism, for a world free from all evil. But this is a misleading way of stating the issue. The sceptic is not asking *for* anything: he is merely asking *whether* an apparent inconsistency in the theist's position can be cured. The demand for a world free from all evil is one that seems to be implicit in the set of doctrines that make up orthodox theism— though, as we have seen, such theism *also* stresses and trades upon the fact that the world is *not* free from evil. No doubt a created world—and particularly what Gruner calls 'a real, earthly, "this-worldly" world—as opposed to a realm of pure spirit'—could not be free from what might be seen as mere limitations and deficiencies: it could not, like God, be infinitely perfect; but nothing has been said to show that real, deplorable, unabsorbed evils, such as theists themselves constantly condemn, are logically necessary in an earthly world.

---

[7] Luke 15: 7.

(c) *The Paradox of Omnipotence*

We shall have to come back, then, to the free will defence as the only hope for a reasoned theodicy. But there is a preliminary problem about the relation between omnipotence and free will. Are men supposed to be free in the sense merely that God *does not* control their choosing, or in the sense that he *cannot* do so? The second alternative poses the paradox of omnipotence: can an omnipotent being make things which he cannot control?

When I originally raised this question, I thought that it was a genuine paradox, that the question could not be answered satisfactorily either in the affirmative or in the negative. I argued that we should distinguish between orders of omnipotence: first-order omnipotence would be unlimited power to act, second-order omnipotence unlimited power to determine what powers to act things should have. (And so on, if required.) But then if a god had second-order omnipotence he could use it so as to give certain things a power to act that was independent of his own power to act, so that he would not then have first-order omnipotence. Omnipotences of different orders can thus come into conflict with one another, and I concluded that nothing could have omnipotences of all orders at once.[8]

However, this was a mistake. Clearly, a god might *have* both first- and second-order omnipotence, so long as he did not *exercise* his second-order power in such a way as to limit his first-order power. But, further, it has been argued that the phrase 'things which an omnipotent being cannot control' is self-contradictory, so that to make such things is logically impossible, and therefore that God cannot make such things, but that this is no defect in omnipotence of any order, since it has been agreed all along that omnipotence does not include the power to do what is logically impossible. Hence the negative answer to the paradox question is satisfactory after all.[9]

But is there not an equally plausible defence of the affirmative answer? If a being with second-order omnipotence confers on certain beings a power of making uncontrollable choices, then to control their choices would be to control things that are omnipotently made uncontrollable, and *this* is logically impossible. Hence, even a being with (first-order) omnipotence is unable to control such things, and failure to control them does not count against his omnipotence, since, as before, this is admittedly limited by logical impossibilities.

[8] Cf. my 'Evil and Omnipotence' in *Mind* 64 (1955).
[9] B. Mayo, 'Mr Keene on Omnipotence', in *Mind* 70 (1961), pp. 249–50.

Thus an omnipotent being *can* make things such that he cannot control them.

But if both the affirmative and the negative answers are thus defensible, the paradox is reinstated. We no longer have a contradiction within the notion of unrestricted omnipotence, omnipotence of all orders at once, but we have instead an undecidable question about it.[10]

This problem is related to another question: does omnipotence entail omnificence? If there were an omnipotent (and omniscient) being, would everything that happens be his doing? We might argue as follows: if God can make it to be that not-X, but it is that X, then he has knowingly allowed it to be that X; and is this not equivalent to making it to be that X? Against this, it might be argued that there is a clear everyday distinction between positively bringing something about and merely letting it happen when one could have prevented it. Letting someone die when one could have saved him is not quite the same thing as killing him, though it is a point in dispute among moralists whether the one is as bad as the other. But we must also consider on what this everyday distinction rests. If we bring something about, we exert effort, but if we merely allow it to happen we do not; rather, we spare ourselves the effort it would have cost us to prevent it. There is a passage of force between agent and result when we do something, but not when we merely allow it to happen. Also, merely allowing something to happen, even though we know in some sense that it will, is commonly associated with some degree of inadvertence; bringing something about (intentionally) usually involves some conscious attention. But the more completely the matter is within our power, the less clear does the first ground of distinction become. If it is something that we can either bring about or prevent with negligible effort, allowing it to happen is less clearly differentiated from bringing it about. Similarly, the more completely the matter is within our knowledge and at the focus of our attention, the less clear does the second ground of distinction become. It seems, then, that as power and knowledge increase without limit, this everyday distinction fades out, and for a being with unlimited power and unlimited vision it would not hold at all.

In short, it seems that omnipotence and omniscience together entail omnificence: God does everything. Of course this need not

---

[10] This is analogous to the 'truth-teller variants' of the Liar and other paradoxes; cf. my *Truth, Probability, and Paradox* (Oxford University Press, 1973), pp. 240–1, 260–2.

mean that no one else does anything. A man does whatever we ordinarily take him as doing; but if there is a god whose omnipotence means that he is in full control of the man's choices, then he does it too. It would follow that if men sin, then God is also the author of that sin.[11] Consequently the free will defence cannot detach evil from God unless it assumes that the freedom conferred on men is such that God *cannot* (not merely does not) control their choosing. That is, it has to adopt exclusively the affirmative answer to the question in the original paradox of omnipotence, despite the fact that there is nothing in the concept of omnipotence that justifies a preference for this over the negative answer.

Plainly, these are difficulties for theism. But let us suppose (simply in order to complete the discussion) that they can somehow be surmounted, and assume that the freedom invoked in the free will defence is a freedom of choice that even God cannot control.

(d) *The Free Will Defence*

It is customary to disguinguish natural evils, such as pain, from moral evils, the various forms of wickedness. Moral evils, it is suggested, consist in the misuse of freedom of choice; they are thus directly covered by the free will defence. Some natural evils are due partly to human wickedness—for example, cruelty—or to human mistakes; but only partly, for something else must have provided the opportunities for cruelty and the conditions in which mistakes can do harm. But the vast majority of natural evils cannot be ascribed to human choices at all, and it seems, therefore, that the free will defence cannot cover them even indirectly. But Alvin Plantinga argues that it can cover them, since they can be ascribed to the malevolent actions of fallen angels.[12] Formally, no doubt, this is possible; but it is another of what Cleanthes called arbitrary suppositions. While we have a direct acquaintance with some wrong human choices—our own—and our everyday understanding extends to the recognition of the like choices of other human beings, we have no such knowledge of the activities of angels, fallen or otherwise: these are at best part of the religious hypothesis which is still in dispute, and cannot be relied upon to give it any positive support. This is at most a

[11] Cf. Hume's *Enquiry concerning Human Understanding*, Section 8, Part 2.

[12] *The Nature of Necessity* (see n. 1 to Chapter 3, p. 41, above), p. 192. As Swinburne points out, in *The Existence of God*, p. 202, this is an *ad hoc* hypothesis the addition of which tends to disconfirm the hypothesis that there is a god.

possible explanation of natural evils: it could not be said actually to explain them, even if the free will defence as a whole were in good order.

This fact is all the more important, because the boundary between natural and moral evils is not simple or clear-cut. Even the worst human behaviour has a somewhat mixed character. 'Here we shall find', says Francis Hutcheson, 'that the basest actions are dressed in some tolerable mask. What others call avarice, appears to the agent a prudent care of a family, or friends; fraud, artful conduct; malice and revenge, a just sense of honour and a vindication of our right in possessions, of fame; fire and sword, and desolation among enemies, a just thorough defence of our country; persecution, a zeal for the truth, and for the eternal happiness of men, which heretics oppose. In all these instances, men generally act from a sense of virtue upon false opinions, and mistaken benevolence; upon wrong or partial views of public good, and the means to promote it; or upon very narrow systems formed by like foolish opinions. It is not a delight in the misery of others, or malice, which occasions the horrid crimes which fill our histories; but generally an injudicious unreasonable enthusiasm for some kind of limited virtue.'[13] This is surely right. Hutcheson was writing in 1725, but what he says here applies equally well to the horrors of the twentieth century. Wars, great or small; Stalin's tyrannies and persecutions; the Nazi holocaust; the unleashing of firestorms on German cities; Hiroshima and Nagasaki; Vietnam; Cambodia; terrorism of all varieties; Islamic fanaticism; in all of these some kind of idealism has played a significant part, providing some justification or excuse, however misguided, that falls under one or more of Hutcheson's headings. Where several parties start with what seems a reasonable pursuit of their legitimate aspirations, they can be and often are trapped in states of conflict where to do terrible things to one another—and, incidentally, to innocent bystanders—appears justifiable or even obligatory. We cannot put this down simply to human failings: a large part of the fault lies in the way these conflict traps arise from human interactions, indeed, but not as the fulfilment of any human intentions. There are *circumstances of injustice*: situations in which people are led to the extremes of inhumanity by steps each of which seems reasonable or even unavoidable. These circumstances of injustice are, therefore, an important variety of *natural* evils which are constantly intertwined with moral ones. There

[13] F. Hutcheson, *Inquiry* (see n. 10 to Chapter 6, p. 117, above), Section IV, pp. 124-5.

is more than Plantinga may have noticed for which his fallen angels would have to be given the discredit.

If the free will defence is to be of any use to theism, then, it must be extended to cover natural evils, presumably in Plantinga's way, arbitrary though that is. However, I shall leave this extension aside, and examine the argument simply with reference to human free will.

Here we must take account of the omniscience that traditional theism ascribes to God. Is he supposed to know in advance, when he creates men with free will, all the uses they will actually make of it? Let us assume, first, that he does know this; we shall come back later to the alternative assumption that he does not. Given that God does know this, anyone who uses this defence must say that it is better on the whole that men should act freely, and sometimes—indeed, quite often—err, as they do, than that they should be innocent automata, acting rightly in a wholly determined way. But he must also say that only these alternatives were open to God, that foreseeable human wrongdoing was an unavoidable accompaniment of freedom of choice—unavoidable even for a being whose powers were limited only by logical impossibilities. But how can this be so? If God has made men such that in their free choices they sometimes prefer what is good and sometimes what is evil, why could he not have made men such that they always freely choose the good?[14] Since there seems to be no reason why an omnipotent, omniscient, and wholly good god would not have preferred this alternative, the theist who maintains that there is such a god, and yet that he did not opt for this—since by his own account human beings make bad free choices—seems to be committed to an inconsistent set of assertions.

For at least some theists this difficulty is made even more acute by some of their further beliefs: I mean those who envisage a happier or more perfect state of affairs than now exists, whether they look forward to the kingdom of God on earth, or confine their optimism to the expectation of heaven. In either case they are explicitly recognizing the possibility of a state of affairs in which created beings always freely choose the good. If such a state of affairs is coherent enough to be the object of a reasonable hope or faith, it is hard to explain why it does not obtain already.

Nevertheless, it is often thought that this suggestion, that God

---

[14] This was the central thesis of my 'Evil and Omnipotence' (see n. 8, p. 160, above) and of A. Flew's 'Divine Omnipotence and Human Freedom', in *New Essays in Philosophical Theology*, edited by A. Flew and A. C. MacIntyre (SCM Press, London, 1955 and 1963).

could have made men such that they would always freely choose the good, is not coherent. Sometimes this objection rests merely on a confusion. It would, no doubt, be incoherent to say that God makes men freely choose the good: if God had made men choose, that is, forced them to choose one way rather than the other, they would not have been choosing freely. But that is not what was suggested, which was rather that God might have made—that is, created—beings, human or not, *such that* they would always freely choose the good; and there is at least no immediate incoherence or self-contradiction in that.

Again, it may be objected that the notion of beings such that they would always freely choose the good assumes that these beings would be free from temptations, that they would have only innocent inclinations, and so could not exemplify the moral value of resisting and overcoming temptations to do wrong. But it is not for me to make assumptions about this either way. Since I am charging the theist with holding incompatible beliefs, it is *his* conceptions of good, evil, and so on that are in play here. He can take his pick about which he considers to be the better state of affairs, either there being agents with free will but only innocent inclinations—that is, with what Kant calls a holy will—or there being free agents who have a mixture of good and bad inclinations but who always control their bad inclinations, resist temptations, and always act well after all for that reason—that is, who are governed by what Kant calls a sense of duty. The trouble is that, whichever of these he takes to be the ideal state of affairs, he also asserts or admits that it frequently fails to occur.

Having dismissed these two objections, we come to the serious question whether it might for some reason have been logically impossible that a god should create beings such that they would always freely choose the good. Let us consider this in a series of steps.[15]

(i) Granted that it is logically possible that one man should on one occasion freely choose the good—which the theist undoubtedly concedes—might it be logically impossible that all men should always do so? Some objectors have thought this, suggesting that whatever is done freely must be sometimes not done. But there is no reason why this should be so, unless 'freedom' is actually defined so as to include or entail variation. And then we have a problem. Freedom, we remember, is supposed to be a higher good which outweighs the badness of the bad actions, and of their results, which it is alleged to

[15] Cf. my 'Theism and Utopia' in *Philosophy* 37 (1962).

bring with it. But in so far as freedom *definitionally* involves variation, it is quite implausible to regard it as such a higher good. What special value could there conceivably be in the variation between good and bad choices as such? This variation aspect of freedom cannot be what makes it so very well worth while. And surely whatever the valuable, other, aspects or consequences of freedom may be, it is at least logically possible that they should exist without such variation, that is, without bad choices actually being made. So in any sense of 'freely' that is of use for the free will defence, it must be logically possible that all men should always freely choose the good; and, as we know, it is only logical possibility that matters here.

(ii) Granted this, might it be logically impossible that men should be *such that* they always freely choose the good? If determinism and freedom are compatible, there can be no difficulty about this step. On a determinist view, what agents choose to do results causally from what they antecedently are, and the ascription of freedom denies external constraints which would make their actions depend on something other than their natures; it may also deny certain internal, mental, conditions which would prevent their choices from being proper expressions of their natures. So what a determinist calls free choices flow determinedly from the nature of the agent, and it follows that if it is possible that men should always freely choose the good, it must be equally possible that they should be *such that* they do so. But if compatibilism is rejected, this step becomes controversial. And many thinkers have asserted incompatibilism. Some, accepting determinism, have therefore adopted 'hard determinism', explicitly rejecting what they take to be our ordinary notions of freedom, choice, responsibility, and desert, while others have denied determinism, partly in order to be able to maintain the applicability of these other notions. We must therefore digress to consider this issue.

(e) *Digression: the Nature of Free Will*

For our purposes, it is the second, libertarian, kind of incompatibilist that matters, the thinker who claims that we do indeed have contra-causal free will. There are two great difficulties for this position, that of giving any evidence for it, and that of even saying just what contra-causal free will would be. The libertarian may try to meet both difficulties at once by appealing to our ordinary belief, or knowledge, that an agent frequently *could have done otherwise* than he did. Now if we can say truly, at time t_2, that although A did X he could have done Y, the following statement must have been true at some earlier time t_1: 'A can do X and he can do Y'. So let us concentrate on this supposed present situation at t_1, that the agent can do either of these two things. Unfortunately, the word 'can' is indeterminate in meaning. Typically, it denies the presence of obstacles, constraints, or restrictions; but in different contexts it refers to obstacles, etc., of different kinds. In this case, it may mean that there are no external barriers to A's doing X or to A's doing Y, and hence that what he does is up to him. It may also mean that there is no abnormal psychological condition from which A is suffering (such as agoraphobia, or having been hypnotized) which would, say, prevent his doing Y or ensure his doing X. Or, again, it may mean that there is nothing at all that excludes either possibility, in particular, no set of antecedent sufficient causes for his doing X rather than Y, or vice versa. The causal determinist will in most ordinary cases agree that A can do X and can do Y in the first two senses, but deny this in the third; the libertarian will assert it in the third sense, and therefore also in the other two. But since 'can', and hence also 'could have done otherwise', are systematically indeterminate in meaning between what the determinist accepts and what he rejects but the libertarian asserts, the everyday belief that agents often could have done otherwise does not even begin to settle the issue between them. Even if the libertarian could show that the ordinary use commonly expresses a belief that an agent could have done otherwise in the most comprehensive sense, that there was, antecedently, nothing at all that excluded the doing of Y, it would still be easy for the determinist to argue that this belief may itself rest on a confused transition from the one sense of 'can' and 'could have' to the other.

Perhaps the libertarian will appeal to a 'sense of freedom', to some direct awareness that an agent has that he is choosing between (say) two courses of action that are both open to him in the most comprehensive sense: he knows that he can (without qualification) do X, and equally that he can do Y, that he is not even causally bound to go one way rather than the other. But how could he be aware of this? One can have a pretty direct awareness of external obstacles: one commonly knows, or can easily find out, if one is tied up, locked in, being swept away by a torrent, or indeed if someone is holding a pistol to one's head. Rather less reliably, one may be able to find out if one has been hypnotized or is suffering from some phobia or obsession. By contrast, one can therefore be fairly directly aware that there are, at the moment, no such constraints on one's choice or action. But in normal cases, where there are no such constraints as these, one would not be directly aware of any antecedent causes of one's choosing, and equally, therefore, one could not be directly aware of the absence of antecedent causes. Contra-causal freedom, or the lack of it, simply is not the sort of thing of which we could have any 'sense', any immediate introspective evidence. And in fact some of the thinkers who have argued most energetically in favour of contra-causal freedom, such as C. A. Campbell, restrict it to cases where there is a struggle between the (moral) self and its so far formed character, and do not claim that it occurs in the most obvious everyday situations where people feel free to do one thing or another, for example, in deciding whether to have boiled potatoes or chips.[16]

Campbell argues that the self is conscious, in cases of struggle, of '*combating* his formed character', and therefore 'knows very well indeed—from the inner standpoint—what is meant by an act which is the *self's* act and which nevertheless does not follow from the self's *character*'. Admittedly one can be aware of struggling against what one takes to be one's character as so far formed; but one cannot be immediately aware that what thus struggles lacks a causal history.

On the other hand, it is true that there is no conclusive evidence or argument for causal determinism about human actions. The most weighty argument on this side relies on the assumption that all mental occurrences are either identical with neurophysiological ones or so closely correlated with their neurophysiological bases that determinism would carry over from the latter to the former, and hence to choices and actions. But this argument is somewhat weakened by the indeterminism that is currently accepted in quantum physics, together with the fact that triggering relations would allow an indeterminacy that belongs primarily to micro-phenomena to carry over into ordinary large-scale affairs. And in any case there would be an *ignoratio elenchi* involved in relying on a physicalist argument for a fundamental criticism of theism, since a theist would deny the physicalism, being committed to the view that spirit or consciousness is somehow prior to material things. Let us not, therefore, assert that causal determinism holds, but rather leave the possibility of indeterminism open, and see whether the libertarian can make any use of it.

Let us grant, then, that human choices and actions may not have antecedent sufficient causes; in what other ways might they come

<hr>

[16] C. A. Campbell, *On Selfhood and Godhood* (Allen & Unwin, London, 1957), pp. 167–78, and *In Defence of Free Will* (Allen & Unwin, London, 1967), pp. 41–4.

about? They might be purely random, subject to no cause and no explanation. Or there might be some element of randomness within limits set by prior causes. Or they might be brought about by events which are themselves subject only to statistical laws, such as those of quantum physics are supposed to be. But none of these possibilities is of the least use to a libertarian who is hoping to use the free will defence. For that defence requires that human free will should either be, or be necessary for, something of such great value that it outweighs the badness of such wrong choices as are made, and we can discern no such value in any of these kinds of complete or partial randomness. We can indeed discern value in freedoms of other sorts, for example in doing something because one so wishes, rather than through constraint or duress, or in choosing a pursuit because one values it, or in rationally weighing the merits and demerits of alternative courses of action that are, as far as external constraints are concerned, open to one, and choosing accordingly, or in not being subject to a neurotic compulsion, and so on. But freedoms of all these, and all similar, sorts are entirely compatible with causal determinism, and *a fortiori*, what matters for our present purpose, with an agent's being antecedently such that he will do one thing rather than another. We can, therefore, shelve the question of what evidence there is for the libertarian's view; it is an even greater problem for him to say clearly what sort of freedom he wants and believes that we have. What could count as a freedom that both is of supreme value (either in itself or in what it makes possible) and is incompatible with an agent's being such that he chooses freely in one way rather than another?

There may be a hint in the account given by John Lucas of why we are reluctant to accept determinism. 'If my decision is predictable in this way'—that is, specifically, infallibly, and from temporally antecedent causes—'it is no longer ... the starting point of action. The action no longer can be said to stem *from* my will, even though it be mediated *through* it. And therefore it seems it is not really mine.'[17] But at most this could explain why each agent values his own cause-free status, rather self-centredly, not how contra-causal freedom might be of value from a divine point of view. In any case, the thought that Lucas correctly reports here is confused. The action *does* stem from my will: why would it be *more* mine if I and my will had no causes that would make them predictable (in principle)? In such a line of thought there is often a hint that there is a real *me*, distinct from the

[17] J. R. Lucas, *The Freedom of the Will* (Oxford University Press, 1970), p. 28.

one that is believed to have a causal history, and that if determinism held this real *me* would be helpless, an idle spectator of the course of events. But there is no reason for supposing that there is such an extra-causal self, and no account has been offered of how its operation would differ from that of a causal self. We have here a confused reason for disliking determinism, but no positive account of what non-causal action would be like, or how it would be of value. The mere deleting of causes and predictability, without some other change in the choosing itself, could not confer a new value upon it.

Does Kant help us here? 'Will', he says, 'is a kind of causality belonging to living beings so far as they are rational. *Freedom* would then be the property this causality has of being able to work independently of *determination* by alien causes; just as *natural necessity* is a property characterizing the causality of all non-rational beings— the property of being determined to activity by the influence of alien causes.'[18] Kant thinks that a will is subject to alien causes if and only if it chooses or acts as it does because of *inducements* of some kind— desired ends, temptations, threats, rewards, and so on—whereas it is not subject to alien causes if it chooses simply in accordance with its own rational ideal of universal law or of humanity (or rational nature generally) as an end in itself. But though Kant himself thought he was asserting the contra-causal freedom of some human actions, what he says fails to give any substance to this view. The real distinction he draws is between *alien* causes and the *autonomous* operation of the rational will. But this is entirely compatible with the two suppositions, that there are antecedent sufficient causes of a certain agent's having a rational will with a certain strength, and that what such a rational will does on any occasion, how it responds to its circumstances and struggles against contrary inclinations, depends causally on its character and its strength. Autonomy as contrasted with heteronomy is completely distinct from contra-causal freedom as contrasted with having had a causal history. Though Kant meant to assert both, he succeeded in describing only the former.

These comments apply to the *Groundwork of the Metaphysic of Morals*. In a later work, the *Metaphysic of Morals*, he recognized this distinction. He there contrasted *Wille*, the good, autonomous, will, with *Willkür*, the will in the ordinary sense, the faculty of making choices, some right, some wrong, and ascribed contra-causal freedom

---

[18] I. Kant, *Groundwork of the Metaphysic of Morals*, Third Section; also Introduction to the *Metaphysic of Morals* both in Abbott (see n. 3 to Chapter 6, p. 106, above). Kant's view of freedom is criticized by R. C. S. Walker in *Kant* (Routledge & Kegan Paul, London, 1978), pp. 147–50.

only to the latter. But this emphasizes rather than resolves our present difficulty. The value of freedom has been located in the autonomy, the self-legislative character, of the *Wille*; Kant adds nothing to our vague ordinary views about the value of the Willkür's being uncaused, of the absence of a causal history behind our choices.

In the *Groundwork*, however, he adds a second argument. In the sphere of speculative or theoretical reason 'we cannot possibly conceive of a reason as being consciously directed from outside in regard to its judgements; for in that case the subject would attribute the determination of the power of judgement, not to his reason, but to an impulsion. Reason must look upon itself as the author of its own principles independently of alien influences.' Analogously, 'as practical reason, or as the will of a rational being, it must be regarded by itself as free; that is, the will of a rational being can be a will of his own only under the Idea of freedom ...' This argument has been echoed by many later writers; but it is unsound.[19] The truth is that in the speculative area one cannot make a serious rational judgement, or express a genuine belief, and at the same time see oneself as being *induced* to hold that belief. No one can coherently say 'I believe X because I was bribed to do so' or 'I believe the quantum theory because otherwise I won't get a degree in physics' or—and this will come up again in Chapter 11, in connection with Pascal's wager—'I believe in God because I might go to hell if I didn't'. Equally one cannot have a serious rational belief and at the same time see it as having been caused wholly by irrational causes: for example, no one can coherently combine a serious religious belief with the admission that his own belief is caused wholly by indoctrination in childhood. But what this amounts to is that a rational theoretical judgement cannot be seen by the person who makes it as having been caused *in any of the wrong sorts of way*, that is, in ways irrelevant to the truth or justification of the belief. But there is no difficulty in holding a serious rational belief and at the same time seeing it as having been caused in a proper way. The simplest cases are where the state of affairs which is believed to obtain has caused the belief by affecting the believer's sense-organs and interacting with his innate or developed perceptual capacities. It is the presence of a table that has caused my belief that there is a table in front of me. But the same holds for more complicated reasons for belief. Lucas mistakenly assumes that someone who 'is open-minded towards the truth, and

19 E.g. Lucas, op. cit., pp. 115-16, where other references are given.

can be moved by new arguments that occur to him' cannot also see himself as 'determined by antecedent physical factors'; but there is no conflict between these, provided that those physical factors are (or will be) the bases or neural counterparts of good arguments. Analogously, a serious rational practical judgement does not need either to be or to see itself as uncaused; it needs merely to see itself as not being *improperly* caused. Exactly what this means will depend upon the rest of the moral theory: for Kant, anything other than pure reason's itself being practical would be improper. But, whatever the proper operation is taken to be, no reason has been given why this should not itself have a causal history.

In short, Kant completely fails to supply any description of contra-causally free choosing that might be held to be of high value, nor have his followers been any more successful. *A fortiori*, we have not been shown any valuable kind of freedom that is incompatible with an agent's being such that he chooses freely in one way rather than another.

(f) *The Free Will Defence—continued*

We can, then, return from this digression to our main argument, confident that it is *not* logically impossible that men should be such that they always freely choose the good.

(iii) Granted that this is possible, might it not be logically possible that God should create them so? Since the god in question is, by hypothesis, both omnipotent and omniscient, the creation of any contingent natures whatever should be within his power, and he must know exactly what natures he is creating. Might it be objected that to have been created by God with a certain nature would itself destroy an agent's freedom? No doubt 'freedom' might simply be defined as requiring the sheer springing up from nowhere of an agent's nature, and therefore as excluding that nature's having been created, with knowledge of it, by another agent: then for God to create free agents would be for him to create beings without any specific natures, leaving those natures to spring up from nowhere. But once again it is quite obscure what value there could be in freedom thus defined.

There is, then, no incoherence in the proposed alternative, that God should have made men (and perhaps other free agents) such that they would always act well rather than badly; and, if so, the alleged overriding value of freedom provides no explanation of the occurrence of evils in a universe with a supposedly perfect creator.

But would it not be a rather dull world where everyone always acted rightly? Would not I myself find it boring if there were no confused theodicies to refute? Perhaps. But, as I have said before, it is for the theist, not for me, to say what he counts as good. If he says that a fair amount not only of mistake and folly but also of dishonesty, deceit, injustice, cruelty, hatred, malice, treachery, murder, genocide, and so on is all right, that these are appropriate components in what, taken as a whole, is an optimum state of affairs—that is, are wholly absorbed evils—then that is, indeed, for him a solution of the problem. If there are no unabsorbed evils, then theism is in the clear. But the free will defence was an attempt to reconcile theism with the admitted existence of *unabsorbed* evils, and it fails to do this.

However, Alvin Plantinga has restated this defence with the help of his technical apparatus of possible worlds and individual essences. His argument has at its core a criticism of what he calls 'Leibniz's lapse'. Leibniz thought that if God is omnipotent he could have created any possible world he pleased, provided that it was a world that contained God himself. From the assumption that God is omnipotent in this sense, together with his omniscience and complete goodness, Leibniz inferred that the actual world must be the best of all possible worlds. (Strictly speaking, it would follow only that no possible world is better than this one: there might be others equally good.) This, of course, laid him open to Voltaire's satire in *Candide*. But Plantinga argues that Leibniz need not have got into this trouble: there are possible worlds which even an omnipotent god is not able to create.[20]

He illustrates this thesis with a story about one Curley Smith, a fictional mayor of Boston. Suppose that there is a certain concrete situation in which Curley may be offered a bribe, and he will be free either to take it or to reject it. Perhaps the truth is that if Curley is offered the bribe he will reject it. Then God was not able to create a possible world in which in this situation Curley is offered the bribe and takes it. Less happily, suppose that the truth is that if Curley is offered the bribe he will take it. Then God was not able to create a possible world in which in this situation Curley is offered the bribe and rejects it. Either way, there is at least one possible world which God cannot create, and consideration of other free choices shows that there must be many more. So far so good, and this disposes of Leibniz's lapse. But the crucial step comes next. Plantinga assumes

[20] *The Nature of Necessity*, pp. 173-89.

that Curley is so corrupt that 'Every world God could have actualized is such that if Curley is significantly free in it, he takes at least one wrong action'. Curley Smith suffers from what Plantinga calls 'transworld depravity': in whatever world he exists, if he is significantly free he commits some wrong actions: this Plantinga takes to be a fact about Curley's individual essence. Now God, being omniscient, knows all about Curley's essence. There then seems to be a simple answer: whatever persons God creates, he had better not create Curley Smith. But what, asks Plantinga, if it is not only Curley who suffers from transworld depravity, but every other possible created person too? 'Now the interesting fact here is this: it is possible that every creaturely essence (i.e., every essence entailing *is created by God*) suffers from transworld depravity', and therefore 'it is possible that God could not have created a world containing moral good but no moral evil'.

But how is it possible that every creaturely essence suffers from transworld depravity? This possibility would be realized only if God were faced with a limited range of creaturely essences, a limited number of possible people from which he had to make a selection, if he was to create free agents at all. What can be supposed to have presented him with that limited range? As I have argued, it is not logically impossible that even a created person should always act rightly; the supposed limitation of the range of possible persons is therefore logically contingent. But how could there be logically contingent states of affairs, *prior to the creation and existence of any created beings with free will*, which an omnipotent god would have to accept and put up with? This suggestion is simply incoherent. Indeed, by bringing in the notion of individual essences which determine— presumably non-causally—how Curley Smith, Satan, and the rest of us would choose freely or would act in each hypothetical situation, Plantinga has not rescued the free will defence but made its weakness all too clear. The concept of individual essences concedes that even if free actions are not causally determined, even if freedom in the important sense is not compatible with causal determination, a person can still be *such that* he will freely choose this way or that in each specific situation. Given this, and given the unrestricted range of all logically possible creaturely essences from which an omnipotent and omniscient god would be free to select whom to create, it is obvious that my original criticism of the free will defence holds good: had there been such a god, it would have been open to him to create beings such that they would always freely choose the good.

Yet one more attempt may be made to patch up the free will defence.[21] In spite of all that has been said above, let us suppose that there is a concept of a kind of freedom which is of great value and which entails that an agent who is free in this sense chooses one way rather than another, and yet is not antecedently such that he chooses this way rather than that. Let us suppose that, contrary to Plantinga's theory, there are no truths about Curley which entail that if he is offered a bribe in such and such circumstances he will take it, nor any which entail that he will not. Even an omniscient god does not know in advance what Curley would do if the bribe were offered, nor does he know, even when the bribe has been offered, what he will do until he does it. To suppose this is to take sides in the great debate about 'future contingents': God does not know these things, although he knows everything that there is to be known, because until Curley, for example, has made his decision, there *is* no truth about what he will decide to do. When God created free agents—free in this sense— he had to do so without knowing how they would use their freedom.

This development of the defence succeeds better than any other in detaching moral evils, the wrong choices of free agents, from God. But it does so at the price of a very serious invasion of what has commonly been meant by the omniscience ascribed to God. If he does not know future contingents, and, in particular, does not know what free choices human agents will make, it follows that in 1935, for example, he knew little more than we did about the catastrophic events of the twenty years to 1955, and equally that he knows little more than we do now about the next twenty years. And such a limitation of his knowledge carries with it a serious effective limitation of his power. Also, this account forces the theologian to put God very firmly inside time. It could only be *before* God created Adam and Eve that he could not know what they would do if he created them, and the theologian cannot, without contradiction, give God also an extra-temporal existence and extra-temporal knowledge. This may, indeed, have some advantages: it would make things more interesting for God, and eliminate the sheer mystery of extra-temporal existence and action. But it abandons important parts of the ordinary religious view.

But even this is not the end of the matter. Although, on this

---

[21] A. N. Prior develops this view about future contingencies, with many references to earlier, especially medieval, discussions of the issue, but does not use it for a free will defence, in 'Formalities of Omniscience', originally published in *Philosophy* 37 (1962), reprinted in his *Papers on Time and Tense* (Oxford University Press, 1968).

account, God could not have known what Adam and Eve, or Satan, would do if he created them, he could surely know what they *might* do: that is compatible even with this extreme libertarianism. If so, he was taking, literally, a hell of a risk when he created Adam and Eve, no less than when he created Satan. Was the freedom to make unforeseeable choices so great a good that it outweighed this risk? This question must be answered not only with reference to the degree of human wickedness that has actually occurred: men might (strange as it may seem) have been much worse than they are, and God (on this account) was accepting that risk too. He would not then be the author of sin in the sense of having knowingly produced it; he could not be accused of malice aforethought; but he would be open to a charge of gross negligence or recklessness.

But in any case we must withdraw the concession that we made provisionally in introducing this final version of the defence. No concept of freedom has yet been proposed that both requires that free choices should be isolated from the antecedent nature (or essence) of the agent and from the possibility of divine foreknowledge, and at the same time shows this freedom to be, or to be logically necessary for, a good so great that it outweighs the certainty of all the unabsorbed evils that occur, or the risk of all those that might occur. Nor, as we saw at the end of section (c), is there any ground for the required assumption that God could confer on men a freedom that put them beyond even his control.

In short, all forms of the free will defence fail, and since this defence alone had any chance of success there is no plausible theodicy on offer. We cannot, indeed, take the problem of evil as a conclusive disproof of traditional theism, because, as we have seen, there is some flexibility in its doctrines, and in particular in the additional premisses needed to make the problem explicit. There *may* be some way of adjusting these which avoids an internal contradiction without giving up anything essential to theism. But none has yet been clearly presented, and there is a strong presumption that theism cannot be made coherent without a serious change in at least one of its central doctrines.

This conclusion may seem to be a very modest reward for our labours. It leaves open several possibilities for revised religious views. But it may be of some practical use, not only for its exposure of some typical attempts to escape the problem, but also because each of the changes that would make theism more coherent would also do away with some of its attraction.

10

Religious Experience and Natural Histories of Religion

(a) *The Varieties of Religious Experience*

SINCE the early nineteenth century, and particularly through Kant's influence, the traditional 'proofs' of theistic doctrines have been widely rejected or abandoned—though, among Christian thinkers, such abandonment is less characteristic of Catholics than of Protestants. Also, we have seen how the problem of evil poses a very awkward question for anyone who wants to assert, literally, the full traditional set of theistic doctrines. A widespread response to these difficulties has been a shift of emphasis away from proofs and even from doctrines of a metaphysical sort, and a growing reliance instead upon religious experience.

This reliance, however, can take either of two very different forms. First, it may be held that religious experience itself is all that really matters. Believers, and, significantly, people at the moment of conversion, of transition from unbelief to belief, have experiences which are, to them, intrinsically valuable and all-important, which shape and colour their whole lives. It is of this, it may be said, that religion fundamentally consists: any formulated doctrines, biblical or metaphysical, whether they are the peculiar teachings of a particular faith or sect or a very general theism or supernaturalism, are simply beside the point. Although they may seem, to this or that group of believers, to be vital, the experiences would be essentially unchanged even if the associated doctrines were different, and whether those doctrines are true or false the experiences remain valid in their own right. But, alternatively, it may be held that the religious experience, as well as being valuable in itself, is also evidence, or even proof, of the objective truth of some associated beliefs. That is, there may be an argument *from* religious experience *to* something further. But there are sub-divisions of this second alternative. The something further may be taken to be the central doctrines of traditional theism, which we have been examining in relation to many other arguments. Or the something further may be the special teachings of a particular faith, for example the divinity of Jesus Christ and the availability of salvation through him alone. Or it may indeed be just *something further*, the reality of *some* higher but potentially friendly power.

The contrast between these two approaches may be drawn in another way. The verb 'to experience' is indeed transitive: any experience must have an object, it must be *of* something. But it may have an intentional object only, as does a dream experience or the experience of pain. The pain, or the dream, will no doubt have causes; but the pain itself has no existence apart from the experience of it, nor do the events which constitute the manifest dream content. Alternatively, an experience may have a real object: we ordinarily suppose our normal perceptual experience to be or to include awarenesses of independently existing material spatio-temporal things. The question then is whether specifically religious experiences should be taken to have real objects, to give us genuine information about independently existing supernatural entities or spiritual beings, or whether all that matters is their intrinsic character, their intentional objects, and, of course, their influence on the rest of the lives of those who have them.

In considering either approach, it will be essential to have some understanding of what sorts of experiences these are. For this, we can hardly do better than resort to William James's classical work, *The Varieties of Religious Experience*.[1] Like Hume's *Dialogues*, this is one of the few masterpieces among books *about* religion. Drawing upon a great many first-hand reports, both published and unpublished, it not only surveys very different sorts of experience that can all be counted as religious, but also considers, in a balanced, tentative, and yet enterprising way, how they should be explained and evaluated, and what arguments can in the end be properly based upon them.

James's interest is particularly focused on the experiences, especially the solitary experiences, of individual men and women, and on their more extreme, rather than their milder and more conventional forms. He assumes—though this, as we shall see, is controversial—

---

[1] W. James, *The Varieties of Religious Experience* (Collins, Fontana, London, 1960). References in the text to this work are to the numbered Lectures and to pages in this edition.

that all organized, institutional, religion, and all theology, are secondary outgrowths from these solitary experiences: the gods of the churches, the gods of tribes and states, as well as the god of the philosophers, are derived from and ultimately dependent upon the god encountered in solitude by the individual worshipper or convert or mystic. Religions, James thinks, are both founded and repeatedly revived by those who have overwhelming personal experiences of some religious sort. (See Lectures II, XIV, and XV, especially p. 328.)

Being a psychologist, and sub-titling his work 'A Study in Human Nature', James is greatly concerned with the causal origin of these peculiar states of mind and their resemblances to other mental phenomena. But he insists (in Lecture II) that the question of the 'value' of these experiences—in which he includes the question whether what they reveal is an otherwise inaccessible realm of truth—is quite independent of the question of their origin, and in the end (in Lecture XX) he defends not only what *we* would call their value but also, tentatively and in some measure, their objective truth.

One of James's main themes, as his title suggests, is just how varied religious experiences are. He describes (in Lectures IV and V) 'the religion of healthy-mindedness' which 'looks on all things and sees that they are good', perhaps to the point of denying evil, in the style of Christian Science and other forms of 'mind-cure'. Radically different from this is the deeper sort of experience in which a 'sick soul' is miraculously healed, where someone is first overwhelmed by a sense of sin or guilt or inner conflict or perhaps, like Tolstoy, of the sheer meaninglessness of life, and then experiences a revelation, a conversion, in which he feels saved, free, unified, and happy. Different again are the experiences of mystics, whose content is commonly said to be inexpressible and uncommunicable, but which nevertheless seem to those who have them to be states not only of intense emotion but also of profound knowledge; the knowledge in question can, for many cases at least, be roughly expressed as an awareness of the cosmos as unified and beautiful and of the mystic's own unity with it. And experiences of these varied sorts may or may not involve the literal seeing of visions, either of bright lights or of supernatural beings, the hearing of voices, or the sense of being guided about what to do.

But from this bewildering complexity we can, with James's help, sort out some leading themes and principles. One of these is the close resemblances between religious experiences and other well-known mental phenomena. We are all familiar with dreams. Waking visions and hallucinations are relatively infrequent, but still common enough. Many people have occasionally had the impression of hearing words spoken when there have been no such physical sounds in the neighbourhood. Many religious experiences closely resemble, even in their sequences of contrasting phases, the almost universal human experience of being in love. Hysteria, delusions, cycles of mania and depression are known and reasonably well understood psychopathic phenomena in innumerable cases where there is no religious component; but experiences which have such components, which count as religious *par excellence*, share many features with these pathological ones. Experiences of the mystical kind are often induced by certain drugs. Some of the experiences reported by mystics almost irresistibly invite interpretation as expressions of violent sexual passion. From a psychological point of view, as James himself makes clear, the phenomena of conversion, 'mind-cure', sensory or motor automatisms (such as hearing voices), inspiration, mysticism, and so on lend themselves very readily to being understood in terms of the operation of unconscious or subconscious parts of the mind. 'Let me propose', he says, therefore, 'as an hypothesis, that whatever it may be on its *farther* side, the "more" with which in religious experience we feel ourselves connected is on its *hither* side the subconscious continuation of our conscious life' (Lecture XX, p. 487; but see also pp. 125, 237, 267, and 462).

Also, despite James's own insistence that the question of the origin of a religious experience is quite distinct from those of its value and truth, there is an important indirect connection between them. Since these experiences are of kinds which are psychologically understandable without the help of any specifically religious assumptions, they do not in themselves carry any guarantee of a supernatural source. There is nothing intrinsically very remarkable or distinctive about them. This obviously holds for any single 'religious' experience. Peter Sutcliffe, the 'Yorkshire Ripper', who recently murdered at least thirteen women, heard voices which he took to be of divine origin urging him to kill. Theologians themselves have long recognized that it is not easy to decide, about particular visions and messages, whether they come from God or from the devil. As James says, reporting both Jonathan Edwards and St. Theresa, 'No appearances whatever are infallible proofs of grace . . . The good dispositions that a vision, a voice, or other apparently heavenly favor leave behind them are the only marks by which we may be sure that they are not possible deceptions of the tempter' (Lecture I, pp. 41-2). Admittedly these alternatives, God and the devil, would both fall under the broad heading of 'some supernatural source'. But it will be fairly readily admitted today that the experiences initially ascribed to the devil are fully explicable in terms of purely human but subconscious motives; since it is also admitted that those which the theologian would ascribe to God are not *intrinsically* distinguishable from those which he would initially ascribe to the devil, it follows that even what he classes as genuinely religious experiences do not intrinsically resist explanation in purely human terms. And this in itself seems fatal to any argument *from* religious experience *to* any supernatural conclusions whatever.

We distinguished, above, three different forms that such supernatural conclusions might take: the central theistic doctrines, the special teachings of a particular faith, and the existence merely of *some* higher but potentially friendly power. But any argument from religious experience to a conclusion of the second of these kinds would be extremely weak. It is true that the detailed content, the intentional objects, of particular experiences often involve or presuppose such special beliefs. When St. Paul, on the road to Damascus, heard the question 'Saul, Saul, why persecutest thou me?', he was told, within the vision, who was addressing him. James's 'Oxford graduate' (like innumerable others who have experienced conversion) was equally sure that it was both Jesus Christ and God the Father who had worked on him (pp. 222-4). When George Fox saw a channel of blood running down the streets of Lichfield, he was able to connect this with the martyrdom of a thousand Christians there in the time of Diocletian (pp. 30-1). But it is obvious that such interpretations depend either on the context of the experiences or on the believer's independently acquired knowledge and beliefs. Even if the special doctrines are somehow represented in the content of the experiences, it is all too easy to understand them as having been fed in from the religious tradition by which the experiencer has been influenced. Visions of the Virgin Mary may come to those who already pray to her; those who focus on the Bible as the word of God may find new meaning and force in a biblical phrase (pp. 195-8). James also refers to a number of cases of conversion which, though otherwise like religious ones, are purely ethical, involving no theological beliefs or content (Lecture IX, p. 207). Indeed, J. S. Mill's *Autobiography* records a sequence of depression followed by regeneration which had all the marks of a religious conversion except that, not having been brought up in any theistic tradition, Mill read no theistic import into his experiences.[2] Kierkegaard says that one who, living in an idolatrous community, prays to an idol *in the right spirit* thereby prays, after all, to the true god.[3] But this cuts both ways. It entails that one who prays, intentionally, to a specifically Christian god, and who has an experience as of Christ or the Virgin Mary, may, by the same token, be receiving a response from some quite different true god who is sufficiently broadminded to make allowances for the trivial errors of his worshippers. When the Christian says 'I know that my redeemer liveth', we must reply 'No, you don't: certainly not if you mean, by "my redeemer", Jesus as distinct from Osiris or Ashtaroth or Dionysus or Baldur or Vishnu or Amida'. But equally the response may be coming from no god beyond the experiencer's own unconscious mind.

Religious experience is also essentially incapable of supporting any argument for the traditional central doctrines of theism. Nothing in an experience as such could reveal a creator of the world, or omnipotence, or omniscience, or perfect goodness, or eternity, or even that there is just one god. On this James is very firm and obviously right: 'I feel bound to say that religious experience, as we have studied it, cannot be cited as unequivocally supporting the infinitist belief. The only thing that it unequivocally testifies to is that we can experience union with *something* larger than ourselves and in that union find our greatest peace ... It need not be infinite, it need not be solitary' (p. 499). Thus he is prepared to return to 'a sort of polytheism', which, he remarks, 'has always been the real religion of common people, and is so still today' (pp. 499-500). Moreover, it is a 'piecemeal supernaturalism' that, on his view, these experiences support. God, or the gods, do not merely create and sustain the whole natural world; the supernatural must enter into 'transactions of detail' with the natural—in other words, the sorts of interventions that we have defined miracles to be (pp. 496-8). Here James's empiricism is at work. It is only if the supernatural makes some such specific differences that a supernaturalist hypothesis could be confirmed in contrast with a purely naturalistic rival.

The very most, then, that an argument from religious experience could give us is much less than either the philosophical theist or the adherent of any specific faith demands. Even if these experiences were witnesses to some further truth, it could only be, as James says,

[2] J. S. Mill, *Autobiography* (see n. 4 to Chapter 9, p. 156, above), Chapter 5.
[3] S. Kierkegaard, *Concluding Unscientific Postscript*, translated by D. F. Swenson and W. Lowrie (Princeton University Press, 1941), Book I, Part II, Chapter 2.

the existence of *some* greater friendly power, whose precise identity and character are left wholly indeterminate. But this, James thinks, is enough for religion. He finds a common core of intellectual content underlying all the discrepancies of the varied and conflicting creeds, namely the combination of an 'uneasiness' and a 'solution'. The uneasiness is that 'there is *something wrong about us* as we naturally stand'; the solution is that '*we are saved from the wrongness* by making proper connection with the higher powers'. The individual finds in himself a better part which is '*continuous with a* MORE *of the same quality which is operative in the universe outside of him, and which he can ... in a fashion get on board of and save himself when all his lower being has gone to pieces in the wreck*' (pp. 483-4). All the phenomena, he says, 'are accurately describable in these very simple general terms. They allow for the divided self and the struggle; they involve the change of personal center and the surrender of the lower self; they express the appearance of exteriority of the helping power and yet account for our sense of union with it; and they fully justify our feelings of security and joy. There is probably no autobiographic document, among all those which I have quoted, to which the description will not well apply' (pp. 484-5).

However, 'So far ... as this analysis goes, the experiences are only psychological phenomena' (p. 485). Whether their content has any objective truth is the crucial further question. Certainly no demonstrative argument will establish this. The issue is whether the hypothesis that there objectively is a something more gives a better explanation of the whole range of phenomena than can be given without it. James himself thinks that it does; yet he gives no real argument to support this opinion. This is, obviously, a less economical hypothesis than its naturalistic rival, and in fact such argument as James gives undermines it: 'the theologian's contention that the religious man is moved by an external power is vindicated, for it is one of the peculiarities of invasions from the subconscious region to take on objective appearances, and to suggest to the Subject an external control. In the religious life the control is felt as "higher"; but since on our hypothesis it is primarily the higher faculties of our own hidden mind which are controlling, the sense of union with the power beyond us is a sense of something, not merely apparently, but literally true' (p. 488). But clearly this 'vindicates' the theologian's contention only by reducing it to the rival naturalistic view. Our 'ideal impulses', James says, originate in 'an altogether other dimension of existence from the sensible and merely "understandable" world ... we find them possessing us in a way for which we cannot articulately account', and this region 'is not merely ideal, for it produces effects in this world' (p. 490). However, all that has been shown goes against even this modest and indeterminate supernaturalism. The undeniably real causal source of these impulses may be normally 'unseen' and not understood or articulately reported; but it is eminently understandable, and it belongs well within the same 'dimensions of existence' as other, wholly familiar, mental phenomena.

This conclusion is corroborated by an examination of what James says about the question whether 'the mystic range of consciousness' furnishes 'any *warrant for the truth* of the twice-bornness and supernaturality and pantheism which it favors'. Mystical states, he says, are 'absolutely authoritative over the individuals to whom they come'; yet 'No authority emanates from them which should make it a duty for those who stand outside of them to accept their revelations uncritically'; nevertheless, 'They break down the authority of the non-mystical or rationalistic consciousness, based upon the understanding and the senses alone. They show it to be only one kind of consciousness. They open out the possibility of other orders of truth, in which, so far as anything in us vitally responds to them, we may freely continue to have faith' (p. 407). But this is incoherent. Since, as he rightly says, no authority emanates from mystical experiences—because they can be so easily explained in purely natural, psychological, terms—for anyone who stands outside them to accept their revelations (the word 'uncritically' is redundant: to accept them at all in these circumstances would be uncritical), they cannot be authoritative in an objective sense even for those who have them. Though such people commonly do subjectively take their revelations as authoritative, this is no more than a sign that they are insufficiently critical. There is no reason why they too, in their more sober moments, should not realize that their experiences are open to explanations which accord them no veridical force. Consequently, these experiences do not show that what is based on the understanding and the senses is only one 'order of truth' among others: there may indeed be more than one kind of consciousness, but the one familiar order of truth can accommodate them all.

We may now turn to the other issue, whether we can take religious experience as sufficient in itself, without attempting to base on it any argument for any further, supernatural, reality. What sort of value have these experiences in themselves? Here, too, however, there are several more specific questions. First, what value is found in these experiences by those who take them as what they purport to be, revelations of a deeper, supernatural, realm? Secondly, what value should *we* assign to these experiences, if we abandon any truth-claims that they involve, but still consider the experiences as they are, containing those truth-claims? Thirdly, are these experiences more valuable as they are than otherwise similar ones that lacked those truth-claims would be? Fourthly, would they remain valuable if they had still the very same religious content, the same intentional objects, but those who had them no longer believed this content to be objectively true?

Undoubtedly those who have these experiences and take them seriously find immense value in them. Yet even they will sometimes allow that this value is conditional upon their further fruits. St. Theresa herself argues that her visions are genuinely heavenly ones, not the work of the devil or the sport of her own imagination, on the ground that they have yielded 'a harvest of ineffable spiritual riches, and an admirable renewal of bodily strength' (quoted, pp. 41–2). But James's assessment is rather different:

She had a powerful intellect of the practical order. She wrote admirable descriptive psychology, possessed a will equal to any emergency, great talent for politics and business, a buoyant disposition, and a first-rate literary style. She was tenaciously aspiring, and put her whole life at the service of her religious ideals. Yet so paltry were these, according to our present way of thinking, that (although I know that others have been moved differently) I confess that my only feeling in reading her has been pity that so much vitality of soul should have found such poor employment.

... in the main her idea of religion seems to have been that of an endless amatory flirtation ... between the devotee and the deity. (pp. 338–9)

In other words, St. Theresa's experiences fail by the very test that she herself proposed: the harvest was not, in James's opinion, one of spiritual riches. Similarly, James describes St. John of the Cross as 'a Spanish mystic who flourished—or rather who existed, for there was little that suggested flourishing about him—in the sixteenth century' (p. 300), and he shows how the 'characteristic practical consequences' of saintliness, namely devoutness, asceticism, strength of soul, purity, charity, and the cult of poverty and obedience, while some measure of them may be valuable, can all run to absurd extremes (pp. 270–320 and 333–65). 'When their intellectual outlook is narrow, [the saints] fall into all sorts of holy excesses, fanaticism or theopathic absorption, self-torment, prudery, scrupulosity, gullibility, and morbid inability to meet the world. By the very intensity of his fidelity to the paltry ideals with which an inferior intellect may inspire him, a saint can be even more objectionable and damnable than a superficial carnal man would be in the same situation' (p. 358). Yet James also allows (p. 364) that the greatest saints are immediate successes. In short, once we give up the assumption that the content of religious experience is true, we cannot reach any unequivocal estimate of their worth: whether their fruits are good or evil depends very much on other, surrounding factors.

Our third question, whether these experiences would be more or less valuable without the specifically religious truth-claims that they contain, is also hard to answer. We have noted that J. S. Mill and others display non-religious analogues of the sequence of depression followed by an inspiring conversion. There can be little doubt that John Bunyan would have undergone cycles of misery and elevation even if he had not been caught up in the movement of religious thought that gave his experiences their specific character (pp. 163-5, 191-3). On the other hand the religious tradition itself, like the medical one, often helps to create the diseases that it boasts of curing. Religious teachings, taken all too literally by some who are exposed to them, help to generate the extreme sense of sin and failure which characterizes the sick soul and gives it an overwhelming need for salvation. Without the associated religious beliefs, both the antecedent misery and the subsequent relief would probably be, in general, less extreme. On balance, this might be a gain more often than a loss.

The answers to both our second and third questions must also be affected by this consideration: if the religious experiences do not yield any argument for a further supernatural reality, and if, as we have seen in previous chapters, there is no other good argument for such a conclusion, then these experiences include in their content beliefs that are probably false and in any case unjustified. This, it seems, must be scored as a disvalue against them. However, this judgement must remain provisional until we have considered, in Chapter 11, whether belief without reason, without intellectual justification, can nevertheless be defended.

Our fourth question was whether these experiences would remain valuable if the experiencers themselves were more critical about them, and abandoned the belief that their specifically religious content is objectively true. Could they keep them just as experiences, but still with significance for and power over the rest of their lives? That seems unlikely. Such a change is more likely to be equivalent to replacing these experiences with their non-religious counterparts, as envisaged in our third question. Systematically to withdraw the claim to objective truth would in time significantly alter the internal quality of the experiences, and reduce, though not necessarily cancel, their influence. But this question anticipates our consideration, in Chapter 12, of the possibility of religion without belief.

(b) *Natural Histories of Religion*

William James thought that the religious experiences of individuals were the nucleus and root of all religion, and that all factual claims going beyond what such experiences themselves contain, all metaphysical theology, and all socially organized and institutionalized religion, are merely secondary outgrowths from this root. But this is controversial. As we have seen, particular religious experiences are in general very much coloured by or even parasitic upon, the traditions in or near which they occur. This *might* mean only that each single experience is affected by a residue from earlier religious experiences; but it leaves not merely open but far more likely the alternative possibility that religion has sources other than any such experiences, that experiences in the sense in which James has surveyed them interact with other currents of thought and feeling to generate religion as a whole.

This possibility has a bearing on the arguments of the last section. As we have seen, the general character of religious and mystical experiences invites us to assimilate them to otherwise familiar and explicable mental phenomena; but such an explanation of their *general* character would leave unaccounted for just those elements in their content which make them *specifically* religious. For any single experience, it is easy to explain these further elements as having been drawn in from a surrounding religious tradition—even a convert like St. Paul or Alphonse Ratisbonne (see James, pp. 225–8) will already be in touch with, although hostile to, the movement to which he is converted, and is likely to have been brought up in some related tradition. But this explanation obviously cannot account for these elements in the whole body of religious experience, unless we postulate some source for them other than those experiences themselves. If no other source could be found, there would be more plausibility in James's view that although 'on the hither side' the supposed objects of these experiences can be understood as belonging to the subconscious continuation of our conscious life, we need to postulate something 'on the farther side' as well, that the natural psychological mechanisms may be a route by which we have access to an otherwise unseen supernatural reality, and that 'If there were such a thing as inspiration from a higher realm, it might well be that the neurotic temperament would furnish the chief condition of the requisite receptivity' (p. 45).

In fact, several other sources have been proposed, most notably perhaps by Hume (in association with whom we can take such anthropologists as E. B. Tylor, Sir James Frazer, and R. R. Marett), Feuerbach, Marx, and Freud. Hume entitled his work on this topic *The Natural History of Religion*,[4] implying that he would describe religion as a natural phenomenon, with an origin in human nature, in much the same way as botanists describe plants or zoologists describe animals in their branches of 'natural history'. We can borrow this title as a general name for the whole class of projects of this sort.

In the *Natural History*, which was published soon after it was written, not held in reserve, like the *Dialogues*, until after Hume's death, Hume pretends to take as established truth a philosophical theism rationally based on the argument for design. But, he argues, this pure theism is not the ordinary religion of mankind. The first religion was, he says, polytheism or idolatry. Literary records show that (apart from Judaism, which he rather surprisingly ignores) 'about 1700 years ago all mankind were idolaters'; but he also argues *a priori* that theism could not have been the primary religion of the human race, because the sort of reasoning that would lead to it does not come naturally to most people. They do not in general look for a cause or explanation of the overall order in the world, or of the 'marks of design' in plants and animals, for these are all familiar and are so taken for granted. It is irregularities, prodigies, and unpredictable calamities that suggest supernatural powers, and still more the particular needs and uncertainties in human life: 'the first ideas of religion arose not from a contemplation of the works of nature, but ... from the incessant hopes and fears, which actuate the human mind', and these lead men to acknowledge 'several limited and imperfect deities'. (pp. 30-1) And although monotheism has now arisen and spread very widely, Hume argues that its success is due not to

[4] D. Hume, *The Natural History of Religion*, edited by A. W. Colver in *David Hume on Religion* (see n. 1 to Chapter 8, p. 133, above). References in the text are to pages in this edition.

the (supposedly) cogent reasoning in the design argument, but to a curious development from polytheism. A nation comes to give special adoration to some one tutelary deity chosen from the pantheon, or, modelling the society of gods and goddesses on human monarchies, it makes one the ruler over the rest. In either case, competition in flattery of this chosen god elevates him ultimately to the status of a perfect being, creator and absolute monarch of the universe. (pp. 51-3) Yet there is, Hume says, 'a kind of flux and reflux in the human mind'; contrary tendencies lead from idolatry to theism but also back again from theism to idolatry (pp. 56-7). The one trend could be illustrated by the transition from 'Thou shalt not make unto thee any graven image . . . Thou shalt not bow down thyself to them, nor serve them' and 'Thou shalt have no other gods before me' to the dictum that 'There is no god but God'. In the opposing trend, men seek particular objects of devotion, closer to them than the one perfect and universal god, and more attentive to their special needs: this is illustrated by the role of the saints in Catholicism. Whereas William James *advocates* 'piecemeal supernaturalism', Hume thinks that it is rationally much less defensible than monotheism, but in some ways better adapted to the emotional needs of mankind.

Hume's main purpose in this work is to drive a wedge between the religions that actually flourish and secure people's allegiance—whether polytheist or monotheist, or, by recognizing saints, angels, and so on, a compromise between the two—and the pure philosophical theism, verging on deism, that alone seemed to him likely to command any rational support. He wants to show that philosophy cannot be used to defend any ordinary popular religion. If philosophy is incorporated into a theology, 'instead of regulating each principle, as they'—that is, philosophy and theology—'advance together, she is at every turn perverted to serve the purposes of superstition' (p. 65). He concludes:

What a noble privilege it is of human reason to attain the knowledge of the supreme being; and, from the visible works of nature, be enabled to infer so sublime a principle as its supreme Creator. But turn the reverse of the medal . . . Examine the religious principles, which have, in fact, prevailed in the world. You will scarcely be persuaded, that they are other than sick men's dreams: Or perhaps will regard them more as the playsome whimsies of monkeys in human shape, than the serious, positive, dogmatical asseverations of a being, who dignifies himself with the name of rational. (p. 94)

'Playsome whimsies', however, describes only some of the less important embroideries on religious thought, and 'sick men's dreams' sums up rather that side of religion that is based on the sorts of experience that James has surveyed. Neither phrase is adequate to the most important themes in Hume's own discussion, the way in which piecemeal supernaturalism expresses and satisfies needs that arise from all the varied uncertainties of human life, from hopes and fears about events which are largely uncontrollable and whose causes are largely unknown, and the way in which a special relation to a particular chosen deity may lead from idolatry to monotheism.

It is surely beyond question that these are real tendencies in human thinking, and that they have contributed, along with the religious or mystical experiences of individuals, to the religious tradition. Moreover, these tendencies naturally find expression in social, organized, forms of religion. It is in groups that people commonly face and try to cope with life's uncertainties or significant changes—birth, adolescence, marriage, and death—and it was, notably, a tribe or nation which having first seen itself as his chosen people, then turned Jehovah into a universal god.

Later anthropologists inserted animism and magical belief as a stage preceding the worship of departmental deities (though still later workers in this field have cast doubt on any simple evolutionary pattern). This would not seriously affect Hume's argument; but it lends itself to exaggerations which are open to criticism. Tylor and Frazer saw magic as essentially a kind of pseudo-science and pseudo-technology, the imagining of causal relationships in many places where there are none (based on just those principles of resemblance and contiguity which Hume saw as the principles of the association of ideas) and the attempt to use these imagined causal connections to bring about desired results. But D. Z. Phillips, following Wittgenstein, protests that such an account 'asks us to believe that so-called primitive men were ignorant of elementary natural facts and elementary causal connections', whereas 'the facts easily refute this suggestion. The peoples concerned possessed considerable technical skills and knowledge. They had a thriving agriculture and ... had to take advantage of the regularity of the seasons ... They were also skilled hunters. They made their own weapons, knew where to look for their prey and how to stalk it ... how could any of this be possible if they were imprisoned by the kind of ignorance ascribed to them by Tylor and Frazer?'[5] This comment would apply only to a suggestion that among these peoples the belief in magical pseudo-

[5] D. Z. Phillips, *Religion without Explanation* (Basil Blackwell, Oxford, 1976), pp. 32–3.

causation replaced and excluded all recognition of genuine causal relations; otherwise there is no problem. These peoples, like the rest of us, knew of some genuine causal connections but not others, and like us often felt the need to control things that they could not control by natural means. As Phillips himself admits, 'Tylor and Frazer saw [the rituals] as supplementations to the purposive activities ... which we have already referred to'. There is no implausibility in supposing that people who use rational and efficient methods of achieving their purposes *also* believe in, and *to some extent* rely upon, the direct causal efficacy of magical devices or religious ceremonies. We need only recall the extent to which quack medicine, fringe medicine, and indeed large parts of respectable medicine have constantly flourished and been relied upon, in the most civilized societies, even where there has been no significant causal connection, by the intended routes, between their treatments and recovery. They are believed to be efficacious in ways in which they are not, partly because we very much want help and reassurance that are not otherwise available, and partly because, either by chance or through the psychological effect of the comfort they give, their treatments are followed by recovery often enough to yield apparent confirmations of their claims. And exactly the same has been true of the causal claims of magic and of primitive (and not so primitive) religion.

The real mistake made by these anthropologists was to suggest that magic functioned *only* as pseudo-science and pseudo-technology. No doubt the rituals had genuinely beneficial, if not explicitly intended, effects in sustaining morale and co-operation. Also, as Phillips says, they would have an expressive character. But he is quite wrong in saying that 'When rituals are seen as expressions of this kind, it can also be seen that in no sense are they based on hypotheses or opinions' (p. 36). They can easily be *both* expressive *and* causally purposive. And, curiously, Phillips is equally critical of R. R. Marett's view that these rituals have the function of relieving emotional stress (pp. 49–55). Yet when he says 'the ritual is not performed in *order* to express anything; it *is* the expression of something' (p. 52), he is not denying anything that Marett, or any similar theorist, asserts: of course it is not being suggested that the savage first recognizes his emotional stress as such and then deliberately invents a ritual to discharge it. Phillips's other criticism is that the emotions cannot explain the religious (or magical) thinking, because they themselves arise only within a religious or magical tradition; but again all that is being criticized here is an absurdly over-simplified causal model. Of course there is interaction between the emotions and the religious thought. But this in no way tells against the hypothesis that feelings which have their sources partly in other aspects of life contribute, both as originating and as sustaining causes, along with mistaken but understandable causal beliefs, to the tradition of magical or religious practice and thought.

Men's hopes and fears, their practical and emotional needs, supply most of the force and help to determine the character of religion; but we must look elsewhere for the source of what we may call its pictorial or descriptive content. Magical relations are, perhaps, merely pseudo-causal and impersonal; but the supernatural, whether in animism or polytheism or monotheism, has usually been conceived as personal. Men have made not only their first but also their last gods in their own image. Being conscious of personality in themselves and in one another, they imagined innumerable spirits as persons with thoughts, desires, and purposes somewhat like their own, responding to men somewhat as men respond to one another, and actively fulfilling intentions through such control over material things as men sometimes have and more often wish to have. Ludwig Feuerbach argues that what was thus obviously true of earlier religions remains true of the most sophisticated, for example of Christianity with its metaphysical concepts of infinite perfection, of the *ens realissimum*, and the doctrines of the incarnation and the trinity.[6] All such descriptive content is borrowed from human nature. 'Man— this is the mystery of religion—projects his being into objectivity, and then again makes himself an object to this projected image of himself' (p. 29). 'What was at first religion becomes at a later period idolatry; man is seen to have adored his own nature ... But every particular religion, while it pronounces its predecessors idolatrous, excepts itself ... it imputes only to other religions what is the fault, if fault it be, of religion in general' (p. 13). Anthropomorphism is not really, Feuerbach thinks, a fault, for its complete avoidance would be a denial of religion; a thoroughgoing negative theology 'is simply a subtle, disguised atheism' (p. 15). 'Religious anthropomorphisms ... are in contradiction with the understanding; it repudiates their application to God ... But this God, free from anthropomorphisms, impartial, passionless, is nothing less than the nature of the understanding itself regarded as objective' (p. 35). 'Thus the understanding is the *ens realissimum* ... What ... is the nature conceived without

[6] L. Feuerbach, *The Essence of Christianity*, translated by Marian Evans (Kegan Paul, London, 1893). References in the text are to pages in this edition.

limits, but the nature of the understanding releasing, abstracting itself from all limits' (pp. 38–9). Again, 'God as a morally perfect being is nothing else than the realised idea, the fulfilled law of morality, the moral nature of man posited as the absolute being'; but by adding the notion of God as love man 'delivers himself from this state of disunion between himself and the perfect being, from the painful consciousness of sin, from the distressing sense of his own nothingness' (pp. 46–8). The incarnation and the trinity represent human tenderness and social union. Thus various aspects of the Christian god are projections of human understanding, will, and affection. In the end, 'God is the self-consciousness of man freed from all discordant elements' (pp. 97–8).

Feuerbach is, indeed, concerned not only to explain religion but also to recommend a religion of his own. He suggests that we can find in humanity as a whole, in man as a species, the freedom from the limitations of individuals which traditional religions have fictionally postulated in God. We can find a satisfying religious object by eliminating the errors of supernaturalism and making explicit the human aspirations of which previous religions have been distorted expressions. But this proposal is unpersuasive. Though mankind as a whole may be free from many of the limitations of individuals, it is certainly not free from all limitations, it is not omnipotent or omniscient or morally perfect, and many of the needs that religion expresses and purports to fulfil will not be satisfied by mankind as a whole, even on the most optimistic view of its future. But such defects in Feuerbach's proposal do not entail that there are errors in his explanation. No doubt it, like others, only *helps* to account for religion; but the projection of human nature, especially of the moral aspirations which themselves arise from the social interactions between human beings, certainly contributes significantly to the content of religious ideas.

An important variant of Feuerbach's approach is to see religion less as a projection of forms of individual thought and feeling than as a representation of human society. A body of religious practice, with its associated beliefs, is a way in which a social group copes as a unit with the various crises that confront it or its members. Taking the beliefs as being essentially subordinate to this function, we can think of Jehovah as a personification of a certain movement or tradition or spirit (in the metaphorical sense) in which the Israelites were to some extent caught up, though other tendencies repeatedly drew them away from this one. Similarly, we can think of Pallas

Athene not just as the tutelary deity of Athens, but as a personification of the spirit of political unity and joint purpose in the Athenian people. In John Anderson's phrase, God is the social movement.[7] Such movements, traditions, and institutions are both external and internal to the individual, as God in religious experience is felt to be. They are larger, independent, realities, objectively existent though not directly perceivable. The individual is not merely governed by them but also caught up in them: they enter into him and help to constitute his nature. This is, therefore, another way in which we can not merely explain but make true the believer's conviction that he is moved by an external power, that (in James's summary) he finds in himself a part which is 'continuous with a MORE of the same quality which is operative in the universe outside of him'. But, obviously, we must add that the god or gods of traditional religion are distorted representations of such social realities: we must still account otherwise—by reference to the other side of Feuerbach's theory, or to Freud's—for the element of personification.

Any adequate social explanation of religion must take account of social division and conflict as well as co-operation. Here the classic statement is that of Karl Marx:

Religion ... is the self-consciousness and the self-feeling of the man who either has not yet found himself, or else (having found himself) has lost himself once more. But man is not an abstract being ... Man is the world of men, the State, society. This State, this society, produce religion, produce a perverted world consciousness, because they are a perverted world ... Religion is the sigh of the oppressed creature, the feelings of a heartless world, just as it is the spirit of unspiritual conditions. It is the opium of the people.

The people cannot be really happy until it has been deprived of illusory happiness by the abolition of religion. The demand that the people should shake itself free of illusion as to its own condition is the demand that it should abandon a condition which needs illusion.[8]

This is echoed by Engels:

All *religion* ... is nothing but the fantastic reflection in men's minds of those external forces which control their daily life, a reflection in which the terrestrial forces assume the form of supernatural forces ... when *society, by taking possession of all means of production and using them on a planned basis*, has

---

[7] John Anderson, Professor of Philosophy at the University of Sydney, 1927–58, made this remark more than once in discussion, though I have not been able to find it in his published works.

[8] K. Marx, *Introduction to a Critique of the Hegelian Philosophy of Right*, in K. Marx and F. Engels, *Collected Works* (Lawrence & Wishart, London, 1975 onwards), Vol. 3.

freed itself and all its members from the bondage in which they are now held by these means of production which they themselves have produced but which confront them as an irresistible alien force ... only then *will the last alien force which is still reflected in religion vanish; and with it will also vanish the religious reflection itself*, for the simple reason that then there will be nothing left to reflect.[9]

This view has several different facets. Most directly, it means that those who are deprived and exploited find, or are given, an illusory consolation in religion (either in the prospect of happiness in an afterlife or in the immediate joys of corporate religious experience) which reconciles them to their material poverty and helplessness, and so weakens their resistance to oppression and prevents them from resorting to revolution. Less directly, it means that the system of religious thought is part of an ideology through which the ruling class sees its position and procedures as justified, and, in so far as this ideology is transmitted to the lower classes, they too are encouraged to accept the existing order as right and proper, and to see any revolt against it as being also a rebellion against God. In particular, some of the typical Christian virtues, such as meekness, humility, obedience, non-resistance, and non-retaliation are well adapted to keeping subordinates in their place, while their betters are content to recommend these virtues rather than practise them. More generally still, it means that religion is an expression of an alienated human nature, of a situation where men are cut off both from one another and from the economic resources and forces which they have brought into existence, and can be expected to disappear when such alienation ceases.

There are elements of truth in this view, and it too is a contribution to a natural history of religion. But it also contains wild exaggerations. It is easy to point out that there have been revolutionary religions as well as ones that have defended the established order, and that religiously influenced movements have worked with some success for the material betterment of oppressed and deprived classes, and have not merely provided other-worldly consolations. Equally, the 'sighs' that religion expresses arise not only from economic deprivation and political oppression, but also from psychological tensions with various other causes. Again, Engels's theory of 'reflection' is far too crude, and if it were seen merely as a metaphor it would not sustain the conclusion he draws from it. Once the religious tradition has arisen—and obviously it arose long before class conflicts took

[9] F. Engels, *Anti-Dühring* (Lawrence & Wishart, London, 1969), pp. 374-6.

their present form—it has naturally a force and a history of its own: it is not a mere epiphenomenon but interacts with the politico-economic order: nor is it merely used by other social forces. There is therefore little reason to suppose that religion would disappear if politico-economic alienation were removed. What is more, the characteristic Marxist over-optimism of expecting social conflict and alienation themselves to disappear after a proletarian revolution is itself best understood as a kind of secularized salvationism, the expression of a consoling illusion different, indeed, in specific content but not in general character from the vision of a supernatural ideal realm.

Another influential natural history of religion is that proposed by Freud and other psychoanalysts. The central theme in psychoanalysis is that a great many phenomena—dreams, neuroses, psychoses, mistakes and slips, but also large parts of culture, including religion—can be understood in terms of the fulfilment of unconscious and often repressed wishes. Freud saw an analogy between religious rituals and the elaborate and repeated performances of obsessional neurotics. In *Totem and Taboo* he explained both these primitive systems of thought and later religions, especially Christianity, as having arisen from events in the Darwinian 'primal horde', where the sons killed the father whom they not only hated but also loved and admired.[10] He saw religion as one expression among others of the Oedipus complex, the relic of an infant son's ambivalent attitude to his father: man's relation to a god is modelled on the infantile state of helpless dependence on a father who is both a benefactor and a tyrant. Thus religious ideas are 'illusions, fulfilments of the oldest, strongest, and most urgent wishes of mankind'.[11]

The details of Freud's speculations are open to many doubts and criticisms. On the other hand, the general theses that religion expresses and seems to fulfil very strong and persistent wishes, both conscious and unconscious, and that the believer's supposed relation to God (or the gods) is significantly like that of a child to its parents, and is probably influenced by the adult's memory of that relation, will hardly be disputed. What is disputable is the claim that individual psychology (even aided by a very dubious sort of race memory) can *on its own* provide a full explanation of religious phenomena.

[10] S. Freud, *Standard Edition of the Complete Psychological Works* (Hogarth Press, London, 1953 onwards); see especially *Totem and Taboo* (Vol. XIII, 1957) and *The Future of an Illusion* (Vol. XXI, 1961).

[11] *The Future of an Illusion*, p. 30.

Two main conclusions emerge from this survey of some proposed natural histories of religion. First, it would be a mistake to think that any one of them, by itself, can fully account for religion; but it is very likely that each of them correctly identifies factors which have contributed to some extent to religion, whether to the content of its beliefs, or to its emotional power, or to its practices and organization, both as originating and as sustaining causes. But, secondly, even an adequate, unified, natural history which incorporated all these factors would not in itself amount to a disproof of theism. As William James and many others have insisted, no account of the origin of a belief can settle the question whether that belief is or is not true. Not that any of our theorists thought that it did. Hume, in his *Natural History*, pretended to assume that a pure theism, and only a pure theism, was true; his aim was to separate popular, living, religion from this defensible philosophical view of the world. Feuerbach, Marx, and Freud all assumed that the explicit doctrines of religion, taken literally, were false; but they also assumed that this falsity had been established already, before they offered their accounts of the origin of religion. Marx was an atheist long before he became a socialist or communist or economic theorist; Freud was an atheist long before he discovered psychoanalysis. This whole natural-history approach neither is nor purports to be a *primary* case against theism.

Nevertheless, as we have already noted, it contributes indirectly and subordinately to the case against theism. Our reply to the argument from religious experience to further, supernaturalist, claims, even when these are as tentative and unorthodox as those put forward by William James, was that we need not postulate any supernatural source or sources for these experiences, since they can be fully explained on purely natural grounds, by reference to otherwise familiar psychological processes and forces. But this explanation, as we originally sketched it, was incomplete. Any single religious experience could be understood, given the context and background of the religious tradition within (or in the neighbourhood of) which it occurred. But such traditions themselves were in need of further explanation. If no independent further explanation were on offer, there would be some plausibility in James's suggestion that the whole body of religious experience should be seen as a series of contacts with an objective unseen realm, the 'neurotic temperament' merely providing 'receptivity' to messages from that realm. But if there is, as we have seen, a set of factors which between them provide an adequate explanation of all those elements in the religious tradition which are not covered by the familiar psychological analogues of religious experience, then James's suggestion loses all its plausibility. Here, as elsewhere, the supernaturalist hypothesis fails because there is an adequate and much more economical naturalistic alternative.

It is, indeed, surprising that popular defenders of religion so often argue that man has a natural, psychological, need for religious belief. For, in so far as this is so, it tells not for but against the truth of theism, by explaining why religious beliefs would arise and persist, and why they would be propagated and enforced and defended as vigorously as they are, even if there were no good reason to suppose them to be true.

There is, however, one further loose end to be tied up. We have noted D. Z. Phillips's criticisms of such thinkers as Tylor, Frazer, and Marett. He is similarly critical of Feuerbach, Durkheim, and Freud. But we have not yet examined his main objection to all such explanations of religion, which underlies his contrary advocacy of 'religion without explanation'. They all presuppose that what is essential to religion, and is therefore in need of explanation, is belief in an objective supernatural reality. Phillips is ready to concede, as his opponents hold, that such beliefs would be either false or meaningless, or at least ungrounded: this, he admits, has been established by Hume and his successors, provided that the religious statements are interpreted, as Hume and his successors have assumed, as making literal, factual, claims. But Phillips, following Wittgenstein, thinks that religion need not and should not be thus understood. If he is right, then our natural histories do, indeed, miss the mark. What they seek to explain is at any rate not the vital heart of religion. We shall consider this way of escape in Chapter 12, when we examine the possibility of religion without belief.

11

Belief without Reason

IT would appear, from our discussion so far, that the central doctrines of theism, literally interpreted, cannot be rationally defended.
Even those who have enjoyed what they take to be religious experiences have no good reason to interpret them as they do, as direct
contacts with literally divine or supernatural beings, nor can any sort
of revelation justify such beliefs. There may be enough flexibility in
those central doctrines for even the conjunction of them to escape
conclusive disproof by the problem of evil, but the overall balance of
evidence and argument is against each of those doctrines on its own,
and strongly against the conjunction of them.

But does this matter? 'Our most holy religion', Hume said, 'is
founded on *faith*, not on reason', and though Hume meant this
ironically, there have been many religious believers who have held
this literally.[1] Can theism, then, dispense with rational support, and
rely on faith alone?

Obviously it can, since for many believers it does so rely. There are
any number of adherents not only of Christianity but also of many
other religions who just accept their various faiths, never thinking
seriously of the possibility that they might be mistaken, and therefore
never feeling any need for rational support for the central doctrines
of those religions. No doubt their belief has causes: it has been taken
over from parents or teachers or a whole cultural tradition; but these
causes do not involve reasons. They may be traced by a natural
history of religion which shows how belief can flourish not merely
without rational support but even in opposition to the weight of the
evidence.

It is, therefore, not in doubt for a moment that belief without
reason is causally possible. What is of interest is rather the

[1] *Enquiry concerning Human Understanding*, Section 10, Part 2.

paradoxical question whether belief without reason may none the less be intellectually respectable, whether, although there are no reasons which would give a balance of direct support to theistic doctrines, there are reasons for not demanding any such reasons. Various arguments for this initially surprising thesis have been advanced by Pascal, Kierkegaard, and William James.

(a) *Pascal's Wager*[2]

Either God exists or he does not; but reason, Pascal says, is unable to decide the question either way. So you are forced to play a game of chance: you must, in effect, bet on one or the other. You cannot simply suspend judgement. Since it is a practical choice, you should consider what your various interests are. What you may stand to gain is knowledge of the truth and happiness; what you risk, if you should lose, is error and misery; the resources with which you wager are your reason and your will. There is no more damage to your reason if you bet one way rather than another, so it does not count. If you bet on God's existing, then, if it turns out that he does exist, you gain infinite happiness; while, if it turns out that he does not exist, you lose nothing. But if you bet on God's not existing, then, if it turns out that he does exist, you will have lost your chance of everlasting happiness; while, if it turns out that he does not exist, you gain nothing. So it is overwhelmingly practically reasonable to bet on God's existing, although you have no more intellectual reason to suppose that he exists than that he does not.

This is Pascal's first formulation of the choice before us; but he adds others. Perhaps it is not true that you lose *nothing* in betting on God's existing: you lose the worldly happiness that you could gain in this life if you were free from religious commitments. So, if you bet on God's existing, then, if you lose, you will have lost one happy life, while, if you win, you will have won an infinity of happy lives. But if you bet against God's existing, then, whether you win or lose, you will have only one happy life, while, if you lose, you will have lost the opportunity of an infinity of happiness. Pascal adds that he does not need to assume that the chance of God's existing is equal to the chance of his not existing. Even if the odds against his existing are n to 1, your expectation in betting on his existing, measured in units of happy lives, is infinity divided by $n + 1$, which is still infinity,

[2] B. Pascal, *Pensées*, in *Œuvres*, edited by L. Brunschvigg (Hachette, Paris, 1925), Section III, No. 233.

while your expectation in betting on his not existing is one such unit; so long as n is finite, the former is infinitely greater than the latter: 'il y a ici une infinité de vie infiniment heureuse à gagner, un hasard de gain contre un nombre fini de hasards de perte, et ce que vous jouez est fini'. The decision would become problematic only if n equalled infinity—that is, only if the odds against God's existing were infinite—so that the expectation in betting on God's existing were infinity divided by infinity, which is indeterminate.

The accompanying table, therefore, would express Pascal's final view of the betting problem.[3] (Results and expectations are here measured in happy life units.)

Bet on God's existing

Chance of winning $\dfrac{1}{n+1}$ Chance of losing $\dfrac{n}{n+1}$

Result of winning ∞ Result of losing 0

Expectation $\dfrac{\infty}{n+1}$ $+\,0$

$$=\dfrac{\infty}{n+1}$$

Bet against God's existing

Chance of winning $\dfrac{n}{n+1}$ Chance of losing $\dfrac{1}{n+1}$

Result of winning 1 Result of losing 1

Expectation $\dfrac{n}{n+1}$ $+$ $\dfrac{1}{n+1}$

$$=1$$

All this is a paraphrase of Pascal's argument, not an exact translation. It is clear that, given his assumptions, the argument goes through. Everything turns, therefore, on the acceptability of those assumptions. Of these the most basic is the very formulation of the problem as one of a practical decision in uncertainty. What, one might ask, would it be to wager that God exists? One can decide, on the grounds of various probable advantages and disadvantages, to act in one way or another, but can one, for such practical reasons, decide to believe something? Although there are voluntary actions, there seems to be no possibility of voluntary belief. However, Pascal has anticipated this objection. Perhaps, for the reasons he has given, you would like to believe in God but find yourself initially unable to

---

[3] This is a modification of tables given in Notes on pp. 147–50 in the edition referred to in n. 2, p. 200, above.

do so. Since it is not reason that is now an obstacle to belief—for, by hypothesis, intellectual considerations were unable to settle the question either way, and practical reason, in view of the wager argument, favours belief—the obstacle must lie in your passions. You can work on these as others have done who have found the way to faith, by using holy water, having masses said, and so on: 'Naturellement même cela vous fera croire et vous abêtira'. Although you cannot believe by simply deciding to do so, you can come to believe by deciding to cultivate belief. Indirectly voluntary belief is possible, though directly voluntary belief is not.

No doubt Pascal is right about this; but it goes against his earlier claim that to bet one way or the other about God will do no injury to your reason. Deliberately to make oneself believe, by such techniques as he suggests—essentially by playing tricks on oneself that are found by experience to work upon people's passions and to give rise to belief in non-rational ways—*is* to do violence to one's reason and understanding. As Pascal himself says, 'cela . . . vous abêtira': it will make you stupid. Others have put it more mildly: to acquire faith, you must become as a little child. But, however it is expressed, the point remains: in deliberately cultivating non-rational belief, one would be suppressing one's critical faculties. Of course it will be said that to do this is to reject only a false reason, a superficial understanding, in order to attain a true wisdom, a deeper understanding. But to say this is to beg the question. We have as yet no reason to suppose that this 'true wisdom' is anything but a hopeful delusion, a self-deception. Nor could we come to have any reason to suppose this except by exercising those despised critical faculties.

Here, too, we should remember that in his discussion of the wager Pascal moves from the assumption that the odds for and against the existence of God are equal to the assumption that the odds against his existence are n to one, where n is any finite number. With the latter assumption, he is still able to argue that the expectation of happiness is greater in betting for than in betting against God's existence; but he can no longer argue that there is no greater cost to one's reason in the former than in the latter. To decide to cultivate belief in God, when, epistemically, the odds are n to one against his existing, and n is some large number, is deliberately to reject all rational principles of belief in uncertainty. There is, in Pascal's proposal, a real cost which he has tried to conceal.

Still, it may be thought that even if this cost is properly allowed for, the case for a practical choice based on comparative expectations holds good. But here we must bring out, and challenge, his other assumptions. He considers only these alternatives: first, that there is a god who will reward with everlasting happiness all those who believe in him for whatever reason, and, secondly, that there is no god and that one's existence simply ends completely when one dies. But obviously there are other possibilities. One, to which a Christian thinker might well have paid some attention, is that people are predestined to salvation or to non-salvation—perhaps to damnation—no matter what they now decide, or try to decide, to do. If so, nothing one does now will make any difference with regard to one's prospects for an afterlife, so one should try to do whatever gives the best chance that the present life will be happy. Another possibility is that there might be a god who looked with more favour on honest doubters or atheists who, in Hume's words, proportioned their belief to the evidence, than on mercenary manipulators of their own understandings. Indeed, this would follow from the ascription to God of moral goodness in any sense that we can understand. The sort of god required for Pascal's first alternative is modelled upon a monarch both stupid enough and vain enough to be pleased with self-interested flattery. Again, even if there were a god of Pascal's sort, there are various sub-possibilities to be taken into account: perhaps this god is not satisfied with the mere belief that there is *a* god, but adopts the principle *nulla salus extra ecclesiam*, where the church within which alone salvation is to be found is not necessarily the Church of Rome, but perhaps that of the Anabaptists or the Mormons or the Muslim Sunnis or the worshippers of Kali or of Odin. Who can say? From the position of initial ignorance and non-reliance on reason in which Pascal starts, no such possibility is more likely than any other.

Once the full range of such possibilities is taken into account, Pascal's argument from comparative expectations falls to the ground. The cultivation of non-rational belief is not even practically reasonable. Indeed, the true position is the exact opposite of what he has presented. Whereas Pascal says that speculative reason is neutral with regard to the existence of a god, and that belief must therefore, and can, be based on practical reason alone, the truth is rather that practical reason is here neutral, and that we can and must therefore do the best we can with speculative reason after all.

(b) *William James and the Will to Believe*[4]

William James's discussion in his essay 'The Will to Believe' is both intellectually and morally far superior to Pascal's. Indeed, he anticipates one of our criticisms of Pascal: 'if we were ourselves in the place of the Deity, we should probably take particular pleasure in cutting off believers of this pattern [that is, those who follow Pascal's advice] from their infinite reward'. But he also develops some of Pascal's ideas, and he, too, sees the problem as one of rational choice in uncertainty.

James distinguishes the options with which he is most concerned, which he calls 'genuine' options, as those which are (for the agent or thinker in question) *living, forced*, and *momentous*. A living option is one where the agent sees both the alternatives as serious possibilities. A momentous one is one that matters, and in particular one where the agent has a unique opportunity, where his decision is not easily reversible, and if he lets this chance go it will not recur. An option is forced where the choice is between two exclusive and exhaustive alternatives, where there is no real third possibility such as suspense of judgement. For choices in the area thus defined, he argues against the view of W. K. Clifford, that 'It is wrong always, everywhere, and for every one, to believe anything upon insufficient evidence'.[5] He maintains, on the contrary, that *'Our passional nature not only lawfully may, but must, decide an option between propositions, whenever it is a genuine option that cannot by its nature be decided on intellectual grounds'*.

To show this, James first insists, and rightly, that 'our non-intellectual nature does influence our convictions'. Though 'talk of believing by our volition seems ... simply silly', the truth is that 'It is only our already dead hypotheses that our willing nature is unable to bring to life again. But what has made them dead for us is for the most part a previous action of our willing nature ...' 'There are passional tendencies and volitions which run before and others which come after belief, and it is only the latter that are too late for the fair; and they are not too late when the previous passional work has been already in their own direction.'

He combines this with another correct thesis, that most of what anyone believes, he believes on authority, through the influence of

[4] W. James, *The Will to Believe and Other Essays* (Longmans, London, 1896).
[5] Quoted by James from W. K. Clifford, *Lectures and Essays* (Macmillan, London, 1886).

the intellectual climate around him. He could say, at Brown University, and again at Yale, 'Here in this room, we all of us believe in molecules and the conservation of energy, in democracy and necessary progress, in Protestant Christianity and the duty of fighting for "the doctrine of the immortal Monroe", all for no reasons worthy of the name'.

Secondly, James distinguishes between absolutism or dogmatism—the view that we can achieve not merely knowledge but certainty, that we can know when we know—and empiricism, that is, fallibilism, the view that objective certainty is in general unattainable. While firmly endorsing empiricism, he says that this does not mean giving up the quest for truth and the hope of gradually getting closer to it. This is correct, though we must query his characteristically pragmatist remark that 'if the total drift of thinking continues to confirm [a hypothesis], that is what [the empiricist] means by its being true'. We may well hope that the results of investigation will converge upon the truth, and their convergence with one another will be evidence for their truth, but the truth of a hypothesis does not consist in convergence, but rather in things simply being as the hypothesis supposes that they are.

James's third step is to distinguish between the two purposes of knowing the truth and avoiding error, and to say that he himself regards 'the chase for truth as paramount, and the avoidance of error as secondary'. Clifford's view, by contrast, treats the avoidance of error as more important than the attaining of truth. 'Clifford's exhortation . . . is like a general informing his soldiers that it is better to keep out of battle forever than to risk a single wound. Not so are victories either over enemies or over nature gained. Our errors are surely not such awfully solemn things. In a world where we are so certain to incur them in spite of all our caution, a certain lightness of heart seems healthier than this excessive nervousness on their behalf.' But he admits that this principle bears differently upon questions of various sorts.

In the consideration of scientific questions, James allows that suspense of judgement may be in order: here options are not forced. But even here less caution, more passionate involvement, is favourable for discovery. 'The most useful investigator, because the most sensitive observer, is always he whose eager interest in one side of the question is balanced by an equally keen nervousness lest he become deceived. Science has organized this nervousness into a regular *technique* . . .' What James says here is closely related to some of Karl

Popper's doctrines. James speaks of 'verification', whereas Popper speaks only of 'corroboration' when a hypothesis stands up to severe tests and resists attempts to falsify it; but James rightly assumes what Popper is very reluctant to concede: this outcome tells positively in favour of a hypothesis, and gives us some reason to believe that it is at least approaching the truth.[6] James's account of the typical motives of the good investigator is also sounder than Popper's.

Moral questions, unlike scientific ones, 'present themselves as questions whose solutions cannot wait for sensible proof'. James wants to hold on to the objectivity of morals, while denying that moral questions can be empirically settled. I would agree with his dictum, but for a different reason, namely that categorically imperative statements, purporting to give people directives to do this or to refrain from that, directives that are unconditional and in no way dependent upon the desires or purposes of the agent, are not capable of being simply true, nor are statements about what is good or bad in senses that would entail such directives.[7]

There are also 'truths dependent upon our personal action'. 'Whenever a desired result is achieved by the co-operation of many independent persons, its existence as a fact is a pure consequence of the precursive faith in one another of those immediately concerned.' Hence there are 'cases where a fact cannot come at all unless a preliminary faith exists in its coming'; in such cases 'it would be an insane logic' to forbid faith to run ahead of evidence.

Almost all of these initial steps in James's argument are not only eloquently expressed but also correct and important. Most of our beliefs do rest on authority, and our 'passional nature' does play some part in many, perhaps all, of them. In almost all areas judgements are fallible in varying degrees, and while we aim at truth we can claim at most that tested and confirmed hypotheses are likely to come close to the truth. In science it is reasonable not only to make enterprising guesses but also to combine critical testing of them with the hope and tentative belief that they are not too far from truth. In social and political affairs it is reasonable—since it is a necessary condition for co-operation—to trust others in advance of any certainty that they are trustworthy. Moral judgements of some central sorts are not capable of being true, and *a fortiori* cannot be shown to

[6] See, in P. A. Schilpp, editor, *The Philosophy of Karl Popper* (Open Court, La Salle, Illinois, 1974), Popper's 'Replies to my Critics', especially pp. 1013-41.

[7] See my *Ethics: Inventing Right and Wrong* (Penguin, Harmondsworth, 1977), Chapter 1.

be true; but it is not contrary to reason to make them, and the sentiments and ways of thinking that they express are essential to any tolerable human and especially social life. In all these ways we must at least qualify Clifford's dictum; but the crucial question is, How do these principles relate to religion and in particular to theistic belief?

According to James himself, religion says essentially two things. 'First, she says that the best things are the more eternal things, the overlapping things, the things in the universe that throw the last stone, so to speak, and say the final word ... The second affirmation of religion is that we are better off even now if we believe her first affirmation to be true.' Now two things are plain about this summary. The first affirmation is extremely vague, and the main content of both affirmations is evaluative, though the first may presuppose some factual claims. James goes on to say that 'The more perfect and more eternal aspect of the universe is represented in our religions as having personal form'. From this he concludes that the only practical way of taking the religious hypothesis seriously is to meet it half way. One who refused to make advances until he had proof 'might cut himself off forever from his only opportunity of making the gods' acquaintance'.

The problem of religious belief is thus assimilated on the one hand to that of morality (in a broad sense) and on the other to the need, in social co-operation, to trust others before one is sure that they are to be trusted—that is, to two spheres in which we have already agreed that it is reasonable for decision to run ahead of evidence. That is why James rejects 'the agnostic rules for truth-seeking', saying that '*a rule of thinking which would absolutely prevent me from acknowledging certain kinds of truth if those kinds of truth were really there, would be an irrational rule*'. In this field, therefore, as in some others, not only is it a fact that 'our passional nature' influences our opinions, it is also legitimate that it should do so. In effect, James is saying about faith, as the Samnite, Gaius Pontius (in Livy, Book IX) said about war, that it is justified when you cannot avoid it: *Iusta est fides, quibus necessaria*.

This is a persuasive and powerful case. But three strands can be distinguished within it. One concerns what are essentially moral choices. These are, indeed, free in the sense that they need not and cannot wait for the intellect to determine them. They escape Clifford's rigid agnosticism. But this fact leaves us with, as yet, no guidance about what choices to make. Whatever choice lies concealed in the obscure claim that the best things are the more eternal things, we should have to test this by seeing how it fits in and coheres with our other moral views and our purposes as a whole. This question will come up again in Chapter 14.

The second theme is that of passion as a tie-breaker. Even on factual questions, issues of truth and falsehood, James says that where intellectual considerations are evenly balanced—and where the option is living, forced, and momentous, so that suspense of judgement is impossible—passion can lawfully decide. This is more questionable. It is all too close to Pascal's view that, when speculative reason cannot decide, self-seeking practical reason can act as a tie-breaker. Admittedly passion *will* frequently so decide in an impasse; we must accept this as inevitable, and we can do so with the less unease when we admit, as we must, that at all times many of our beliefs rest partly on passion. But James has exaggerated the dependence of belief on passion by putting under this heading the very many beliefs which we hold on authority. Some of these, I grant, belong under the heading of passion, where our acceptance of a supposed authority itself rests on nothing more than custom and our tendency to go along with other people. But sometimes what passes for an authority really is an authority; that is, we may have good reason to suppose that the 'authority' has knowledge, or a well-founded opinion, about the matter and has no strong motive for deceiving us. Sometimes we even have evidence from our own experience that the 'authority' is generally reliable in the area in question. In such cases, what we accept on authority is thereby given, though only indirectly, some degree of rational support. No doubt we still are constantly deceived in many ways, often on matters of the greatest importance. But this is no reason for happily accepting the determination of belief by passion; rather it is a reason for trying to be more critical, and for extending into other fields, if possible, those practices of mutual criticism and testing which in lawsuits and in science, for example, provide some check on error and deceit. In any case, we need a tie-breaker only where there is a tie to be broken; and it is far from clear that rational consideration about what is the best overall explanatory hypothesis does reach such an impasse with regard to the central questions of theism.

The third strand in James's argument is the most important. Given that there is, inevitably, a 'passional' component in thought, and, equally inevitably, a great and constant risk of error, and given also that, about many matters, the chance of being right has a value not outweighed by the disvalue of the chance of being wrong, we must reject Clifford's principle of never believing anything on insufficient evidence. We must be willing not only to frame hypotheses and test them, but also to give a tentative acceptance to hypotheses which have some plausibility and have received some confirmation through testing. This is a principle which an atheist can endorse as readily and whole-heartedly as any theist. It is James's next step that is crucial: there may be for us a live hypothesis that 'the more perfect and more eternal aspect of the universe' is personal in form, and then the only proper way to test this hypothesis will be to try to enter into conversation with this person (or persons): to have a chance of 'making the gods' acquaintance', we must be prepared to meet them halfway. In view of all that has been said in earlier chapters, I doubt whether this should still be a live hypothesis for us. But let us suppose that it is. Let us agree with James that a rule of thinking which would absolutely prevent me from acknowledging certain kinds of truth if those kinds of truth were really there would be an irrational rule. What follows is that we shall be intellectually better placed in relation to theism—whether in the end we accept it or reject it—if we have at least once made the experiment of playing along with it, if we have genuinely opened not only the intellectual but also the passional side of our minds to the possibility of conversing with 'the gods', if there are any gods and they are willing to converse with us. But it follows also that since our object is to ascertain whether 'those kinds of truth are really there', we must maintain in this area also the tension of which James himself has spoken (with reference to science) between the eager interest of the optimistic speculator and the critical 'nervousness lest he become deceived', the balanced consideration whether our observations really confirm our hypothesis or disconfirm it. An experiment whose aim is to ascertain the truth must be so conducted as to allow the hypothesis in question to be falsified or at least disconfirmed. A hypothesis is confirmed only by surviving severe tests, that is, tests which, if it is false, are likely to show that it is false. While we must, as James says, reject as irrational a rule of thinking which would prevent us from acknowledging certain kinds of truth even if they were really here, we must equally reject as irrational a rule of thinking which would prevent us from denying such supposed truths even if they were not really there. And this is not only in order to avoid error: it is an essential part of the method of confirming truth. If faith is to be defended as an experiment, it must conform to the general principles of experimental inquiry. The result of any such experiment, of trying to converse with 'the gods', will presumably be some 'religious experience'. But, as we saw in Chapter 10, the credentials of any such experience are themselves doubtful. A favourable result of the experiment would have to be a series of experiences which somehow resisted the kinds of psychological explanation indicated in that chapter.

With this proviso, we can accept this third strand in James's argument, his case for what we may call an experimental faith. But how different this is from anything that would ordinarily be advocated as religious faith! In particular, how different this is from the way in which Pascal proposes that we should cultivate religious belief—'cela ... vous abêtira'—and also, as we shall see, from Kierkegaard's view that reason has no place in the sphere of faith. According to this third strand in James's argument, a kind of tentative faith is a move in the game of rational investigation. It may be objected that such employment is inconsistent with the very spirit of religious belief, that the latter requires an intellectual unconditional surrender, an abandonment of autonomous investigation. That is, it may be said that 'experimental faith' is a contradiction in terms. I shall argue, against Kierkegaard, that this is not so; but if it were so, its effect would be to destroy James's case for antecedent belief. We could not retain his argument for faith while rejecting the empiricist assumptions and the experimental principles on which that whole argument depends.

(c) *Kierkegaard and the Primacy of Commitment*[8]

In Kierkegaard the move from reason to faith is more extreme than in either Pascal or James. 'The inquiring subject,' he says, 'must be in one or the other of two situations. *Either* he is in faith convinced of the truth of Christianity, and in faith assured of his own relationship to it; in which case he cannot be infinitely interested in all the rest, since faith itself is the infinite interest of Christianity, and since every other interest may readily come to constitute a temptation. *Or* the inquirer is, on the other hand, not in an attitude of faith, but objectively in an attitude of contemplation, and hence not infinitely interested in the determination of the question.' From this he concludes that 'the problem cannot in this manner decisively arise; which means that it does not arise at all, since decisiveness is of the essence of the problem'.

[8] S. Kierkegaard, *Concluding Unscientific Postscript* (see n. 3 to Chapter 10, p. 182, above), Book I, Part II, Chapter 2.

If this were sound, it would mean that the rational discussion of theism, at least in the form of Christianity, is impossible, and (for example) that all the arguments, on either side, reported or offered in our previous chapters have failed to come to grips with any real issue. But is it sound? Let us try to spell out Kierkegaard's argument more fully. In saying that decisiveness is of the essence of the problem, he is claiming, first, that the question of the truth of Christianity is such that it is part of the question itself that the questioner should be infinitely interested in the determination of it. But secondly, he alleges, one cannot be infinitely interested in this determination unless one is infinitely interested in Christianity, and, thirdly, one can be infinitely interested in Christianity only if one is already convinced of its truth, that is, if one is already in a state of faith which precludes the *consideration* of the question. Thus expanded, the argument is valid: given the premisses, the conclusion follows. But there is no reason why we should accept any one of these premisses, let alone all three. The second and third are just dubious empirical assertions; the first of the three is more discussable. How *could* a questioner's interest in a question be part of the essence of the question itself? If there is an issue of truth and falsity about Christianity, that is, if there is any such thing as even the possibility that Christianity is true, then there must be the two possible states of affairs, its being so and its not being so. Then anyone who can think about or envisage these two possibilities can consider also the possibility of a decision between them, and to do this is to raise the question. Thus the question of the truth of Christianity arises for such a thinker, quite irrespectively of his degree of interest in the question or of his commitment to either side. To deny this is to cast serious doubt on whether there is any question of truth here at all; and, as we shall see, Kierkegaard's argument drives him in that direction.

He develops his thesis by contrasting 'objective' and 'subjective' reflections, or ways of raising the question of truth. '*When the question of truth is raised in an objective manner, reflection is directed objectively to the truth, as an object to which the knower is related ... When the question of the truth is raised subjectively, reflection is directed subjectively to the nature of the individual's relationship; if only the mode of this relationship is in the truth, the individual is in the truth even if he should happen to be thus related to what is not true.*' Again, 'subjectively, reflection is directed to the question whether the individual is related to a something *in such a manner* that his relationship is in truth a God relationship'. He contrasts one who prays in the house of the true God and with the true conception of God in his knowledge, but prays in a false spirit, with one who, living in an idolatrous community, prays with the entire passion of the infinite, although his eyes rest upon the image of an idol: 'The one prays in truth to God though he worships an idol; the other prays falsely to the true God, and hence worships in fact an idol.'

This suggests that according to Kierkegaard what matters is not the truth or falsity of *what anyone believes*—that would be 'objective truth'—but rather the nature of the believing relationship.

'Objectively *what* is said is stressed; subjectively *how* it is said.' But what is it for this relationship to be 'in the truth'? Apparently all that is required is that it should be one of infinitely passionate personal interest and commitment. But if the nature of this relationship is all that matters, does not the second term of the relationship simply drop out? Is it not a loose cog that does no work? And might it not then be anything at all, or indeed a mere fantasy object? This is strongly suggested by Kierkegaard's thesis that 'truth is subjectivity'; but it seems not to be what he intends. For (as quoted above) he contrasts 'the true God' with 'an idol'; he takes the life of Christ quite literally as a revelation given to men by this true God; and he even speaks of the Christian as being passionately interested *on behalf of his own eternal happiness*; one so interested would be a victim of deception (perhaps self-deception) if the Christian doctrines were not literally true. When someone prays in (subjective) truth to an idol, this is somehow converted into prayer to the 'true God'; the proper second term of the relationship is there, and the worshipper is related to it, after all. Again, 'The object of faith is the reality of another ... it is the reality of the teacher, that the teacher really exists'. Yet there is also support for the 'loose cog' interpretation: Kierkegaard also speaks of one who 'embraces an uncertainty with the passion of the infinite', and uses Socrates as an illustration. Although Socrates regards immortality as problematic, 'On this "if" he risks his entire life, he has the courage to meet death, and he has with the passion of the infinite so determined the pattern of his life that it must be found acceptable—*if* there is an immortality'. This *might* be read as saying that Socrates had based his plan of life on an anticipation of Pascal's wager; but this would be so fantastic a distortion of Socrates' thoughts and motives, as Plato presents them, that I cannot believe that it is what Kierkegaard meant. He must have meant rather that Socrates' total commitment to philosophical, especially moral, inquiry, and to the criticism of unfounded claims to knowledge, itself involved 'the passion of the infinite'. If so, there must be a great deal of free play with respect to the intentional object of commitment.

The two interpretations between which we are hesitating, and between which Kierkegaard himself seems to oscillate, reflect upon his attempt to show that the problem of the truth of Christianity, or perhaps of theism in general, cannot arise. If *all* that matters is the mode of relationship, and it can have almost any object at all, including an imaginary one, then, indeed, although a question may arise about the reality of this or that specific object, it will be trivial and it will not be the problem of the truth of Christianity in general, or of theism in general: there will, indeed, be no such problem. But if Christianity, or theism, essentially involves some literal claims about the existence of a god and his relationship to and dealings with men, then, even if the mode of relationship *also* matters—so that the relationship's being 'in truth' can somehow forge a connection with its proper object even where the believer is himself unaware of that object or uncertain about it—there is a real question which arises and can be investigated, and which is not foreclosed by Kierkegaard's dilemma.

More important, however, to Kierkegaard than the claim that this question cannot arise is his view that even if it arises the 'objective' consideration of it is worse than useless. Not, apparently, because it cannot establish the truth of religion, but rather because it might come close to doing so. The 'objective approximation-process' is incompatible with faith. 'Anything that is almost probable, or probable, or extremely and emphatically probable, is something he can almost know, or as good as know, or extremely and emphatically almost *know*—but it is impossible to believe. For the absurd is the object of faith, and the only object that can be believed.' Kierkegaard stresses and welcomes the paradoxical character of Christianity—especially in its claim that God has literally existed as an individual human being—and explicitly rejects any interpretations that would make it more rationally acceptable: 'Christianity is therefore not a doctrine, but the fact that God has existed'. It is vital for him that the absurd should 'stand out in all its clarity—in order that the individual may believe if he so wills'.

Like Pascal in his wager, and like James with his experimental faith, Kierkegaard makes belief a matter of will. But unlike both of these, he is not arguing on any general grounds in favour of such belief. He seems to be arguing *from* a position, not *to* a position. His dominant aim is expository, to show what Christianity is. Of course this means that he is really showing what Christianity *as he conceives it* is, although he would not concede this qualification. Rather, he would insist that this is what Christianity *really* is, and this would include—but would not be exhausted by—the historical claim that his is the original type of Christianity. Since Christianity was in his day, and still is, in a very broad sense an *established* religion, since many people think that it is good to be Christian, and many more give Christianity formal adherence or lip service or at least some considerable degree of respect, it is in practice a way of recommending a position to say that it is the truly Christian one. (This is an instance of the propaganda device that Charles L. Stevenson analysed under the name of 'persuasive definition'.[9]) Perhaps, then, Kierkegaard is, after all, arguing for a position, but only by trading upon that conventional, respectable, nominal Christianity which he despises and condemns.

Leaving this piece of trickery aside, we can say that what Kierkegaard does is to present for his readers' acceptance a picture of a purely voluntary faith, a faith which relies on no intellectual support and spurns intellectual questioning and criticism. 'Faith constitutes a sphere all by itself, and every misunderstanding of Christianity may at once be recognized by its transforming it into a doctrine, transferring it to the sphere of the intellectual.'

This contrasts sharply with a view which Anselm, for example, summed up in the phrase 'faith seeking understanding': *fides quaerens intellectum*. Anselm begins from a position of faith. He believes in a god, and indeed addresses God as a person. Nevertheless he would like to add understanding and intellectual conviction, or even logical proof, to that initial belief. This project is not incoherent or misguided. We saw, in Chapter 3, that it fails; but that does not mean that it was misconceived. And in fact there are plenty of other reasonable and in some cases successful instances of *fides quaerens intellectum*: many of the philosophical replies to various forms of scepticism come under this heading. Our beliefs in an external world, in other minds, and in the general reliability of inductive reasoning are all initially non-rational. We merely find ourselves believing these things, as James would say, for no reasons worthy of the name. That is why, when the sceptical doubts are raised, we at first, and perhaps for quite a long time, find them unanswerable. Not having reached these beliefs by any process of reasoning, we have no arguments prepared and ready with which we could reply to the sceptic. Never-

[9] C. L. Stevenson, 'Persuasive Definitions', in *Mind* 47 (1938).

theless, such arguments can in the end be found. In these cases faith can seek and find the understanding to support it. And when understanding has thus supported it, our belief in these matters is not thereby undermined or corrupted.

For all that anyone could have told in advance, the same might have been true of Anselm's project. He, of course, was looking for, and thought he had found, an *a priori* demonstration of God's existence. But the same might equally have been true of Swinburne's project of seeking an empirical, inductive, argument for this conclusion, or of James's project of seeking experimental confirmation. Indeed, the two latter are, at least today, more sensible projects than Anselm's, in so far as we have good general grounds for denying that demonstration is possible about such a matter of fact as the existence of a god. But the main point is that faith can seek for understanding, whether demonstrative or inductive or experimental. One does not abandon one's initial belief when one sets out to look for confirmation, nor, if one found it, would one have to give up the belief. A test pilot, flying a new type of plane for the first time, must have plenty of faith in its designers and manufacturers. None the less, his task is to confirm what he initially believes, and he does so only by taking the risk of disproving it, and only by being on the lookout for any weaknesses and faults. And Kierkegaard himself, in his commendation of Socrates, implicitly admits that a commitment of the kind he values can be shown in an inquiry that sees its own outcome as uncertain.

Why, then, does Kierkegaard also take the contrary view, that commitment must be uncritical, and that the absurd is the only possible object of faith? Is he, perhaps, falling into the fallacy of supposing that because someone would need a particularly strong commitment or will to believe in order to accept an absurd or paradoxical belief with no objective reasons in its favour, it is only a belief of this sort that can retain the commitment that he values? Or is he finding a special merit in *gratuitous* faith, which would be lost if the faith were supported by reason, or even if it sought such support? There are, indeed, some analogous judgements of value. We may admire someone whose loyalty to a friend lets him go on believing that the friend is innocent of some crime although all the evidence seems to show that he is guilty; we might even admire the patriot whose slogan is 'My country, right or wrong'. Certainly there is merit in loyalty that does not give way too easily; but there is also room for the concept of misplaced loyalty and misguided devotion. Or is

Kierkegaard looking at the matter from what he takes to be God's point of view? Would God want an unquestioning faith in himself, and value it the more highly the more resistant it was to adverse evidence? But this suggestion, like Pascal's, presupposes a god to whom we cannot ascribe moral goodness in any sense that we can understand. We are, in effect, back with the god of the Book of Job, and, whatever we may think of Job himself, there can be no doubt that Jehovah comes out of that story very badly.

At the same time, we cannot deny the psychological attraction of Kierkegaard's emphasis on gratuitous faith. His writings have fathered a whole family of existentialisms, whose common quality is just this advocacy of the making of dramatic choices unbacked by reasons. Here we find a practical analogue of the human mind's tendency (pointed out by Hume, as we saw in Chapter 1) to believe what is strange and marvellous in an extreme degree, just because surprise or wonder is such an agreeable emotion. Just as we may believe reports for the very reason that makes them less worthy of belief, so we may choose actions for reasons that might well rather warn us against them. It is fun to take risks, and there is a thrill in making an indefensible and apparently unmotivated choice. But this can hardly be recommended as a general plan of life, and what Kierkegaard himself is advocating is a sort of intellectual Russian roulette.

We set out to inquire whether belief without reason could, paradoxically, be intellectually respectable. Kierkegaard has certainly not shown that it is. Though he disdains rational considerations, he is, nevertheless, exposed to rational criticism. As we have seen, he is not free from inconsistencies. He hesitates over the question whether faith is compatible with a critical outlook, and also over the question whether it matters that theism, or Christianity, should be true. If it does matter, then we cannot dismiss as irrelevant the only sorts of inquiry that could determine its truth. If it does not matter, then it would be better to admit this openly, and try to defend religion as a form of commitment that does not require belief.

12

Religion without Belief?

THE phrase 'religion without belief' may seem—and may indeed be—a contradiction in terms. But 'belief' is ambiguous. In modern English its dominant meaning is what we may call factual belief: to believe is to be (fairly firmly) of a certain opinion. Believing is primarily cognitive, it is *believing that*; even if we speak of believing *in* something—ghosts, say, or fairies, or God—we are likely to mean simply believing that there are ghosts, or fairies, or that there is a god. But the original meaning of 'belief' was rather what we now mean by 'faith'. God was the primary object of belief, and to believe in (or 'on') him was to trust him and rely on him. Even today 'belief' covers more than factual belief: to believe in socialism, or in Margaret Thatcher, or in family planning, is not merely to believe that there are such entities. However, in raising the possibility of religion without belief, I intend to ask whether something which might be called specifically religious belief can be understood, and perhaps defended, as not including factual belief about the typically central religious doctrines. I am thinking not so much of cases where the adherents of some religion—the Jains, for example, or some Buddhists—explicitly reject factual belief in a personal god, or perhaps any sort of god, as of cases where although the religious believers themselves speak in ways that seem, at least on the surface, to involve such factual claims, theologians or philosophers interpret their belief as not including such factual assertions taken literally. Our questions are whether religion is better thus understood, and whether religion, thus understood, is better.

One such approach has its source in some of Wittgenstein's lectures, notes of which have been published.[1] But even where we have

---

[1] L. Wittgenstein, *Lectures and Conversations on Aesthetics, Psychology, and Religious Belief*, edited by C. Barnett (Basil Blackwell, Oxford, 1966). The passages quoted or referred to are all on pp. 53-72.

Wittgenstein's own writings, there is controversy about how they
should be understood; obviously far more caution is needed about
attributing views to him on the basis of a student's notes, and all that
I say here about Wittgenstein is subject to this qualification. D. Z.
Phillips bases his view of religion on that of Wittgenstein, and he
often makes far more explicit what Wittgenstein leaves as hints and
suggestions.[2] Yet his account, too, as we shall see, is not free from
obscurity.

Wittgenstein says that someone who believes in a Last Judgement
and someone who says about this 'Possibly, I'm not sure' are not
close together but are on entirely different planes. The religious
believer is taking something as guidance for his whole life. It is this,
and not any occurrent intensity of feeling, that shows how firmly he
believes, or, perhaps, that constitutes the firmness of his belief. His
belief could go against the best scientific evidence—presumably even
against what he himself acknowledged to be the best scientific evidence. Like Kierkegaard, Wittgenstein suggests that the religious
believer does not even want favourable evidence: 'if there were evidence, this would in fact destroy the whole business'. It was 'ludi-
crous' of a certain Father O'Hara to try to make religious belief
appear to be reasonable, that is, to put it on a par with scientific
beliefs. This was unreasonable, even ridiculous, because he believed,
but based his belief on weak reasons: religion, treated as being on the
same plane with science, becomes superstition. Although Christianity
is said to be a historical religion, the 'historical' claims (especially
about the life of Christ) are not treated as historical, because believers
do not apply to them the sort of doubt which would ordinarily apply
to historical statements about any fairly remote epoch. There is a
distinctively religious use of language, determined by its connections
with other things that the speakers say and do. We might come upon
some island and find people there using sentences which if they had
one set of connections, we should take as (possibly mistaken) scientific statements, but which, if they had a different set of connections,
we should take as religious statements; and in some circumstances
we should not know how to take them.

The problem here is to grasp what is involved in the view that
religious beliefs are on a different plane from scientific or historical
or everyday ones. As Wittgenstein says, the firmness of a belief is not
like the intensity of a pain; it can be measured by the risks that the

[2] *Religion without Explanation* (see n. 5 to Chapter 10, p. 190, above). References to
Phillips in the text are to pages in this work.

believer will take in reliance on it, or again by the extent to which the belief enters into the believer's choices of action and into his inter-pretation of what happens to him. But this is a quite general principle; it applies to many ordinary beliefs as much as to religious ones— though no doubt we also have beliefs which have little or no practical relevance, which do not enter into our active lives, but which are firmly held in so far as we possess evidence which, we suppose, tells strongly in favour of them, and it would take a lot of contrary evidence to make us give them up.

Are religious beliefs distinguished from others by their resistance to contrary evidence? The fact that a religious believer is not shaken by what appears, even to him, to be strong contrary evidence of a scientific or historical or everyday sort, does not show that the *content* of his belief is other than it appears to be, that it is totally different from the content of a scientific or historical or everyday belief. It may well be that he has grounds for his belief which seem to him to outweigh the contrary evidence. Alternatively, it may well be that there are causes, rather than reasons, which make his belief resistant to contrary evidence. Admittedly that would mean that he was being somewhat unreasonable; but what would be surprising in that?

Suppose that we try to use the suggestion that the content of a religious belief is not what it appears to be; how can we spell this out? Wittgenstein is unwilling to say of a believer and a non-believer either that they mean the same by 'There will be a Judgement Day'— which one asserts and the other denies—or that they mean different things: the criterion of *meaning the same* is not clear here. But what ground have we for doubting that they mean the same? The fact that the believer does not allow scientific evidence to tell against the statement does not show that he means anything different, nor does the fact that it plays a role in his life which perhaps, it would not even begin to play in the unbeliever's life, even if he moved from atheism to agnosticism. We should begin to get a difference of mean-ing only if we allowed the theist's conviction, the importance of the belief to him and the firmness with which he holds it, to be part of what the sentence means in his use. But this would be equivalent to the suggestion that we have found, but criticized, in Kierkegaard, that a questioner's interest in a question may be part of the question itself.

Admittedly there are ways in which a theist's response to contrary evidence might show a difference in meaning. For example, he might admit that certain information is evidence against what the atheist or agnostic would mean by 'There will be a Judgement Day', but deny that this is evidence against what *he* means by this sentence. Again, he might be willing to concede that there will never be a Judgement Day in the atheist's or the agnostic's sense, but refuse to give up *his* belief in a Judgement Day. But here it is the theist's specific ways of defending his belief that may reveal a difference in meaning, not his resistance to contrary evidence in itself. Even if someone is determined to go on asserting some formula no matter what happens, this does not in itself make the formula tautologous, though consistency with regard to the use of the formula would then force him to change it into a tautology, so far as its descriptive meaning is concerned.

But suppose that the religious statement 'There will be a Judgement Day' does not mean what, on the surface, it appears to mean; what other sort of meaning could it have? The best clue to this is the hint that 'a certain picture might play the role of constantly admonishing me', and that someone, whenever he had to decide which of two courses to take, might always think of retribution, and again might take whatever happened to him as a reward or a punishment. Then perhaps for such a person statements about divine retribution, whether seen as immediate or as reserved for a final day of judgement, could have as their real meaning *just* their force as guides to choice along with their function as expressions of feelings of responsibility. Similarly, someone's statement that he expects to meet again a friend who is dead might have as its real meaning *just* the expression of his great and enduring affection.

I do not deny that statements might have such non-descriptive meanings as these. But it would be rather surprising if sentences which on the surface have reasonably straightforward factual, descriptive meanings had, in a certain kind of use, *only* such non-descriptive meanings. At least two other possibilities are far more likely. One is that the religious believer is still making the factual claims which his remarks would, if taken literally, convey. These would, after all, serve to justify or support the feelings of responsibility which, by hypothesis, he really has, or to assuage to some extent his grief and sense of loss over his friend's death. He means these statements literally, and believes them with their literal meaning, because, for whatever reason, he emotionally needs to believe them. His belief may then be what Wittgenstein and Phillips describe as superstition; but such may well occur. If the believer none the less admits that these statements lack evidential support, the tensions between these different considerations may simply compartmentalize his thinking. When he looks at the issue from the evidential point of view, he does not believe these statements; but he can also shift from that point of view to another, and believe, quite literally, what he needs to believe. It cannot be denied that many people's thinking does thus separate into compartments insulated from one another.

A second possibility is that though the statements still have, for the believer, their literal meaning, he may not genuinely assert them. Rather he may entertain them, much as we can read what we know to be a work of fiction, and yet find it compelling and deeply moving. It is true that we commonly insulate our reading of fiction from our practical lives, whereas the religious believer may integrate his life and his beliefs. But it is quite possible to treat a system of ideas and statements as having the ontological status of fiction while at the same time it not only expresses sentiments and values which play a large, even dominant, role in one's practical life, but also helps to maintain and strengthen these sentiments and values. This possibility is analogous to the more sceptical of our two interpretations, in Chapter 6, of Kant's suggestion that knowledge of God, freedom, and immortality is given 'only for practical use': in our moral thinking we cannot, on this reading of Kant, help supposing that there is a god, that our wills are free, and that our souls are immortal, but whether there really *is* a god, and so on, is another matter: we have only 'a faith of pure practical reason'.

There are, then, several ways in which we can make sense of the suggestion that religious belief is on a different plane from beliefs of other kinds. As a description of *some* religious thinking the suggestion is plausible; but not as a general account of what is essential to and characteristic of religious belief. Whether we develop it in terms of religious statements, with their literal, factual, meaning, being preserved and protected by compartmental thinking; or of their being not asserted but conserved as expressive and influential fictions; or of their being left with only non-descriptive meanings—or, indeed, of any mixture or confusion of these—we can hardly understand this as being the natural, original, use of religious statements. As Hume said in another context, such a way of thinking 'has no primary recommendation either to reason or the imagination'. It could arise only out of a more basic use in which the statements in question were both taken literally and asserted confidently, without any fear of contrary evidence or of lack of scientific support, not because either of these would have been irrelevant, but simply because they posed no serious threat: the believers thought they had some overwhelming assurance of the literal truth of the statements in question. Each of the suggested ways of putting religious belief on a different plane would be likely to arise only as a compromise formation, when pre-existent beliefs encountered challenges to their literal truth, challenges which religion found it difficult or impossible to meet on its original ground.

D. Z. Phillips would not speak thus of a compromise formation. He refers, indeed, to the 'enormous influence' of Hume on contemporary philosophy of religion, and says that 'given its assumptions, Hume's attack on certain theistic arguments is entirely successful'; but his main thesis is that 'It is equally important to see that many forms of religious belief are free from these assumptions'—and he means, I think, that these are long-standing forms of belief, not ones that have emerged specifically in attempts to avoid the Humean criticisms (p. ix). He maintains, in short, that if the questions whether there is a god, whether we survive bodily death, and so on are taken in a literal, factual, way, then the sceptical or Humean answers to them are correct, but that religious beliefs and statements can and should be taken in another way, to which the Humean criticisms are irrelevant. Phillips concedes to Hume, first, that we cannot infer a god from the world either by a design argument or by a cosmological argument; in fact 'The whole notion of a God and another world which we can infer from the world we know is discredited' (p. 21). But, secondly, he seems to reject not only these modes of inference but also the conclusion. He rejects the construal of the reality of God 'as if it were the reality of an object' (p. 171). ' "God",' he says, 'is not the name of an individual; it does not refer to anything' (p. 148). 'To ask whether God exists is not to ask a theoretical question' (p. 181). He quotes with approval Rush Rhees's dictum, ' "God exists" is not a statement of fact. You might say also that it is not in the indicative mood', and adds ' "There is a God", though it appears to be in the indicative mood, is an expression of faith' (pp. 174, 180-1).

These denials are explicit enough, but Phillips's positive view is much less clear. He develops it by both comparing and contrasting magical and religious beliefs with metaphysical views; but unfortunately his account of metaphysical thinking is seriously defective. His favourite example of a metaphysician is of someone who raises sceptical doubts about the external world or about other people's experiences, say of pain. Since this sceptic's doubt persists in the face of all the evidence that would ordinarily settle such questions, and since his behaviour in practice displays no uncertainty, Phillips thinks that it is not a genuine doubt. The sceptic is still asking how we can be certain 'after we have fulfilled what would normally be called making certain', and therefore 'wants to ask what cannot be asked' (p. 107). But this does not follow, and it is not true. It is true that the sceptic's doubt is in one sense not a genuine doubt. As I said in Chapter 11, he provides an example of *fides quaerens intellectum*. He has, like everyone else, a natural belief in the external world and in other minds, but he sees, rightly, that there is no obvious immediate sufficient justification for this belief, and he quite reasonably looks to see if some more subtle justification can be found. He is not, as Phillips supposes, making some mistake about the meanings of our common language which can be corrected by recalling his attention to the ordinary use of the relevant words. Phillips compares magical and religious statements with metaphysical ones with respect to this supposed feature: what their users, too, want to say cannot be said (p. 109). But since the supposed feature of metaphysical talk is non-existent, the comparison is unilluminating. Phillips also contrasts the magical and religious uses of language with the metaphysical, in that the metaphysical one is non-ordinary, and invites the question 'Why are you speaking like that?', whereas the magical use (in a society where it is at home) and the religious use are the everyday uses of those parts of the language (pp. 118-20). But the fact that a certain way of using sentences, or of thinking, is somewhere conventional is no guarantee that it is unproblematic. Recalling the metaphysician to the ordinary use of language will not solve his quite genuine problems; equally, the fact that the magical or religious use is already ordinary still leaves us with an unsolved problem about what it means, if it does not bear the literal meanings which would make it superstitious.

Phillips's clearest positive suggestions would point to an interpretation of magical and religious language as expressive. 'The magical and religious beliefs and practices are not the confused outcome of deep problems and emotions, but are themselves expressions of what went deep in people's lives. That a man's misfortunes are said by him to be due to his dishonouring the ghosts of slain warriors is itself the form that depth takes here; it is an expression of what the dead mean to him and to the people amongst whom he lives. That a man says that God cares for him in all things is the expression of the terms in which he meets and makes sense of the contingencies of life.' (p.114) This is no doubt true; but it suggests a false antithesis, that since this language is expressive it cannot also be literal and descriptive. Why should it not be both? In fact it most naturally would be both.

Meeting the contingencies of life in a spirit of what we might call ultimate confidence and security would very naturally both support and be supported by a literal belief in an almighty and caring power, and in a world beyond the one we know. Again, when Phillips says that 'The beliefs seem to be ways of looking at fortune and misfortune rather than one way among many of explaining particular fortunes and misfortunes' (p. 106), this too is a false antithesis: they could easily, and would most naturally, be both.

If, despite these objections, we follow these suggestions, we are led to the view of religious belief whose classical exposition was given by R. B. Braithwaite.[3] This corresponds to the 'second possibility' outlined on page 221 above. According to this view, the core of, for example, Christian belief is a determination to live according to Christian moral principles; this intention is associated with thinking of 'Christian stories'; but the believer 'need not believe that the empirical propositions presented by the stories correspond to empirical fact' (Braithwaite, quoted on p. 141). But Phillips seems to find this account too stark, too simple. He thinks that Braithwaite's view is 'a borderline case between conscious and unconscious reductionism' (p. 140). The conscious reductionist is a Humean sceptic who holds that religion is a fiction, whose genesis we can explain, and which we can then eliminate and do without. The unconscious reductionist aims rather at giving an account of religious belief—not at eliminating it—but 'has, in fact, reduced religion to something which lacks some of the fundamental characteristics of religious belief' (p. 140). Phillips thinks that in the account he gives of religious stories 'Braithwaite reduces the status they have in religious discourse', though he does not see that he has done so (p. 142). His weakness is that he 'shares the same conception of truth and falsity' as the philosophers whose inquiries are limited by Hume's terms of reference; he 'does not realize that in these religious beliefs, the grammar of "belief" and "truth" is not the same as in the case of empirical propositions or the prediction of future events' (pp. 142–3).

But now the firm ground beneath our feet has disappeared, and we are stuggling helplessly in a bog. Of course Braithwaite was right to work with the simple, common, conception of truth and falsity. To speak of a different grammar of 'truth' is to demand a licence for

[3] R. B. Braithwaite, 'An Empiricist's View of the Nature of Religious Belief', in *The Philosophy of Religion*, edited by B. Mitchell (Oxford University Press, 1971), reprinted from the Ninth Arthur Stanley Eddington Lecture (Cambridge University Press, 1955).

evasion and double-talk. Braithwaite, Phillips says, 'never considers the possibility that the religious belief is itself the expression of a moral vision. One is taught about a day of judgement, not as just one more matter of fact which is to occur in the future. One is told that it is necessary, unavoidable, something that confronts us all . . . This is not a version of the belief that you will be caught out in the end. On the contrary, it gets its force from the conviction that one is known for what one is all the time . . . The word "God" has its sense in this context from this conviction of a necessary scrutiny by love and goodness, a scrutiny unlike that of any human agency since any idea of its being mistaken or misinformed is ruled out.' (p. 143) This sounds impressive; but what exactly is Phillips saying? Perhaps the talk about an ultimate judgement should be taken as a metaphor which represents rather a continuous scrutiny. But if one is known continuously for what one is, one must be so known by someone or something. If it is not any (other) human agency, it must be either oneself or some supernatural being. If Phillips means that the content of the conviction is literally true, then he must after all defend the literal, objective, existence of a god or something like a god. If, instead, he means that what one is known by is oneself or a part of oneself, then his view is substantially identical with Braithwaite's: the stories, the religious statements, represent and support moral senti-ments and resolves, but they are only metaphorically true. We get a slightly different version of Braithwaite's view if we say that the statement that one is known for what one is all the time is itself not true—one may not be so known even by oneself—but that *this* statement expresses and supports a moral sentiment or resolve. There is, in fact, no coherent alternative other than those which Phillips rejects. Either the believer claims literal truth for the religious state-ments and stories—or at least for some of them—or he does not. Yet if he claims it, Phillips says that he is falling into superstition, while if he does not, then, like Braithwaite, he 'has reduced religion to something which lacks some of the fundamental characteristics of religious belief'. Phillips's talk about a different grammar of 'truth' is a vain attempt to evade this simple but inescapable dilemma.

There follows a series of similarly obscure claims. 'It will not do to characterize such language as a psychological aid to moral endea-vour, since for those who use it and believe what it expresses, the meaning of their endeavours is given in the language' (p. 145). 'This language is not contingently related to the believer's conduct as a psychological aid to it.On the contrary, it is internally related to it in that it is in terms of this language that the believer's conduct is to be understood.' (p. 144) But if this 'internal relation' means that the believer cannot help seeing his conduct in terms of the religious statements—for example as being obedience to God, or as seeking divine guidance—it will follow that *he* cannot help taking some at least of these statements as literally true, and so falling into superstition. And if not even an outside observer can understand the conduct otherwise, he too will have to take those statements as true and so also fall into superstition. Perhaps what is meant is that the observer can adequately describe and understand this conduct only by reporting what it means to the believer, so that he must grasp the believer's concepts but need not endorse their application; but then the observer will be able to characterize the language of belief as a psychological aid to moral endeavour. Perhaps, too, as in our more sceptical reading of Kant, while the believer *in his moral thinking* finds himself compelled to postulate that there literally is a god, and so on, yet even he himself outside that thinking may be able to see that these issues are at least undecided; but then the believer himself is substantially in Braithwaite's position. Phillips adds: 'It is a grammatical confusion to think that this language is referential or descriptive. It is an expression of value. If one asks what it says, the answer is that it says itself' (p. 147). But then if, for some class of users, this language is understood to be purely expressive, these users must be in the position that Braithwaite describes. Phillips swings from one alternative to the other, wrapping both in obscurity, because he is seeking, but cannot find, a view that is different from both. What *he* wants to say cannot, indeed, be said; but this is a symptom not of depth but of incoherence.

So far I have followed Phillips in taking together many different sorts of religious statements and beliefs, and also in linking these closely with the magical beliefs of other cultures. But one distinction at least should be drawn. Many religious statements can be taken as expressing moral views and sentiments and resolves, and what, by Braithwaite's account, they support is a way of life which makes sense in its own right. But, despite what Kant says, this does not hold for the central statements of theism. To talk of 'God', Phillips claims, is not to refer to an individual, an object. But then what is it? Rhees's dictum that 'It is a confession—or expression—of faith' (quoted, p. 174) is of little help. Even if we understand faith as being primarily trust and reliance rather than factual belief it still needs an object: one cannot rely without relying on something. Phillips speaks of a

'sense of the given': the believer sees each new day, talents, opportunities, and so on as gifts from God. 'In face of what is given, the
believer kneels. Talk of "God" has sense in this reaction.' And again
'the praising and the glorifying does not refer to some object called
God. Rather, the expression of such praise and glory is what we call
the worship of God' (pp. 147–9). But now we are at a loss. How does
the expression of praise and glory make sense unless there is a real
object to be praised and glorified? Praise logically requires, it is true,
only an intentional object. One cannot praise without praising something, but what one praises may exist only in one's own thoughts.
But one could not consistently make a big thing of praising and
glorifying a god that one at the same time recognized to exist only in
one's own mind, or even jointly in the minds of many believers like
a figure in a widely current myth or legend.

This difficulty for those who share Phillips's approach comes out
in some extraordinary criticisms of St Anselm. Following Norman
Malcolm, Phillips speaks of Anselm's 'grammatical insight', but the
insight was conceptual rather than grammatical: the concept of God
which Anselm used can, as we saw in Chapter 3, be held to involve
existence. But Anselm is said to have been confused, because he
'abstracted the affirmation [of faith] from the very contexts which
could give birth to it'; his phrase 'a being than which nothing greater
can be conceived' arises out of 'a distorted reading of the words of
praise'; it has been 'torn from the context of praise and presented in
the context of proof'.[4] His proof is condemned on the ground that
it is not, like Kierkegaard's, from the emotions. But Anselm was
right where Phillips thinks that he went wrong, and his real mistake
was quite different. The concept of God which he knew and used in
the context of praise and of faith does involve existence: one could
not praise God in Anselm's way, or the psalmist's, without taking
'God' as the name of an objectively real being, without assuming
that this concept is instantiated. His mistake, as we have seen in
Chapter 3, lay in thinking that the fool could not without contradiction *have* this concept but deny that it is instantiated; but his was,
at least, a very good attempt at a proof, whereas Kierkegaard's
'proof from the emotions' is no proof at all.

But perhaps we can understand 'praising and glorifying' in some
less literal way, so that it can survive without an object. One might,
indeed, still have 'the sense of the given'. One might have a welcoming
and tolerant attitude to life, being pleased and even surprised at

[4] Phillips, op. cit., pp. 175–80; for Malcolm, see n. 8 to Chapter 3, p. 55, above.

anything good that came one's way, rather than assuming that one had a right to it, and not feeling that one had a legitimate grievance whenever anything went wrong. This attitude, however, is as available to the atheist as to the believer; indeed, it is somewhat less available to the theist who sees everything as subject to divine control. Nevertheless, it may be, though it need not be, expressed by some appropriate songs of praise, which one could continue to use, in Braithwaite's spirit, while no longer seriously making the factual claims they appear to contain.

Phillips considers the charge that his conclusions 'are simply a form of disguised atheism' (p. 149). His defence is to appeal to 'the conceptual character of the investigation'. If, *per impossibile*, there were an object corresponding to these pictures or perspectives, it could not be the God of religion . . . anything whose existence could be verified cannot be God.' But a misleading positivism underlies his conceptual investigation. The question is not whether statements about a god could be verified, but whether they are true—simply true, not 'true' with some special grammar. The typical statements about 'the God of religion' are such that (as we saw in the Introduction) they *could* conceivably be true—though they may *also* have expressive and action-guiding aspects with regard to which no issue of truth or falsity arises. They are also open to rational investigation: even if they could not be conclusively verified, they could well be empirically confirmed or disconfirmed, supported or undermined, in less direct ways. Phillips has given no grounds for denying that 'the God of religion' is a possible subject of simple truth or falsehood; in consequence what he offers is either disguised atheism or unsupported theism—since he declines to support its factual claims—or else an unresolved hesitation between the two.

The atheism is very thinly disguised in his discussion of 'perspectives on the dead'. He contrasts John Wisdom's description of a child's belief that his dead father is still alive in another world—and somewhat improved and magnified by the transition—with a view developed by Simone Weil and Peter Winch. 'The remedy,' Weil says, 'is to use the loss itself as an intermediary for attaining reality. The presence of the dead one is imaginary, but his absence is very real; it is henceforth his manner of appearing' (quoted, p. 125). Winch adds (changing the sex of the loved one) that 'she makes a difference to the world by virtue of her absence' (quoted, p. 126). And Phillips himself comments that 'belief in the reality of the dead need not entail an attempt to fill the void by convincing oneself that the one thought to be dead is still alive. Therefore beliefs in the reality of the dead need not entail beliefs which are patently false' (p. 130). 'In Wisdom's example there is a loss of contact with reality, whereas in Winch's example it is precisely reality that is embraced, despite the fact that the reality to be embraced is the longing for a dead one and the realization that the dead can only be present, in this context, in the form of absence' (p. 126).

Stripped of some romantic phrases, this means simply that the dead survive only in the thoughts of those who remember and miss them, but that there is nothing absurd in remembering and missing one's dead friends, though coming to terms with the void created by their deaths. This, however, is the traditional attitude not of the believer but of the atheist—or the Epicurean. ('Sweet is the memory of a dead friend,' Epicurus writes, and 'Let us show our feeling for our lost friends not by lamentation but by meditation.'[5]) It is admirable precisely because it combines genuine affection and feeling for others, and the recognition that people play a real part in one another's lives, with the embracing of reality, with freedom from evasion and self-deception. Phillips contrasts this attitude with one which he ascribes to some unidentified and surely mythical philosophers, who can only reiterate *ad nauseam* that the dead are dead, meaning by that not only the denial of an afterlife but also the recommendation that the dead should be quickly forgotten. Phillips means to assign this latter attitude to the atheist or sceptic, and the former to the religious believer. But it is the former that is the traditional view of the unbeliever, and Phillips is trying to take over, in the name of religion, not only the factual beliefs but also the moral attitudes and values of atheism.

There could, then, be a coherent form of religion without factual belief, such as Braithwaite describes. But Phillips is right in saying that this would lack some of the fundamental characteristics of religious belief, and would reduce the status of the religious 'stories' and affirmations of faith. On the other hand, he has not found any coherent alternative which, while dispensing with factual claims, could yet avoid these criticisms; still less has he succeeded in defending the suggestion that such an alternative is a long-standing form of religious belief.

---

[5] Epicurus, Fragment LXVI in the Vatican Collection, in W. J. Oates, *The Stoic and Epicurean Philosophers* (Random House, New York, 1940), p. 43.

13

Replacements for God

THE forms of religion without factual belief that we examined in Chapter 12, the view, considered in Chapter 11, that faith can and should dispense with reason, and even the emphasis on religious experience discussed in Chapter 10, can be seen as different ways in which traditional theism has retreated in the face of philosophical and scientific difficulties. Yet another possible move is to revise the concept of God, and in particular to give up the view of God as a person. This is the conclusion for which Hume's sceptic, Philo, was willing to settle: '. . . the whole of natural theology . . . resolves itself into one simple, though somewhat ambiguous, at least undefined proposition, *that the cause or causes of order in the universe probably bear some remote analogy to human intelligence'.*[1] A somewhat different revision has recently been embraced by theologians; influential thinkers in this vein include Paul Tillich and, in a more popular style, J. A. T. Robinson.[2] When such writers identify God with 'Being-itself' or 'a depth at the centre of life' or 'the object of ultimate concern', it may seem that their claims have been so watered down as to be not only indisputable but uninteresting. If God is simply whatever you care most about, then not even St Anselm's fool will deny that God exists. But so easy a victory is not worth winning. However, this may be a misinterpretation. These writers may mean rather that some thing, or some principle, objectively *is* of ultimate concern and at the same time is *the* ultimate reality. If so, they are continuing a tradition that goes back at least to Plato.[3] Plato's Form

[1] *Dialogues concerning Natural Religion* (see n. 1 to Chapter 8, p. 133, above), Part XII. This passage was added by Hume in his final revision in 1776.

[2] P. Tillich, *Systematic Theology* (Nisbet, London, 1953-63) *The Shaking of the Foundations* (SCM Press, London, 1949); J. A. T. Robinson, *Honest to God* (SCM Press, London, 1963).

[3] *Republic*, Book VI; the quotation is at 509.

of the Good is supposed to be an objective entity or principle which not only governs the universe but is creatively responsible for the existence of everything: 'you may say of the objects of knowledge that not only their being known comes from the good, but their existence and being also come from it, though the good is not itself being but transcends even being in dignity and power'. Plato compares the Form of the Good with the sun, which provides not only the light which enables us to see things but also the creative energy which brings plants and animals to life; similarly, objective value not only makes everything intelligible but also brings everything into existence; but it is itself ἐπέκεινα τῆς οὐσίας, 'on the far side of being'.

This metaphysical theory is a real alternative to the doctrine that there is a personal creator, a divine mind or spirit. Its central idea, that objective value both explains things and creates them, has continued as a strand in philosophical and religious thinking, though often combined with or submerged within personal theism. But it deserves to be separated out and examined in its own right. It has been so separated, and not only clearly stated but also vigorously defended, by John Leslie.[4]

Leslie calls this theory *extreme axiarchism*: axiarchism would cover all theories that see the world as ruled largely or entirely by value (including both the belief in an omnipotent and benevolent creator and the view that all things are animated by desire for good), while extreme axiarchism is the view that 'some set of ethical needs is creatively powerful' (p. 6), or, more epigrammatically, that 'the universe exists because it ought to' (p. 1).

This theory plainly presupposes and requires the objectivity of value. It also interprets this value or goodness as ethical requiredness, or ought-to-be-ness. To say that something is good (in some respect) is to say that it is ethically required that it should be as it is. But, further, this theory proposes that this ethical feature also in another sense requires or necessitates existence, a sense related to that in which a cause requires or necessitates the existence of its effect— whatever that sense may be.[5] It cannot be exactly the same sense as this; for a cause normally, and perhaps necessarily, precedes its effect in time, and is an occurrent event or condition or state of affairs. But

---

[4] J. Leslie, *Value and Existence* (Basil Blackwell, Oxford, 1979); references are to this work, by page or by chapter. Articles which summarize Leslie's view are 'Efforts to explain all existence', in *Mind* 87 (1978), pp. 181–94, and 'The world's necessary existence', in *International Journal for the Philosophy of Religion* 11 (1980), pp. 207–24.

[5] See Chapter 8 of *The Cement of the Universe* (see n. 2 to Chapter 1, p. 20, above).

something's ethical requiredness, the need for it to be, could precede that thing in time only as a hypothetical fact, the fact that this item would be good, that its existence or occurrence would be of value, whereas its continued non-existence would be a pity.

This notion, that the mere ethical *need* for something could *on its own* call that item into existence, without the operation of any person or mind that was aware of this need and acted so as to fulfil it, is, no doubt, initially strange and paradoxical. Yet in it lies also the greatest strength of extreme axiarchism. For Leslie argues that it offers the only possible answer to the question which underlies all forms of the cosmological argument, the question 'Why is there anything at all?' or 'Why should there be any world rather than none?'. It is obvious that no causal explanation can answer this question. Many thinkers, as we saw in Chapter 5, have thought that the postulation of a god could answer it; but an answer of this kind encounters two radical difficulties. First, in giving what Swinburne calls a personal explanation, it has to assume that will alone, without any interme- diary instrumentalities, can somehow bring about its own fulfilment, creating something out of nothing; but this notion has no empirical basis, but seems rather to result from an analogy with a misconstrual of what happens when a human agent's purpose is fulfilled by way of very complicated material intermediaries. Secondly, it invites the reply, 'But then why is there a god with this extraordinary power?' Then we are told that this question is out of order, that a god terminates the regress of explanation as nothing else could; but this requires the at least controversial concept of a necessary being, and, what is more, the concept, which I have argued to be indefensible, of something whose existence is self-explanatory; that is, it has to invoke the notions that provide the core of the ontological argument. But once we allow the (admittedly difficult) notion that something's value, its ethical requiredness, might both give rise to and explain its existence, we have a possible answer to this ultimate question which does not invite these objections. The world's being good, its fulfilling of an ethical requirement, might be an ultimate, necessary, fact which does not itself call for any further explanation. Moreover, the avail- ability of such an answer may make the question itself more respect- able. 'The bare truth that there is any world could be thought to shout for explanation. If people have been deaf to the cry, then a main cause is their thinking it logically absurd to try to explain *absolutely all* existents. Through its sheer availability, however, ex- treme axiarchism may make this deafness, so often called antimetaphysical, into metaphysics as speculative as axiarchism itself.' (p. 64)

Leslie does not claim that there is any analytic connection between ethical requirement and creative requirement. These are, he agrees, two quite distinguishable features, two different ways in which something may be 'marked out for existence'. His suggestion is that there may be a synthetic but necessary connection between them. Necessary, but not *a priori*: he makes no claim that we can know with *a priori* certainty that ethical requiredness is creatively effective. Yet there is some analogy between an ethical requirement and a creative requirement—for example, in their like directedness towards existence—which is enough to give some initial plausibility to the suggestion that they go together. And certainly it would be a gross error to argue *a priori* on the opposite side, that merely because ethical requirement and creative requirement are conceptually or logically distinct there cannot be a real, and perhaps necessary, connection between them.

Although he commonly speaks of creative effectiveness, Leslie is as ready as, for example, Aquinas is to allow that nothing turns upon creation as a beginning of the universe in time. 'A deity would be a creator were a thing a necessary accompaniment of his wish for it, a wish which might be eternal. Similarly, that an ethical requirement "created" the universe says that had there been no such requirement, then the universe would not have existed, even if it has in fact existed always.' (p. 51)

Leslie sums up as follows what is, in effect, his variant of the cosmological argument. 'The choice then seems between (i) the universe, or some part bearing creative responsibility for the rest, just happening to be there, and (ii) the universe (perhaps including a divine person) existing thanks to its ethical requiredness. The one qualification which might be needed is that such requiredness might instead be responsible only for a divine person, leaving it up to him to create all else . . .' (p. 79)

He also develops variants of the design argument and the argument from consciousness. The very occurrence of causal regularities calls for some further explanation. 'Of conceivable universes, the vast majority would be chaotic; what then persuades events in ours to conform to laws?' (p. 106) 'I agree that a universe ruled by chance, if sufficiently huge, would contain large patches easy to describe, much as monkeys with typewriters would in the end compose a few sonnets. But if taking seriously this means of explaining the orderliness which we have so far experienced, we should expect disorder to begin in the very next microsecond.' (p. 109) It is, therefore, not unreasonable to look for a further explanation of there being causal laws, and the proposed candidate is the goodness of there being such laws (Chapter VI). This explanation is particularly appropriate in that the specific laws by which our universe works are suited to the development of life and consciousness, when they might so easily have been otherwise (Chapter VII). But Leslie also considers the objection that value resides only in conscious states, so that it is difficult to appeal to value as an explanation of a universe of which consciousness is, so far as we can tell, only a very small part. He toys with phenomenalism as a possible way of answering this objection—for, if phenomenalism is correct, then minds alone are the fundamentally real substances that make up the universe (Chapter X)—but this is a very implausible way out of the difficulty.

Extreme axiarchism also faces its own variant of the problem of evil (Chapter V). One might not expect this difficulty to arise, since the ascription to God of omnipotence and omniscience is essential to the setting up of this problem for orthodox theism, and a radical revision of the concept of God might well dispense with these features. In particular, there is no reason why a non-personal principle of creative value should be encumbered with omniscience. Nevertheless, Leslie is right to confront this problem. For if goodness, ethical requiredness, is the *sole* creative principle and the only explanation why there is any world at all, we can indeed ask, Whence, then, is evil? It would obviously be less satisfactory, because less simple, to admit that value is, even in principle, only a partial explanation of what there is, that there is also an element of the sheer unexplained brute fact, of things just happening to be there; for the recognition of such unexplained brute facts was the rejected alternative to the hypothesis that ethical requiredness is creative. Leslie's answer to the problem of evil is, in effect, in the terms we used in Chapter 9, to argue that there may well be no unabsorbed evils, when we take account of the value of lives that involve real choices against a background of discoverable causal regularities—whether those choices are causally determined or not, for Leslie allows for a compatibilist view of freedom.

This summary may be enough to show that extreme axiarchism is a formidable rival to the traditional theism which treats God as a person or mind or spirit. As I have noted, it leaves a place open for a personal god—or rather two alternative places. There might be such a god as one component among others of a universe whose ultimate source and explanation is its ethical requiredness; again, it might be that an omnipotent and benevolent spirit was himself the only immediate product of creative value, everything else being created in turn by him. But Leslie remarks that the latter 'looks both untidy and inessential to Christianity, for instance, which worships goodness and not sheer power—not even when it conceives God as a person' (p. 79). In fact, this could have been put more strongly. A divine person would be completely redundant within extreme axiarchism's scheme of explanation, since value alone, without conscious purpose, is supposed to be creative; and the postulation of a directly efficacious will, bringing about its own fulfilment without intermediaries, would, as our discussion of Swinburne's 'personal explanation' in Chapters 5 and 7 shows, be an embarrassingly improbable addition to the theory. There is even less reason for allowing the hypothesized principle of creative value to be *called* God. That would be a device for slurring over a real change in belief, and, in all likelihood, an excuse for moving back and forth between traditional theism and this alternative, adhering in practice to the one while being prepared to defend only the other. Far from being honest to God, this is dishonest to both theism and extreme axiarchism. The latter should be seen and considered as what it is, a radically different alternative and rival to theism, with a distinguished ancestry of its own going back, as we have seen, to Plato's vision of the Form of the Good.

The availability of this alternative should tell against traditional theism with anyone who is dissatisfied, for whatever reason, with the naturalistic, sceptical, view of the world. If, with Leibniz and others, you demand an ultimate explanation, then this may well be a better one than the postulation of a divine mind or spirit. But for us the crucial question is how this suggestion fares in competition with the naturalistic or sceptical view.

As we have seen, extreme axiarchism still encounters the problem of evil. Indeed, it is specially exposed to this problem, in that it cannot shelter, as theism often tries to, behind the contra-causal development of the free will defence. It at first *seems* possible to detach the wrong choices of free agents from even an omnipotent god, whereas, if objective value is the sole creative principle, nothing that is real can be detached from it. (It is true that *in the end* theism is no better off, since, as we saw in Chapter 9, this method of defence fails.) That is, the extreme axiarchist must hold that there are no unabsorbed evils. Leslie does in effect hold this, so his position is at least consistent. Whether it can be thoroughly reconciled both with a realistic picture of the world as it is and with a plausible interpretation of ethical requiredness is another, more controversial, matter.

Paradoxically, however, extreme axiarchism may be embarrassed less by the problem of evil than by what we may call the problem of indifference. This has two aspects. Creative ethical requiredness, like Leibniz's God, could presumably do nothing without a sufficient reason. Leibniz argued that there could not be a Newtonian absolute space, because, if there were, God would have been faced with the choice of creating the universe just where it is or creating it somewhere else, 'preserving the same situations of bodies among themselves', that is, with all the same *relative* positions and motions, and he could have had no reason for preferring one to the other.[6] Creative value, it seems, would be faced with innumerable equally embarrassing choices between alternatives of which neither was better than the other. The other aspect of the problem of indifference we have already noted: there seem to be vast tracts of space-time and material existents that have no value worth mentioning. This problem is acute for Leslie, because he believes that 'only experiences, conscious states, could have intrinsic value' (p. 153), and therefore agrees with Berkeley that to accept the ordinary view of the material world 'is to suppose that God has created innumerable beings that are entirely useless, and serve to no manner of purpose'.[7] To avoid, as he must, any corresponding supposition about creative value, he argues, as we have noted, for phenomenalism. But among hypotheses to explain the whole pattern of our experiences, phenomenalism is much less satisfactory than *some* kind of realism. Experiences, taken on their own, are fragmentary and disorderly, full of unexplained coincidences; it is only by supplementing their contents that we can reach any approximation to a coherent, orderly, world.[8] But further, among realisms, there is, as we have seen in Chapter 4, a strong case for material realism as opposed to Berkeley's scheme of a divine mind which feeds into human minds small fragments of its own complete ideal world. If neither phenomenalism nor a Berkeleian view is satisfactory, then we are forced to recognize the existence of

[6] *The Leibniz–Clarke Correspondence* (see n. 4 to Chapter 5, p. 85, above): e.g. Leibniz's Third Paper.

[7] *Principles of Human Knowledge*, Section 19.

[8] Hume, *Treatise*, Book I, Part iv, Section 2; *cf* Chapter 2 of *Problems from Locke* (see n. 4 to Chapter 4, p. 73, above).

innumerable beings that serve no sort of purpose, and this is a strong point against extreme axiarchism.

An even greater difficulty for this theory lies in the implausibility of its own central principle, the hypothesis that objective ethical requiredness is creative, that something's being valuable can in itself tend to bring that thing into existence or maintain it in existence, and can therefore provide an ultimate explanation of its being there, independently of its being caused or created by any other existing things. Leslie is right both in renouncing any claim that this principle is analytic or otherwise *a priori* and in resisting the contrary prejudice that it can be known *a priori* to be impossible. Yet it remains a sheer speculation. This principle is equivalent to a doctrine of intrinsic immanent teleology (p. 25): things exist, and are as they are, for a goal or end or purpose or final cause; but the purpose is not located in any mind, nor is the goal or end made such by being taken as an end, by being desired or pursued, by any active being, nor even by the fact that it would be so taken as an end or would satisfy some desire. Thinkers have often believed in such pure immanent teleology; but it is a category which has no genuine ordinary applications. Explanations, for example of biological structures, of plant or animal behaviour, or of devices, like homing rockets, that are based on feedback, which are initially or superficially teleological can be shown to rest entirely on processes of efficient causation—either directly, or else mediately by way of reduction to conscious purposive action which itself reduces to a form of efficient causation.[9] Axiarchical creation, therefore, is modelled upon a *misunderstanding* of certain natural processes. Its proposed explanation of the world and its details is in the same position as Swinburne's personal explanation: this, too, as we saw in Chapters 5 and 7, is based on an analogy with a misleading abstraction from the ordinary process of the fulfilment of human intentions. In fact, what look at first like three rival, independent, kinds of explanation—causal, personal, and teleological—are, when their ordinary applications are properly understood, all forms of just one kind of explanation, that based on efficient causation. Ordinary 'personal' and 'teleological' explanations are only telescopings of somewhat complicated examples of causal explanation. We have, therefore, no sound empirical basis from which the axiarchical principle might be developed even by an enterprising extrapolation; it remains a pure, ungrounded, speculation.

Finally, extreme axiarchism rests essentially upon the assumption

[9] This is argued at length in Chapter 11 of *The Cement of the Universe*.

that there are objectively prescriptive values. And this assumption is false.[10] A thorough discussion of this topic would lead us into the foundations of ethics. I have argued elsewhere that the theological frontier of ethics remains open;[11] the same is true of the ethical frontier of theology. Just as we cannot finally settle various ethical questions without deciding whether there is, or is not, a god, so equally we cannot finally settle various theological questions, such as the viability of axiarchism, except with the help of a decision about the status of ethical values.

Leslie is right in arguing (Chapter XII) that neither ethical naturalism nor non-cognitivism (prescriptivism, emotivism, and the like), gives an adequate analysis of what we ordinarily mean when we use moral or in general evaluative language. These theories do not exhaustively interpret—either separately or in conjunction with one another—our ethical concepts. We do think of goodness as a supposedly objective ought-to-be-ness. In calling something good we do commonly imply that it is intrinsically and objectively required or marked out for existence, irrespective of whether any person, human or divine, or any group or society of persons, requires or demands or prescribes or admires it. Some thinkers hold that such a concept—even if we are inclined to use it—is incoherent, that requiring is something that only minds—or something constituted by minds, like a legal system—can do. I do not believe that it is incoherent: I can find no actual contradiction implicit within it. Nevertheless it cannot be denied that it is, when clearly distinguished from various concepts of relative or subjective value, a very strange concept.

Leslie's ontology of values is very like that of Samuel Clarke.[12] Some relations are fully secondary to the related terms. That one box is able to fit inside another does not involve or depend upon anything beyond the intrinsic characteristics (shape and size) of the two boxes, and the same is true of relations of comparative similarity between, for example, colours. Ethical requiredness is, he suggests, similarly a relation fully secondary to the intrinsic characteristics of whatever has it; thus, he argues, value can be connected synthetically but necessarily with the nature of what has value, though this relation need not be, and indeed is not, knowable *a priori*.

[10] This is argued in Chapter 1 of *Ethics: Inventing Right and Wrong* and throughout *Hume's Moral Theory* (see nn. 2 and 7 to Chapter 6, pp. 106 and 115, above).

[11] *Ethics: Inventing Right and Wrong*, Chapter 10.

[12] See, e.g., the extracts from S. Clarke, *The Being and Attributes of God*, in *British Moralists 1650–1800*, edited by D. D. Raphael (Oxford University Press, 1969).

But this analogy is not very persuasive. Objective value seems very different from the other examples of secondary relations, which are less obviously synthetic, and seem far more open to *a priori* determination. We should hesitate to postulate that this strange concept has any real instantiations, provided that our inclination to use it can be explained adequately in some other way. And in fact we can explain this, in a manner that Hume, in particular, has indicated. Moral and evaluative thinking arises from human sentiments and purposes; it involves systems of attitudes developed particularly by interactions between people in societies, and the concept of intrinsic requiredness results from a projection of these attitudes upon their objects, by an abstraction of the requiring from the persons—or institutions built out of persons—that really do the requiring.

This Humean style of explanation of our concept of goodness or objective requiredness is much more acceptable than the rival view that things or states of affairs actually have such objective requiredness as a secondary relation and that we are in some unexplained way able to detect it and respond to it. This approach also explains, or rather explains away, such plausibility as Leslie finds in the axiarchic principle, in the notion that what is ethically marked out for existence may *thereby* also be creatively marked out for existence. For if we require or demand something, we also necessarily have some tendency to bring it about if we can. The simultaneous projection of both of these into supposedly objective features will yield precisely the notion that there is an objective ethical requirement which, by a synthetic necessity, carries creative requirement with it, in other words that value must, at least to some extent, be creatively effective. Since the axiarchic cluster of ideas is so readily explicable in this alternative way, we must reject both the concept of objectively prescriptive value on which it rests and, *a fortiori*, the suggestion that such value is creative.

We cannot, therefore, soften our rejection of theism by the acceptance of this alternative, or by welcoming any less clearly stated views which hover between extreme axiarchism and traditional theism.

14

Conclusions and Implications

(a) *The Challenge of Nihilism*

W E may approach our conclusion by considering Hans Küng's massive work, *Does God Exist?*[1] Sub-titled 'An Answer for Today', this book not only brings together many lines of thought that bear upon this question, but also sets out to interpret our whole present moral and intellectual situation. It displays a fantastic wealth of learning; it is also extremely diffuse. Time and again after raising an issue Küng will slightly change the subject, and often when we need an argument he gives us a quotation, a report of the views of yet another thinker, or even a fragment of biography. I think he is also unduly concerned with contemporary relevance, and is liable to tell us that some statement or argument is out of date, when all that matters is whether it is true or false, sound or unsound. Nevertheless, as we shall find, there is a main connecting thread of argument, and his final answer, at least, is explicit (p. 702):

After the difficult passage through the history of the modern age from the time of Descartes and Pascal, Kant and Hegel,
considering in detail the objections raised in the critique of religion by Feuerbach, Marx and Freud,
seriously confronting Nietzsche's nihilism,
seeking the reason for our fundamental trust and the answer in trust in God, in comparing finally the alternatives of the Eastern religions, entering also into the question 'Who is God?' and of the God of Israel and of Jesus Christ: after all this, it will be understood why the question 'Does God exist?' can now be answered by a clear, convinced Yes, justifiable at the bar of critical reason.

However, the substance of his discussion is far less satisfactory. One crucial question is whether his final 'Yes' is to the god of

[1] H. Küng, *Does God Exist?* (Collins, London, 1980; first published in German as *Existiert Gott?* by Piper-Verlag, Munich, 1978).

traditional theism or to some 'replacement for God'; but the answer to this question is far from clear. For example, in his *Interim Results II: Theses on secularity and historicity of God* we find this (pp. 185–6):

> God is not a supramundane being above the clouds, in the physical heaven. The naive, anthropomorphic idea is obsolete … For man's being and action, this means that God is not an almighty, absolute ruler exercising unlimited power just as he chooses over world and man.
>
> God is not an extramundane being, beyond the stars, in the metaphysical heaven. The rationalistic-deistic idea is obsolete … For man's being and action, this means that God is not now—so to speak—a constitutionally reigning monarch who is bound, for his part, by a constitution based on natural and moral law and who has largely retired from the concrete life of the world and man.
>
> God is in this world, and this world is in God. There must be a uniform understanding of reality. God is not only a (supreme) finite … alongside finite things. He is in fact the infinite in the finite, transcendence in immanence, the absolute in the relative. It is precisely as the absolute that God can enter into a relationship with the world of man … God is therefore the absolute who includes and creates relativity, who, precisely as free, makes possible and actualizes relationship: God as the absolute-relative, here-hereafter, transcendent-immanent, all-embracing and all-permeating most real reality in the heart of things, in man, in the history of mankind, in the world … For man's being and action, this means that God is the close-distant, secular-nonsecular God, who precisely as sustaining, upholding us in all life and movement, failure and falling, is also always present and encompassing us.

And, after rejecting both the 'Greek-metaphysical' and the 'medieval-metaphysical' concepts of God, he adds (p. 188):

> God is the living God, always the selfsame, dynamically actual and continually active in history. Precisely as the eternally perfect, he is free to seize the 'possibility" of becoming historical … For man's being and action, this means that God is the living God who in all his indisposability and freedom knows and loves man, acts, moves, and attracts in man's history.

Later, for comparison with Eastern religions, he reports and seems to endorse 'the Western tradition of a negative theology from Pseudo-Dionysius to Heidegger' (pp. 601–2):

> God cannot be grasped in any concept, cannot be fully expressed in any statement, cannot be defined in any definition: he is the incomprehensible, inexpressible, indefinable.
>
> Neither does the concept of being embrace him … he is not an existent: he transcends everything … but … he is not outside all that is; inherent in the world and man, he determines their being from within …
>
> In God therefore transcendence and immanence coincide … Before God, all talk emerges from listening silence and leads to speaking silence.

Later again, in discussing 'the God of the Bible', he says (p. 632):

God is not a person as man is a person. The all-embracing and all-penetrating is never an object that man can view from a distance in order to make statements about it. The primal ground, primal support and primal goal of all reality ... is not an individual person among other persons, is not a superman or superego.

But also (p. 633):

A God who founds personality cannot himself be nonpersonal ... God is not neuter, not an 'it', but a God of men ... He is spirit in creative freedom, the primordial identity of justice and love, one who faces me as founding and embracing all interhuman personality ... It will be better to call the most real reality not personal or impersonal but ... transpersonal or suprapersonal.

But, despite all this, Küng also accepts in some sense the God of the Bible who, he says, 'is wholly and entirely essentially a *'God with a human face'* (p. 666). It is 'overhasty' to dissociate the God of the philosophers from the God of the Bible, but also 'superficial' simply to harmonize them. Rather, we should *'see the relationship in a truly dialectical way. In the God of the Bible, the God of the philosophers is the best, threefold sense of the Hegelian term* 'sublated' (aufgehoben)—at one and the same time affirmed, negated, and transcended.' What is more, he 'venture[s] without hesitation to declare: *Credo in Jesum Christum, filium Dei unigenitum'* (I believe in Jesus Christ, the only-begotten son of God) and 'can confidently say even now: *Credo in Spiritum Sanctum'* (I believe in the Holy Spirit) (pp. 688, 699). That is, for all the contrary appearances, he affirms his own orthodoxy.

Küng is obviously fond of having it all ways at once. This is further illustrated by his remarks about miracles (pp. 650-1). Miracles recorded in the Bible 'cannot be proved historically to be violations of the laws of nature'; a miracle is merely 'everything that arouses man's wonder', not necessarily a divine intervention violating natural law. The miracle stories are 'lighthearted popular narratives intended to provoke admiring faith'. (If so, we may comment, they have no tendency to support any kind of supernaturalism or theism.) Yet 'no one who links belief in God with miracles is to be disturbed in his religious feelings. The sole aim here is to provide a helpful answer to modern man for whom miracles are a hindrance to his belief in God.' That is, if your belief in God is supported by miracles, Küng will endorse them for you; but if you find them an obstacle to belief, he will explain them away! Similarly he quotes with approval Bultmann's remark: 'By faith I can understand an idea or a decision as a divine inspiration, without detaching the idea or decision from its link with its psychological justification' (p. 653).

One main strand in Küng's thinking brings him close to Hume's Demea, who stands for an infinite and incomprehensible god against the anthropomorphism of Cleanthes. But then we should recall how Hume uses Demea's view to prepare the way for Philo's scepticism. A god as indescribable and indeterminate as the one Küng seems to offer provides no purchase for reasoning, nothing of which argument can take hold in order to support the thesis that such a god exists.

Nevertheless, Küng claims to have given an argument. As we saw, he says that his 'Yes' is 'justifiable at the bar of critical reason'. Against such writers as Norman Malcolm and D. Z. Phillips, he says firmly that 'the question of truth cannot be avoided. And this truth can be tested by experience, as we shall see, by indirect verification through the experience of reality.' (p. 505) And again (p. 528):

> No, theology cannot evade the demands for confirmation of belief in God: *Not a blind, but a* justifiable belief: *a person should not be abused, but convinced by arguments, so that he can make a responsible decision of faith. Not a belief devoid of reality, but a belief related to reality.*

Part of his case consists of his replies to the various arguments for atheism, essentially various proposed natural histories of religion, which we considered in Chapter 10. As we saw there, despite the weaknesses of some oversimplified theories, a satisfactory natural history of religion can be outlined. Küng's criticisms come in the end to no more than what we have conceded and stressed, that such an explanation of religious beliefs is not a primary argument against their truth. He still needs a positive argument for theism; and indeed he tries to give one.

He concedes (p. 533) that 'There is no direct experience of God'. Equally he explicitly rejects (though for inadequately stated reasons) the cosmological, teleological, and ontological proofs (pp. 534–5). But he says that though 'the *probative character of the proofs of God is finished* today', yet their 'non-demonstrable content' remains important. For the ontological proof, he offers only the (deplorable) suggestion that it should be 'understood less as a proof than as an expression of trusting faith'; but, as we shall see, he really uses the cosmological and teleological arguments in an altered form—indeed, in a form that has some resemblance to Swinburne's, in that he proposes that 'belief in God is to be verified but not proved' (p. 536). Küng, however, combines this with echoes both of the moral proofs and of the will to believe: *'an inductive lead does not seem impossible, attempting to throw light on the experience of uncertain reality, which is accessible to each and everyone, in order thus—as it were, by way of "practical reason", of the "ought", or (better) of the "whole man"—to confront man as thinking and acting with a rationally justifiable decision that goes beyond pure reason and demands the whole person'.* Since his argument thus brings together several different strands, we may be able to use discussion of it to introduce the fulfilment of the undertaking I gave in the Introduction, not merely to examine separately the various arguments for the existence of a god, but also to consider their combined effect, and to weigh them together against the various arguments on the other side, before reaching our final conclusion. This conclusion will be reached in section (b) below.

For Küng the question is not whether we can or cannot advance from an already established knowledge of the natural world, or of consciousness, or of morality, to further, specifically theistic, hypotheses or conclusions. His strategy is rather to argue that in present day thought rationality, both speculative and practical, is threatened along with theism by a pervasive tendency to nihilism. This nihilism, of which he finds the most powerful exponent in Nietzsche, is summed up as the denial of the three classical transcendentals: there is no unity, no truth, no goodness. Man deludes himself in thinking he has found any totality, system, or organization in events; he has sought a meaning in events that is not there; there is no absolute nature of things nor a 'thing-in-itself'; the world is valueless and purposeless. Nihilism presents itself 'as insight into the nothingness, contradictoriness, meaninglessness, worthlessness, of reality' (p. 421).

Küng insists that *'The thoroughgoing uncertainty of reality itself makes nihilism possible, whether in practical life ... or in philosophical or unphilosophical reflection'.* Moreover, it is irrefutable: *'There is no rationally conclusive argument against the possibility of nihilism. It is indeed at least possible that this human life, in the last resort, is meaningless, that chance, blind fate, chaos, absurdity and illusion rule the world'* (p. 423). On the other hand, nihilism is not provable. It is not *a priori* impossible that *'in the last resort, everything is nevertheless identical, meaningful, valuable, real'* (p. 424). Consequently the basic question is, 'Can nihilism be overcome, and, if so, how?' (p. 425).

The fundamental alternative, Küng says, is between trust and mistrust, 'in which I stake myself without security or guarantee ... either I regard reality ... as trustworthy and reliable—or not'—a choice which he explicitly compares with Pascal's wager (p. 438). Fundamental trust, he adds, is natural to man, it makes us 'open to reality', and *'The Yes can be consistently maintained in practice'*, whereas the opposite of each of these holds for fundamental distrust (pp. 443–6). There is a *'way of critical rationality'* which is *'a middle way between an irrational "uncritical dogmatism" and a "critical rationalism" that also, in the last resort, rests on irrational foundations';* it is a *'completely* reasonable *risk, which, however, always remains a risk'* (p. 450).

So far so good, though Küng has rather exaggerated the threat. That there is *some* reality is beyond doubt. The extreme of nihilism would be to deny that reality is discoverable or understandable; but there is no serious case for this denial. Küng differentiates the critical rationality which he defends from the 'critical rationalism' which he rejects (and which he finds, perhaps mistakenly, in Karl Popper and Hans Albert), on the ground that the latter dispenses, as the former does not, with any critical examination of the foundations of our knowledge and so involves an irrational faith in reason. We can agree that nothing is to be exempt from criticism, not even the critical method itself, though of course not everything can be criticized at once: while we are examining any one issue, we must take various other things for granted. This precludes the attainment of certainty, and it should exclude the search for certainty. But there is no great mystery about this, nor any great modernity. Some of the essential points, as we saw in Chapter 11, were made by William James in defence of a fallibilist, experimental, but optimistic and risk-taking empiricism. As James says, a risk which gives us our only chance of discovering the truth, or even approaching it, is indeed a reasonable risk.

Further, the assumption that there is some order, some regularity, to be found in the world—not necessarily strict causal determinism—both is a regulative principle which we can and do use in developing and testing other hypotheses and also is itself a hypothesis of a very broad kind, which in turn is open to testing and confirmation.[2] This seems to be the main thing that Küng means by 'unity', so this too is covered by 'critical rationality', that is, by a fallibilistic but optimistic empiricism. Such an approach, whatever name we give it, can thus be seen to be reasonable in itself, and not in need of any further justification or support.

[2] See the Appendix to *The Cement of the Universe* (see n. 2 to Chapter 1, p. 20, above) and 'A Defence of Induction' (see n. 9 to Chapter 8, p. 148, above).

The reply to nihilism about unity and truth is therefore straight-forward, and we can agree with the substance of what Küng says about this. His reply to nihilism about goodness or value is trickier and more controversial. He quotes with approval the view of H. Sachsse that there is a present and pressing need for the development of 'relevant and practical norms' (p. 466). He concedes that *Today less than ever can we call down from heaven ready-made solutions*, or deduce them theologically from an immutable universal essential nature of man'. He concedes, too, that 'There is in fact what Nietzsche called a "genealogy of morals"'—that is, that concrete existing ethical systems have been developed by a socio-historical process—and that today we have to *work out "on earth" discrimi-nating solutions* for all the difficult problems. We are responsible for our morality' (p. 469). All this is strikingly similar to the main theme of my *Ethics: Inventing Right and Wrong*[3]—and, what is more im-portant, it is in itself an adequate *reply* to nihilism about value. But then Küng seems to slide to a very different thesis (p. 470):

Any acceptance of meaning, truth and rationality, of values and ideals ... presupposes a fundamental trust *in uncertain reality: by contrast with nihilism, an assent in principle to its fundamental identity, meaningfulness and value ... Only if the reality of the world and man, as accepted in fundamental trust, is characterized by an ultimate identity, meaningfulness and value, can individual norms of genuinely human behavior and action be deduced in an appropriate way from this reality and—decisively—from the essential human needs, pres-sures and necessities ...*

This is radically different. Now Küng is suggesting that we must after all postulate an *objective* value from which (along with the empirical facts of human needs, and so on) we might *deduce* specific norms. But this is an error, and in contrast with it we must hold fast to the thesis that value itself is a human and social product. This is not to deny, however, that there is an ethical variety of 'fundamental trust' which is needed at the basis of our moral systems. We require, perhaps, a confident hope that we can find principles of co-operation in the midst of competition. This would be a generalization of the practical 'precursive faith' of which William James speaks: only if people trust one another before each can be sure that the others are trustworthy will they have a chance of establishing effective co-operation.

There is, then, a reply to nihilism about goodness or value, which again can be seen to be reasonable in itself, and not in need of any

[3] See n. 7 to Chapter 6, p. 115, above.

further justification or support. But it is significantly different from the reply that Küng gives. Or rather, he both suggests this reply and slides to a different one.

But where, we may ask, does God come into all this? With comic condescension, Küng allows that *'On the basis of fundamental trust, even an atheist can lead a genuinely human, that is, humane, and in this sense moral, life'*, and that *'Even atheists and agnostics are not necessarily nihilists, but can be humanists and moralists'* (p. 472). Nevertheless, he now makes the crucial step in the direction of theism: 'It must now be obvious that the fundamental trust in the identity, meaningfulness and value of reality, which is the presupposition of human science and autonomous ethics, is justified in the last resort only if reality itself—of which man is also a part—is not groundless, unsupported and aimless' (p. 476).

No. This is not obvious at all. Indeed it is false, and Küng's own argument shows it to be false. The kind of fundamental trust that counters nihilism about truth and 'unity', the 'critical rationality' of which he speaks, is reasonable *in its own right* for the reasons he has given. And the same is true of the motives for the invention of value. There is no need to look for or postulate any 'ground, support, or goal' for reality. The broad hypothesis that there is some order in the world is one which it is reasonable to adopt tentatively, but also to test; and it has been strongly confirmed by the inquiries which have (implicitly) tested it. Likewise, though the inventing of moral values has gone on mainly spontaneously, it is reasonable in the sense that it is only by having the attitudes which that invention expresses that we are able to live together without destroying one another. Each of these is defensible on its own: neither needs any further support.

But it is upon this utterly unwarranted step that Küng bases his further case for a god. He is seeking not, indeed, a demonstrative proof, but an 'indirect verification', of God as the supposedly required primal ground, primal support, and primal goal of all reality.

He first asserts that *'If God exists, then the grounding reality is not ultimately groundless ... the supporting reality is not ultimately unsupported ... evolving reality is not ultimately without aim ...* and *reality suspended between being and not being is not ultimately under suspicion of being a void'*. He adds that while this hypothesis opposes nihilism, it can also explain the *appearance* of nihilism: reality appears to be ultimately groundless, unsupported, and aimless 'Because uncertain reality is itself *not God'*. Similarly, the hypothesis that God exists can give ultimate meaning and hope to one's own life; but it can also explain the *appearance* of meaninglessness and emptiness here 'Because man *is not God*'. (pp. 566–8)

By contrast, he thinks, atheism would imply an ultimately unjustified fundamental trust in reality, and therefore the danger of 'the possible disunion, meaninglessness, worthlessness, hollowness of reality as a whole' (p. 571).

Küng concludes that '*Affirmation of God implies an* ultimately justified *fundamental trust in reality. If someone affirms God, he knows why he can trust reality.*' Hence 'there is no stalemate between belief in God and atheism' (p. 572). Though this affirmation 'rests, in the last resort, on a *decision*' (p. 569), because there is no conclusive argument either for or against it, yet 'trust in God is by no means irrational ... I know ... *by the very fact* of doing this, that I am doing the right thing ... what cannot be proved *in advance* I experience *in the accomplishment*', and this provides '*a fundamental certainty*'. Thus understood, '*Belief in God ... is a matter not only of human reason but of the whole concrete, living man*' (pp. 573–4).

I have summarized Küng's argument as far as possible in his own words, because a paraphrase would not only detract from its eloquence but also risk distorting a view that contains so many complexities and contrasts. My criticisms must, and can, be briefer.

Küng's final step seems to claim that the very act of believing in God is self-verifying; but he gives no reason at all for this claim. The act may carry with it a conviction of certainty: the relief of ceasing to doubt is pleasantly reassuring. But this is purely subjective: to rely on this would be merely another form of the assumption that there is a kind of experience which guarantees the objective validity of its content or intentional object, which we have criticized in Chapter 10 and which Küng himself has rightly dismissed (p. 533). Alternatively, the suggestion may be that in postulating a god one is postulating *that which grounds both itself and everything else*. But to claim that the very content of this postulation gives it objective certainty is to employ yet again the ontological argument, and Küng has rightly dismissed this too (pp. 533, 535).

If we delete this unsound final step, Küng's argument turns essentially upon the confirming of a hypothesis, and in particular upon the relative confirmation of the god-hypothesis as against that of an objective natural world (including human beings) which has no further ground or support or goal. As for the explanation of the *appearance* of nihilism, the god-hypothesis is in exactly the same position as its naturalistic rival. The one says that though there is a god, this god is not obvious, and 'uncertain reality' is not this god, that is, is not its own primal ground, support, or goal; the other says simply that there is no such primal ground, support, or goal. In either case the lack of any obvious primal ground leaves room for nihilism. The two rival hypotheses are equal also in their explanations of the *appearance* of meaninglessness in human life. But though they are equally able to explain the appearance of nihilism, the god-hypothesis is the less economical. Its merits, if any, must be due to the other aspect, to its allegedly providing reality with a ground, support, and goal, and man with an objectively valid aim. But Küng has said nothing to explain *how* the god-hypothesis is supposed to do this. Indeed, the Demea-like indeterminacy of his account of God would make it hard for him to do so. But what he hints at is, in fact, a set of suggestions which we have already explicitly stated and examined, especially in Swinburne's inductive versions of the cosmological and design arguments, in Leslie's extreme axiarchism, and in the various moral arguments discussed in Chapter 6. To avoid assuming 'the groundlessness and instability of reality as a whole', Küng suggests that it may be reasonable to assume 'a cause of all causes'; and to avoid assuming the meaninglessness and aimlessness of reality as a whole it may be reasonable to assume 'an end of ends' (pp. 534-5), or again *'a God who will bring to perfection the world and man'* (p. 657). 'Believing in God as Finisher of the world means coolly and realistically—and even more, without succumbing to the violent benefactors of the people—to work for a better future, a better society, in peace, freedom and justice, and at the same time to know without illusions that this can always only be sought but never completely realized by man' (p. 659).

But the explanations at which Küng hints are completely undermined by the criticisms we have given of the specific arguments in Chapters 5, 6, 7, 8, and 13. As I have said, we have no empirical basis, in a knowledge of direct, unmediated, fulfilments of will, from which we might extrapolate to anything like Swinburne's personal explanation as a way of using a god to explain the world or its details. Nor, correspondingly, do we have any empirical basis for the axiarchist's suggestion that value as such may be intrinsically creative. Nor, again, could we find any ultimately plausible account of how moral values might rest upon or be created or sustained by a god. Still less do we need anything like a god to counter the supposed threat of aimlessness. Men are themselves purposive beings. In their own nature they unavoidably pursue aims and goals; they do not need these to be given them from outside. To be sure, their purposes are limited, specific, and above all conflicting: diverse strivings do not automatically resolve themselves into any grand harmonious everlasting Purpose. That is why there is a real and continuing task of inventing norms and principles through which we can achieve some rough approximation to harmony or at least contain within tolerable limits the inescapable conflicts of purpose.[4] We can welcome Küng's realistic appreciation of this task and his readiness to take part in it. But neither participation in this task, nor the generalization of William James's 'precursive faith' which we may need to bring to it, depends in any way on a belief in 'God as Finisher'; rather, their reasonability arises directly out of a human appreciation of the human situation, as Küng's own argument shows. Nor are the difficult details of this task made any easier by postulating any sort of god.

If the specific suggestions of personal explanation, creative value, and the various forms of the moral argument fail, we are left with the postulation of a god as merely *that which* somehow supplies a ground, support, or goal for reality. But to postulate an entity as *that which* does something gives us no real additional explanation. If we say, for example, that reality is supported because there is something that supports it, the alleged explanation merely repeats what was to be explained; at best, we have a place-holder for a real explanation. Moreover, even if this god-hypothesis did somehow explain the world or moral values or human purposes, we should face again the familiar objection: Why is this (uncertain) god not as much in need of further explanation or support as 'uncertain reality'? To say that God is introduced by definition as that which explains itself, that which terminates the regress of explanation, is again empty and useless; but any attempt to explain and justify the claim that he has such a special status leads us, as we have seen, to the concept which underlies the ontological proof, and we have seen in detail, in Chapter 3, how this fails.

Küng's strategy, as we have seen, is to incorporate the question of the existence of a god within the wider question of how modern man is to meet the challenge of nihilism, and to suggest that the latter can be solved only by a decision in favour of an affirmative answer to the former. But this is wrong. Ironically, he has himself supplied all the

[4] Cf. Chapter 6 of *Hume's Moral Theory* (see n. 2 to Chapter 6, p. 106, above), and my 'Cooperation, Competition, and Moral Philosophy', in *Cooperation and Competition in Animals and Man*, edited by A. Colman (Van Nostrand, London, forthcoming).

materials for showing that the challenge of both intellectual and moral or practical nihilism can be met in purely human terms, by what Küng calls a 'fundamental trust' which is reasonable in its own right—that is, equivalently, by a fallibilist empiricism on the intellectual side and on the practical side by the invention of value. The further postulation of a god, even as indeterminate and mysterious a god as Küng's, is a gratuitous addition to this solution, an attempted underpinning which is as needless as it is incomprehensible.

(b) *The Balance of Probabilities*

We can now bring together the many different arguments for theism which we have discussed, and consider their combined effect. But some of them cannot be combined with one another. The thesis that there is a Berkeleian god is so different from any view that adds a god, either immanent or transcendent (or both immanent and transcendent, like Küng's), to the ordinary material or spatio-temporal world, that arguments for the one cannot assist those for the other. There is a similar discrepancy between Swinburne's (or Cleanthes') explicitly personal god and the creative value proposed by extreme axiarchism, though Küng's god is perhaps so medially placed between these that he could share some arguments with each of them. Moreover, the ontological argument, in all its forms, has been shown to be simply unsound; it can contribute no weight at all to the case for theism. On the contrary, its failure does, as Kant said, though not exactly in the way that Kant thought, undermine the various forms of cosmological argument: even if the concept of a being whose essence includes existence is admissible, such a being would *not* exist in all logically possible worlds, and its existence in the actual world would not be *a priori* certain or self-explanatory; it would not terminate the regress of explanation. But there is at least one interesting and important possibility of consilience, namely that which would bring together (1) reported miracles, (2) inductive versions of the design and consciousness arguments, picking out as 'marks of design' both the fact that there are causal regularities at all and the fact that the fundamental natural laws and physical constants are such as to make possible the development of life and consciousness, (3) an inductive version of the cosmological argument, seeking an answer to the question 'Why is there any world at all?' (4) the suggestion that there are objective moral values whose occurrence likewise calls for further explanation, and (5) the suggestion that some kinds of religious experience can be best understood as direct awareness of something supernatural. These various considerations might be held jointly to support the hypothesis that there is a personal or quasi-personal god.

In evaluating this possibility, we must note how in principle a hypothesis can be supported by the consilience of different considerations, each of which, on its own, leaves the balance of probabilities against that hypothesis. Suppose that there are several pieces of evidence, e_1, e_2, and e_3, each of which would fit in with a hypothesis h, but each of which, on its own, is explained with less initial improbability on some other grounds, say by g_1, g_2, and g_3 respectively. Yet if the improbability involved in postulating h is less than the *sum* of the improbabilities involved in the rival explanations g_1, g_2, and g_3, though it is greater than each of these improbabilities separately, the balance of probabilities when we take e_1, e_2, and e_3 together will favour the hypothesis h. It is important that it is just the one initial improbability of h that is weighed in turn against the improbabilities of g_1, g_2, g_3, and then against the sum of these.

But the supposed consilience of theistic arguments does not satisfy the requirements of this formal pattern. As we have seen, the first and fifth of these considerations are extremely weak: all the evidence that they can muster is easily explained in natural terms, without any improbabilities worth taking into account. Consciousness and the actual phenomena of morality and valuing as a human activity are explained without further improbabilities, given that the natural world is such as to allow life to evolve, so the only improbabilities to be scored against the naturalistic kind of explanation are whatever may be involved in there being causal regularities, the fundamental laws and physical constants being as they are, and there being any world at all. Against the rival theistic hypothesis we should have to score the (significant) improbability that if there were a god he (or it) would create a world with causal laws, and one with our specific causal laws and constants, but also the great improbability of there being a process of the unmediated fulfilment of will, and, besides, the basic improbability of there being a god at all. For while the naturalist had admittedly no reply to Leibniz's question 'Why is there a world at all?', the theist, once deprived of the illusory support of the ontological argument, is equally embarrassed by the question 'Why is there a god at all?' Whatever initial improbability there may be in the unexplained brute fact that there is a world, there is a far greater initial improbability in what the theist has to assert as the unexplained brute fact that there is a god capable of creating a world.

In the end, therefore, we can agree with what Laplace said about God: we have no need of that hypothesis. This conclusion can be reached by an examination precisely of the arguments advanced in favour of theism, without even bringing into play what have been regarded as the strongest considerations on the other side, the problem of evil and the various natural histories of religion. When these are thrown into the scales, the balance tilts still further against theism. Although we could not (in Chapter 9) rule out the possibility that some acceptable modification of traditional theism might enable it to accommodate the occurrence of evils, we saw that no sound solution of this sort has yet been offered; the extreme difficulty that theism has in reconciling *its own* doctrines with one another in this respect must tell heavily against it. Also, although the clear possibility of developing an adequate natural explanation of the origin, evolution, and persistence of religious belief is not a primary argument against theism, and could be brushed aside if there were any cogent positive case for the existence of a god, yet, since there is no such case, it helps to make the negative case still more conclusive. It removes the vague but obstinate feeling that where so many people have believed so firmly—and sometimes fervently—and where religious thought and organization have been so tenacious and so resilient 'there must be something in it'. We do not need to invoke the 'higher causes' by which Machiavelli (with his tongue in his cheek) said that ecclesiastical principalities are upheld.[5] The occurrence, even the continuing occurrence, of theism is not, in Hume's phrase, a continued miracle which subverts all the principles of our understanding.

The balance of probabilities, therefore, comes out strongly against the existence of a god. Chapter 11 has shown that we cannot escape the implications of this result by making a voluntary faith intellectually respectable. The most that we could allow was James's experimental approach, and, as we saw, it would be very hard for this to yield a favourable result. In Chapter 12 we saw the failure of some popular attempts to free religion from the need to defend its traditional factual beliefs; and in Chapter 13 we considered, but rejected, some replacements for a god of the traditional sort. There is at any rate no easy way of defending religion once it is admitted that the literal, factual, claim that there is a god cannot be rationally sustained.

[5] N. Machiavelli, *The Prince* (many editions), Chapter 11.

(c) *The Moral Consequences of Atheism*

But some readers, I know, even some thoughtful and fairminded readers, will not be satisfied. I suspect that the most lasting obstacle to the acceptance of atheism is a lingering notion that such acceptance would be morally and practically disastrous. It may, therefore, be relevant to end with a brief survey of the moral consequences of atheism.

There are four main kinds of view about the general nature and status of morality. The first of these sees moral rules and principles, whatever other functions they may serve, as being essentially the commands or requirements of a god (or gods), backed up by the promise of rewards and the threat of penalties either in this life or in an afterlife. The second (Kantian, rationalist, or intuitionist) sees moral principles as objectively valid prescriptions, formulated or discovered by human reason or intellect, and autonomously authoritative, independently of any god; if someone who holds this view also believes that there is a god, he will see the goodness of this god as consisting in his exemplifying these independent principles. A third view is that which we considered at the end of Chapter 6, according to which there *are* objectively valid principles as the second view maintains, but they are in some way created and sustained in existence by a god. The fourth (Humean, sentimentalist, subjectivist, or naturalistic) view is that morality is essentially a human, social, product, that moral concepts, principles, and practices have developed by some process of biological and social evolution. Their origin and persistence are due somehow to the fact that they enable human beings, whose natural situation includes a mixture of competitive and co-operative forces, and a need for co-operation, to survive and flourish better, by limiting the competition and facilitating the co-operation. But morality is not, on this view, necessarily understood in this light by those who adhere to it: it is possible that its adherents should hold one of the other three views, and yet that a correct description, from the outside, of their thinking and conduct should be given by this naturalistic account.

Now if some adherent to a morality has held either the first or the third of these views, so that *he* has seen morality as essentially dependent upon some god, then it is indeed possible that if he then ceases to believe in that god his adherence to that morality will be undermined: the immediate moral consequences of *his* atheism may be deplorable. This is a good reason for not tying moral to religious teaching at a time when religious belief is itself fragile. The point is well made by Richard Robinson's story of a priest saying to a pair of well-behaved atheists, 'I can't understand you boys; if I didn't believe in God I should be having a high old time'.[6] But if either our second view (of an autonomous objective ethics) or our fourth (naturalist or sentimentalist) view is correct, there is no reason to suppose that such undermining will be either a lasting or a general effect of the decay of religious belief. Indeed, it is hardly even necessary that either of these views should be *correct*: it is enough that they are available to the atheist. But in particular if, as I have argued elsewhere, the fourth view is correct, then morality has a genuine causal source of its own.[7] It is basically a matter of feelings and attitudes, partly instinctive, developed by biological evolution, and partly acquired, developed by socio-historical evolution and passed on from generation to generation less by deliberate education than by the automatic transmission of cultural traits. Since it has such a source, quite independent of religion, it is certain to survive when religion decays.

However, this may seem to be too abstract, too *a priori*, an argument. Is there any better, more empirical, evidence about the contrasting moral consequences of theism and of atheism? The only simple answer to this question is that there is no simple answer. Neither theists nor atheists have any monopoly of either the vices or the virtues. Nor is any statistical survey likely to establish a clear causal tendency for religious belief, or the lack of it, to encourage either virtue or vice. This is partly because the determination of what is to count as virtue or as vice, or of the relative importance of particular virtues and vices, is itself relevantly controversial; this is one of the issues on which believers and non-believers are divided. Another reason is that there are indefinitely many degrees of belief and disbelief. But even if we confined our survey to an agreed core of virtues on the one hand and of vices on the other, and to unequivocal samples of theists and atheists, any statistical results would still be indecisive. For if there were, as I suspect there would then be, some positive correlation between atheism and virtue, this would still not establish a causal tendency for atheism as such to promote virtue. It

---

[6] R. Robinson, *An Atheist's Values* (Oxford University Press, 1964; paperback Basil Blackwell, Oxford, 1975), p. 137. The story is no doubt apocryphal. This book as a whole gives a very full answer to the question of the moral consequences of atheism. References in the text to Robinson are to pages in this work.

[7] See the works referred to in nn. 3 and 4 (pp. 246 and 250) above.

could be too easily explained away by the fact that, other things being equal, there is likely to be a higher incidence of disbelief among the 'wise and learned', for the reason hinted at by Hume in his essay on miracles.[8]

Since there is little prospect of reliable direct empirical evidence, we must fall back on some general considerations. What differences would it make to morality if there were, or if there were not, a god, and again if people associated, or did not associate, their morality with religious belief?

The unsatisfactory character of the first, divine command, view of morality was pointed out by Plato, whose objections have been echoed many times.[9] If moral values were constituted *wholly* by divine commands, so that goodness *consisted* in conformity to God's will, we could make no sense of the theist's own claims that God is good and that he seeks the good of his creation. However, it would be possible to hold coherently that while the goodness of some states of affairs—for example, of one sort of human life as contrasted with others—is independent of God's will, it is only his commands that supply the prescriptive element in morality. Or they could be seen as supplying an additional prescriptive element. A religious morality might then be seen as imposing stronger obligations.

Both these variants, however, as Kant pointed out, tend to corrupt morality, replacing the characteristically moral motives—whether these are construed as a rational sense of duty and fairness, or as specific virtuous dispositions, or as generous, co-operative, and sympathetic feelings—by a purely selfish concern for the agent's own happiness, the desire to avoid divine punishments and to enjoy the rewards of God's favour, in this life or in an afterlife. This divine command view can also lead people to accept, as moral, requirements that have no discoverable connection—indeed, no connection at all—with human purposes or well-being, or with the well-being of any sentient creatures. That is, it can foster a tyrannical, irrational, morality. Of course, if there were not only a benevolent god but also a reliable revelation of his will, then we might be able to get from it expert moral advice about difficult issues, where we could not discover for ourselves what are the best policies. But there is no such reliable revelation. Even a theist must see that the purported revelations, such as the Bible and the Koran, condemn them-

---

[8] *Enquiry concerning Human Understanding*, Section 10; cf. Chapter 1 above.

[9] Plato, *Euthyphro*. The exact force of 'the Euthyphro dilemma' is considered in Chapter 10 of my *Ethics: Inventing Right and Wrong*.

selves by enshrining rules which we must reject as narrow, out-dated, or barbarous. As Küng says, 'We are responsible for our morality'. More generally, tying morality to religious belief is liable to devalue it, not only by undermining it, temporarily, if the belief decays, but also by subordinating it to other concerns while the belief persists.

There is, indeed, a strain in religion that positively welcomes sin as a precondition for salvation. Jesus himself is reported as saying 'I am not come to call the righteous, but sinners to repentance'. Luther says that 'God is the god of the humble, the miserable, the oppressed, and the desperate', and that 'that pernicious and pestilent opinion of man's own righteousness ... suffereth not God to come to his own natural and proper work'. And William James reports (at second hand) an orthodox minister who said that Dr Channing (the eminent Unitarian) 'is excluded from the highest form of religious life by the extraordinary rectitude of his character'.[10]

It is widely supposed that Christian morality is particularly admirable. Here it is important to distinguish between the original moral teachings of Jesus, so far as we can determine them, and later developments in the Christian tradition. Richard Robinson has examined the synoptic gospels (Matthew, Mark, and Luke) as the best evidence for Jesus' own teaching, and he finds in them five major precepts: 'love God, believe in me, love man, be pure in heart, be humble'. The reasons given for these precepts are 'a plain matter of promises and threats': they are 'that the kingdom of heaven is at hand', and that 'those who obey these precepts will be rewarded in heaven, while those who disobey will have weeping and gnashing of teeth'. Robinson notes that 'Certain ideals that are prominent elsewhere are rather conspicuously absent from the synoptic gospels'. These include beauty, truth, knowledge, and reason:

As Jesus never recommends knowledge, so he never recommends the virtue that seeks and leads to knowledge, namely reason. On the contrary, he regards certain beliefs as in themselves sinful ... whereas it is an essential part of the ideal of reason to hold that no belief can be morally wrong if reached in the attempt to believe truly. Jesus again and again demands faith; and by faith he means believing certain very improbable things without considering evidence or estimating probabilities; and that is contrary to reason. (p. 149)

[10] Matthew 9: 13. The passage from Luther is quoted by James on pp. 244–5 of *The Varieties of Religious Experience* (see n. 1 to Chapter 10, p. 178, above) and the story about Dr Channing in n. 1 on p. 466 of the same work.

Robinson adds:

> Jesus says nothing on any social question except divorce, and all ascriptions of any political doctrine to him are false. He does not pronounce about war, capital punishment, gambling, justice, the administration of law, the distribution of goods, socialism, equality of income, equality of sex, equality of colour, equality of opportunity, tyranny, freedom, slavery, selfdetermination, or contraception. There is nothing Christian about being for any of these things, nor about being against them, if we mean by 'Christian' what Jesus taught according to the synoptic gospels.
>
> The Jesus of the synoptic gospels says little on the subject of sex. He is against divorce. He speaks of adultery as a vice, and perhaps includes in adultery all extramarital intercourse. The story of the woman taken in adultery, which is of a synoptic character though it appears in texts of John, preaches a humane and forgiving attitude towards sexual errors. Jesus shows no trace of that dreadful hatred of sex as such which has disfigured the subsequent history of the Christian churches ... (p. 149)

Robinson goes on to comment on the morality of the Bible:

> Newman said that when non-Christians read the Christian Bible 'they are much struck with the high tone of its precepts' (Sermon on John xiii. 17). That is contrary to my experience. I shall never forget the first time I read the Old Testament after I had acquired the habit of independent judgement. I was horrified at its barbarity, and bewildered that it had been widely held up as a store of ideals. It seemed to describe a savage people, fierce and brutal, no more admirable than the worse of the savage cultures that anthropologists describe to us today, and a great deal less admirable than the gentler cultures they report.
>
> Nor will Newman's words fit the impression made by the synoptic gospels. They are a beautiful and fascinating piece of literature; and they preach the great precept 'love thy neighbour'. But this precept is overshadowed in them both by the harsh unloving behaviour of the preacher, and by its absolute subordination to the unreasonable commands to love God and believe in Jesus. (pp. 150-1)

Robinson urges us to reject these commands and the associated values of piety, faith, and improvidence. He reminds us that 'many of man's most terrible actions have been done out of piety, and that piety is responsible for our shameful wars of religion'. He also characterizes the view that belief, or disbelief, can be sinful as a 'blasphemy against reason'. He says that we should accept the precept to love our neighbours, 'extended as Jesus perhaps extended it to love of all humanity, and still further to love of all life, as he certainly did not extend it' (p. 152), and such consequential attitudes as generosity, gentleness, mercy, and the observance of the golden rule. However, we might well query (though Robinson does not) the precise command to love your neighbour *as yourself*. This seems unrealistically to prescribe a degree of altruism that is in general not humanly possible, and so to make of morality a fantasy rather than something that people can seriously try to practise and can ask of one another. Robinson does query the injunction to be pure in heart, and also the call for humility: it is better to make true estimates both of oneself and of others, and not lie about them, though in public 'the right choice will usually be to refrain from drawing attention either to our superiorities or to our inferiorities' (pp. 153-4).

The later tradition of Christian ethics has tended to add to Jesus' teaching some deplorable elements, such as hostility to sex, and many more admirable ones, such as concern with justice and the other requirements for the flourishing of human life in society, and ideals of beauty, truth, knowledge, and (up to a point) reason. But it has in general retained the concern with salvation and an afterlife, and the view that disbelief, or even doubt, or criticism of belief, is sinful, with the resulting tendencies to the persecution of opponents—including, of course, the adherents of rival Christian sects and rival religions— the discouragement of discussion, hostility (even now in some places) to the teaching of well-confirmed scientific truths, like the theory of evolution, and the propagation of contrary errors, and the intellectual dishonesty of trying to suppress one's own well-founded doubts. Many people are shocked at the way in which the Unification Church ('the Moonies') entraps converts and enslaves their minds and emotions; but the same methods have been and are used by many more orthodox sects. Religion has, indeed, a remarkable ability to give vices the air of virtues, providing a sanctified outlet for some of the nastiest human motives. It is fashionable to ascribe the horrors of Nazism to an atheistic nationalism; but in fact the attitudes to the Jews which it expressed had long been established within the Christian tradition in Germany and elsewhere (sanctioned, for example, by Luther's writings[11]), and the Old Testament itself reports many atrocities as having been not merely approved but positively demanded by God and his spokesmen.[12] And while, following Robinson, I have spoken here particularly of Christian ethics, it is only too obvious that Islamic fundamentalism displays today, more clearly

[11] E.g. *On the Jews and their Lies*, in Vol. 47 of Luther's *Works*, edited by H. T. Lehman (Fortress Press, Philadelphia, 1971), pp. 121-306, recommends the burning of synagogues and of the Jews' houses, confiscation of their books, forbidding of worship and teaching, or alternatively expulsion of the Jews from the country.

[12] E.g. Joshua 8, 10, and 11; Samuel 15.

than Christianity has done recently, the worst aspects of religious morality. We do not need to go back in history to illustrate the dictum of Lucretius: *Tantum religio potuit suadere malorum* (So great are the evils that religion could prompt!)[13] By contrast, there is a long tradition of an essentially humanist morality, from Epicurus to John Stuart Mill and modern writers, including Richard Robinson himself, centred on the conditions for the flourishing of human life and stressing intellectual honesty, tolerance, free inquiry, and individual rights.

There are, then, some marked dangers in a distinctively religious morality. But they are dangers only, not inevitable consequences of associating morality with religion. We can echo, in reverse, Küng's concession: it is possible for even a religious believer 'to lead a genuinely human, that is humane, and in this sense moral life'; even theists are not necessarily narrow-minded dogmatists, intolerant persecutors, or propagators of timid credulity and a crudely calculating selfish version of morality itself. Even within Islam there have been thinkers who have tried to develop its humane and liberal tendencies, and to tone down its cruelty, intolerance, and its unfairness between the sexes, though at present their influence is in decline.

But are there no corresponding dangers in a distinctively non-religious morality? Admittedly, there are. As Robinson says, the Roman Catholic church is only 'The second most intolerant and active body in the world today' (p. 216). Communist parties are expressly anti-religious, and profess an overriding concern with human welfare, but they are also intolerant, ruthless, and, once in power, they too make virtues of tyranny and persecution. And one must recognize that the Catholic church, despite its own illiberal tendencies, sometimes contributes significantly to the resistance to tyrannical states, whether communist or not. More generally, humanist moral thinking is prone either to illusions about necessary progress or to an over-optimistic voluntarism—that is, to assuming that 'we' (whoever that may be) can make or remake the world as we would wish it to be, forgetting that the interplay of many different purposes is liable to result in the fulfilment of none of them.

An alleged weakness, not of non-religious moralities in general, but specifically of moralities explained and understood in the naturalistic way outlined above, is that different groups of people can develop different moral views, which will produce conflict when these groups are in contact with one another, and that there is, on this

[13] *De Rerum Natura*, Book I, line 101.

basis, no clear way of resolving such conflicts. This is true. But it is not a *distinctive* weakness of the naturalistic approach. Absolutist and objectivist moralities, including ones with religious attachments, also differ from one another, and there is no clear way of resolving their conflicts either. That each party *believes* that some one morality is objectively right is no guarantee that they will be able to agree on what it is. Indeed, conflicts between rival absolutists are likely to be less resolvable than conflicts between those who understand morality in a naturalistic way, for the latter can more easily appreciate the merits of compromise and adjustment, or of finding, for the areas of contact, a *ius gentium*, a common core of principles on which they can agree.

Another supposed weakness is this: it may be thought particularly difficult to derive any respect for non-human life, any valuing of nature in general, from a purely secular, human, approach. But it is worth noting that Robinson, for example, specifically includes among his 'atheist's values' a 'love of all life' (p. 152; see also pp. 186–7). In fact there is no question of *deriving* a morality from the facts of the human situation. What we can do is to *understand* how moral thinking can develop and what functions it serves; and we can also understand how it naturally extends itself beyond a quasi-contractual system by the operation of what Hume called 'sympathy'.[14]

In contrast with any such real or supposed weaknesses in non-religious morality, we should note its distinctive merits, in particular its cultivation of a courageous realism in the face of the less palatable facts of life—and of death. But we need not dwell on this merit, since, as we have seen, it is dramatically recognized in Phillips's attempt to take over, in the name of religion, the traditional non-believers' attitude to the loss of one's friends, the attitude of coming to terms with such loss without either denying it or suppressing it. The non-believer comes to terms with the inevitability of his own death in a similar way. Küng has likewise tried to take over in the name of religion the traditional non-believers' view of morality itself: 'We are responsible for our morality'. Robinson says that 'The main irrationality of religion is preferring comfort to truth' (p. 117). Phillips and Küng are implicitly recognizing this traditional weakness in religion, and are proposing that religion should follow atheism in doing without it.

In Phillips, the moral take-over bid is linked with a strong tendency to disguised atheism on the theoretical side, and Küng's concept of

---

[14] See pp. 193–5 of *Ethics: Inventing Right and Wrong*, and the article mentioned in n. 4 above.

God is so complex and so indeterminate that his position, too, may not be really so far removed from atheism. Should we then object to such take-overs? So long as the position adopted is, in substance, atheistic, what does it matter if it is *called* religion? After all, Epicurus was willing to postulate happy and immortal gods safely isolated from all contact with human affairs; Spinoza was willing to speak of *Deus sive natura*, identifying nature with God; and even Hume proposed a compromise:

The theist allows, that the original intelligence is very different from human reason: The atheist allows, that the original principle of order bears some remote analogy to it. Will you quarrel, Gentlemen, about the degrees, and enter into a controversy, which admits not of any precise meaning, nor consequently of any determination.[15]

Today, however, it is more honest and less misleading to reject such compromises and evasions, which can too easily serve as a cover for the reintroduction of characteristically theistic views both on the intellectual and on the moral side.

Alternatively, is there any merit in Braithwaite's approach, in retaining the religious 'stories' as a psychological support for a morality, while explicitly rejecting any suggestion that they are factually true? This we might allow, provided that the morality they support is not of the kind we have been criticizing as distinctively religious. Apart from their other faults, such moralities have a tendency to be dangerously over-optimistic. Particularly in the field of international affairs, leaders who have too strong or too fundamentalist a faith may pursue policies which they know to be reckless, in the expectation that God will prevent the worst—and, for humanity, final—disasters. Such reliance would be quite different from the 'fundamental trust' which Küng has reasonably advocated on purely human grounds. There are inevitable uncertainties in human affairs. Machiavelli speculated that 'fortune is the ruler of one half of our actions, but . . . she allows the other half, or a little less, to be governed by us'.[16] Damon Runyon put it more briefly: 'Nothing human is better than two to one'. If so, the only reasonable plan is to do the best we can, taking all possible precautions against the worst disasters, but *then* to meet the uncertainties with cheerful confidence. 'Trust in God and keep your powder dry', understood as Braithwaite might understand it, may be good practical advice. But to trust God to keep your powder dry for you is the height of folly.

[15] *Dialogues concerning Natural Religion*, Part XII.
[16] *The Prince*, Chapter 25.

Index

absolutist view of spatio-temporal features, 73, 236
absorbed and unabsorbed evil, 154-6, 159, 173, 176, 234, 235-6
Adam and Eve, 175, 176
Albert, H., 245
Anabaptists, 203
analytic and synthetic truths, 4, 6, 44, 45, 47, 88, 115, 116, 117, 118, 237, 238-9
Anderson, J., 194
angels, 32, 33, 189; fallen, 155, 162
animism, 190, 192
Anselm, St., 6, 41, 49-55, 62, 83, 100, 104, 214, 215, 227, 230
anthropomorphism, 108, 192, 243
a priori truths, 10, 19, 35-6, 45, 84-5, 86-7, 89, 93, 113-14, 135, 143-5, 146, 147, 149; *see also* analytic and synthetic truths
Aquinas, St. Thomas, 27, 41, 81, 87-92, 233
Arabic philosophers, 81, 92; *see also* Averroes, al Farabi, al Ghazali, *kalam* argument, Maimonides
Archimedes, 85
Aristotle, 81, 92
asymmetry, causal, 91-2, 231
atheism, distinctive values of, 229, 261
atomic and sub-atomic structures, 126, 140, 142
Averroes, 81
Ayers, M. R., 121n

Barnes, J., 51
'belief', ambiguity of, 217
Berkeley, G., 10, 11, 64-80, 81, 121, 128, 131, 236, 251
best explanation, argument to the, 4-6, 23, and *passim*

Bible, 6, 181, 242, 256, 258
'big bang', 94, 140
brain- and mental events, 78, 168, 122-32
Braithwaite, R. B., 224, 225, 226, 228, 229, 262
brute facts, 86, 91, 131, 149, 234, 252-3
Buddhists, 217
Bultmann, R., 242-3
Bunyan, J., 186

Campbell, C. A., 168
Cantor, paradoxes of, 92, 93
Catholic Church, 13, 203, 260
Catholicism, 189
causal asymmetry, 91-2, 231
causal explanation, 85, 97, 98, 128, 129, 130, 131, 232, 237; of belief, 39, 171-2, 199; of perception, 36; *see also* natural explanation
causal laws, 20, 22, 85, 128, 132, 152-3, 190-1, 233-4, 251, 252; and omnipotence, 153
causation: conservation principles and, 35; efficient, 89-90, 237
causes, regress of, 82, 87-92; *see also* regress of explanation
Channing, Dr, 257
Charon, 9
Christ, Jesus, 11, 12, 15, 178, 181, 182, 212, 218, 240, 242, 257, 258, 259
Christianity, 1, 12, 13, 27, 157, 192, 196, 199, 210-14, 216
Christian morality, 195, 257-60
Christian Science, 179
Cicero, 119, 120, 127
C-inductive and P-inductive arguments, 95-7, 98

circularity in argument, 5–6, 31–2, 44

Clarke, S., 85, 238

Clifford, W. K., 204, 205, 207, 209

cogito, the, 30–2

communism, 260

compartmental thinking, 220–1

conscience, argument from, 103–6, 110, 111, 117–18

consciousness, argument from, 81, 100, 119–32, 233, 244

consilience, 7, 150, 251–3; formal pattern of, 252; of arguments for theism, 7, 150, 251–3

contingency, argument from, 81–7, 143, 145

contingents, future, 175

co-operation, 206, 207, 246, 254

cosmological argument, 81–101, 106, 135, 144, 145, 146, 148, 149, 222, 232, 233, 243, 249, 251; Aquinas's variants of, 87–92; *kalam* forms of, 92–5; Leibniz's version of, 82–7; Swinburne's inductive form of, 95–101

Craig, W. L., 81n, 88n, 92

creative ethical requiredness, *see* extreme axiarchism

creaturely essences, 174

credal statements, 3–4; *see also* disguised atheism, meaning of religious language

credulity, thought to be meritorious, 15–16

cumulative effect of arguments, *see* consilience

Curley Smith, 173–5

Darwin, C., 133, 138, 140, 141, 145, 146, 196

Davidson, D., 123, 126

deductive arguments for and against theism, 4, 30–40, 177, 227, 243, 248; *see also* cosmological argument; evil, problem of; ontological argument

dependence of effect on cause, *see* causal asymmetry

Descartes, R., 6, 10, 11, 27, 30–40, 41–9, 53, 56, 58, 62, 83, 104, 240

design, argument for, 81, 100, 101, 106, 117, 121, 133–49, 157, 188, 189, 222, 233, 249, 251; *a priori* assumptions in, 143–5, 146, 147, 149; Hume's criticisms of, 134–40, Kant's criticisms of,

144–5; modern versions of, 140; Swinburne's restatement of, 146–9

determinism, 21, 22, 86, 87, 164, 166, 167, 168, 170–2, 174, 234, 245; *see also* quantum physics, indeterminism of

devil, the, 180, 181, 185

disguised atheism, 192, 228–9, 261–2

dualism, 127–8, 131; *see also* Descartes

Dunkirk, as miracle, 27–8

Durkheim, E., 198

Edwards, J., 180

efficient causation, 89–90, 237

Einsteinian world, 76

Engels, F., 194–5

ens realissimum, 82, 83, 192

Epicurus, 107, 229, 260, 262

ethical requiredness, *see* prescriptivity, objective; creative, *see* extreme axiarchism

Euclidean space, 75, 76

evil: dependence of faith on, 135, 157–9, 188; problem of 4, 66, 135, 136, 137, 150–75, 177, 199, 234, 235, 253

evolution, theory of, 133–4, 138–9, 140, 143, 146, 259

existential propositions, 45

existential quantifier, 46–7, 48, 49, 83

existentialisms, 216

'exists' as a predicate, 45, 48, 49, 83

experimental faith, 209–10, 253

extreme axiarchism, 86, 231–9, 249, 251

faith, in relation to reason, 6, 92, 109, 135, 199, 206, 207, 209–10, 211, 213, 214–16, 218–20, 225–6, 227, 243–5, 246, 247, 250, 253, 257

fallibilist empiricism, 205, 245, 251

al Farabi, 81, 90, 92

Feuerbach, L., 8, 192–3, 194, 197, 198, 240

finite past time, arguments for, 88, 92–5

first cause argument, 87, 88, 91, 94, 143

Flew, A., 133n, 164n

flying saucers, 15

Forms, Platonic, 38–9, 230–1, 235

Fox, G., 181

Frazer, Sir J., 188, 190, 191

Fred's shoes, 96–7, 99

freedom of choice, experience of, 123, 125, 167–8

free will: as higher-order good, 155, 164,

165–6, 172, 175, 234; contra-causal, 166–72, 174–6, 235
free will defence, 155–6, 160, 162–6, 172–6, 234, 235
Frege, G., 46
Freud, S., 8, 194, 196, 197
fulfilment of intention, direct, *see* personal explanation

Gaunilo, 41n, 49, 53–5
generalizations, reasoning to and from, 24
al Ghazali, 81, 93–4, 100
God, as intentional object, 2, 211–12, 221, 248
God, as *that which* 137, 149, 250, 251
God of traditional theism, attributes of, 1–2; replacements for, 230–9, 241–2
God's goodness, nature of, 135, 151, 156,158, 203, 216
gospels, synoptic, 257–9
grammars of truth, 224–6, 227, 228
Greek philosophers, earliest of, 5
Gruner, R., 157, 158, 159

Hare, R. M., 116
Hartshorne, C., 41, 55
Heber, Bishop, 157
Hegel, G. W. F., 240, 242
Hick, J., 153
humanism, 193, 247, 260, 261
Hume, D., 7, 8, 9, 11, 12, 13–19, 23–6, 27, 28–9, 30, 52, 55, 72, 89, 95, 118, 133–9, 142–3, 144, 145, 147, 178, 188–90, 198, 199, 203, 216, 221, 222, 224, 230, 239, 243, 249, 253, 254, 256, 261, 262
Hutcheson, F., 117, 163
hypotheses: confirmation of, *see* C-inductive and P-inductive arguments; testimony, evaluation of

ibn Rushd, *see* Averroes
idea of God: argument from, 30–40; natural explanation of, 38–9
ideas, as intentional objects, 65, 68, 69, 70, 71, 79
idolatry, 188–90, 192, 212
immaterialism, *see* Berkeley, G.
imperative premisses, 112–13
indifference, problem of, 236
individual essences, 173–4
inductive arguments for God's existence,

95–101, 115–17, 118, 129–32, 134–5, 143, 146–9, 249, 251
inductive reasoning: justification of, 4–5, 95, 147–8, 215; principles of, *see* C-inductive and P-inductive arguments; testimony, evaluation of
innate ideas, 37
'intending to sign a cheque', 126, 127
invention of moral value, 206–7, 246–7, 250, 251, 254, 255
Islam, 1, 261
Islamic fanaticism, 163
Islamic fundamentalism, 259–60
Islamic thinkers, *see* Arabic philosophers
Israelites, 193
iterated modalities, 57, 58, 60

Jains, 217
James, W., 6, 178–86, 187, 190, 197–8, 200, 204–10, 214, 215, 245, 246, 253, 256
Jansenists, 27
Jehovah, 190, 193, 216
Jesuits, 27
Jews, 259
Job, 216
John of the Cross, St., 185
Johnson, S., 65–6, 77–8
Joshua, Book of, 259n
Judaism, 1, 188
Judgement Day, 219, 220, 225
Jupiter, the planet, 93

kalam argument, 92–5, 101
Kali, 203
Kant, I., 11, 41, 43–6, 47, 48, 49, 55, 82–4, 93, 106–11, 112, 113, 114, 118, 133, 134, 144, 145, 149, 153, 165, 170, 177, 221, 226, 240, 251, 254, 256
'Kantian resource, the', 112
Kenny, A., 87
Kierkegaard, S., 6, 182, 200, 210–16, 218, 219, 227
Kneale, W., 46n
Koran, 256
Küng, H., 11, 240–51, 257, 260, 261

Laplace, P.-S. de, 253
last judgement, 3, 218
laws of nature, 16–17, 17–22, 24, 25, 26, 28, 65, 123, 127, 131, 146; *see also* causal laws, laws of working

laws of working, basic and derived, 19–22, 85, 99, 139, 140, 142, 147, 148, 234
Lazarus, 13
Leibniz, G. W., 62, 81, 82–7, 88, 91, 92, 97, 101, 120, 143, 173, 235, 236, 252
'Leibniz's lapse', 173
Leslie, J., 231–9, 249
Lewis, D., 60n
Liar paradox, 161n
Livy, 207
Locke, J., 5, 67, 69, 70, 72–3, 75, 79, 119–21, 126, 127, 128, 131
Lucas, J. R., 169–70, 171–2
Lucretius, 260
Luther, M., 257, 259

McGinn, C., 123n, 124
Machiavelli, N., 253, 262
machine-making machines, 146
Mackie, J. L., *The Cement of the Universe*, 20n, 21n, 92n, 231n, 237n, 245n; 'Cooperation, Competition, and Moral Philosophy', 250n; *Ethics: Inventing Right and Wrong*, 115n, 206n, 238n, 246; 'Evil and Omnipotence', 160, 164n; *Hume's Moral Theory*, 106n, 117n, 238n; *Problems from Locke*, 73n; 'The Riddle of Existence', 47n; 'Theism and Utopia', 165n; 'Three Steps Towards Absolutism', 73n; *Truth, Probability, and Paradox*, 161n
magic, 190–2, 222
magical language, 222, 223
Mahomet, 15
Maimonides, 81, 88, 91
Malcolm, N., 41, 55, 227n, 243
Marett, R. R., 188, 191
'Martian', 42–3
Martians, 124
Marx, K., 8, 9, 194, 196, 197, 240
materialism, 70, 71, 73, 74, 119, 120, 122, 124, 125, 127, 131, 236
maximal excellence, 56–9
maximal greatness, 52, 56–9
Mayo, B., 160
meaning of religious language, 1–4, 11, 156, 213, 217–29, 235, 240–2
metaphysical statements, 223
Michelangelo, 3
Mill, J. S., 20, 151n, 156, 181–2, 186, 260
mind-matter relationship, 30–1, 32, 70,

74, 119–32, 162; *see also* brain- and mental events, dualism, psycho-physical laws
miracles, 11–12, 13–29, 97, 118, 131, 182, 242, 251; concept of, 19–23
modal logic arguments for theism, modern, 55–63, 173–4
morality: divine command view of, 102, 110, 114–15, 118, 256–7; objectivist view of, 106, 115–17, 118, 206, 238–9, 251, 261; subjectivist view of, 117, 118, 206, 239, 254, 255, 261

natural explanation: of conscience, 105–6, 117–18; of idea of God, 38–9; of miracles, 26, 28; of morality, *see* morality, subjectivist view of; of religion, 7–9, 11, 12, 188–98, 199, 243, 253; of religious experiences, 11, 179–81, 183–4, 187
natural histories of religion, *see* natural explanation of religion
Nazism, 163, 259
necessary being, 1, 2, 82–4, 91–2, 231–3, 248, 250, 251; *see also* ontological argument
Newman, J. H., 103–6, 109, 110
Newton, I., 134, 139, 142
Newtonian absolute space, 73, 236
Newtonian gravitational astronomy, 134, 142
Nietzsche, F., 8, 240, 244, 246
nihilism, 11, 240, 244–51
no-maximality, 59, 61

Odin, 203
Oedipus complex, 197
O'Hara, Father, 218
Old Testament, 196, 258, 259
omnificence, 161
omnipotence, *see* evil, problem of; paradox of, 160–1
omniscience, *see* contingents, future; omnificence; idea of, 38
ontological argument, 6, 30, 41–63, 81, 82–4, 94, 106, 144, 145, 232, 243, 248, 250, 251, 252; Anselm's version of, 49–55; Descartes's version of, 41–9; Plantinga's version of, 55–63
'orders of truth', 184

pain, 117, 152, 153, 178, 218, 222
Paley, W., 144

Pallas Athene, 193-4
panpsychism, 171
Pascal, B., 171, 200-3, 208, 210, 212, 213, 216, 240, 243, 244-5
Paul, St., 181, 187
personal explanation, 22, 98, 100, 101, 122, 128-32, 149, 232, 235, 237, 249, 250, 252
'persuasive definition', 214
phenomenalism, 70, 71, 74, 77, 234, 236
Phillips, D. Z., 190-1, 198, 218, 220, 222-4, 225-9, 243, 261
'piecemeal supernaturalism', 182, 189, 190
Plantinga, A., 41, 55-63, 83, 162, 173-4, 175
Plato, 38-9, 86, 114, 115, 212, 230-1, 235, 256
polytheism, 8, 182, 188-9, 192
Popper, K., 205-6, 245
possible worlds, 55-63, 84, 117, 173-4, 251
practical reason, 108, 109, 111-14, 171, 200, 203, 208, 221, 244
predestination, 203
prescriptivity, objective, 86, 115-17, 237-9
Price, J. V., 133n
primary and secondary qualities, 33-4, 36, 37, 69-70, 72-3, 75, 80
Prior, A. N., 175n
probabilistic arguments for God's existence, *see* inductive arguments for God's existence
probability, epistemic, 10, 11, 21, 22, 23; physical, 9, 10, 21, 22; statistical, 9, 10, 21, 24
prophecy, 22-3
Protestant Christianity, 205
Protestant Christian theology, modern, 3
psychophysical laws, 123-7, 131
public opinion polls, 23

quantum physics, indeterminism of, 79, 123, 125, 168, 169

Ratisbonne, A., 187
realism, 36, 64-6, 71, 73-4, 236, direct, 74; immaterialist, 64-6; 74; representative, 73-4
regress of explanation, 33, 36, 40, 82, 86,

87-92, 120, 143, 145, 146, 149, 232, 250, 251
Reid, T., 75
religious experience, argument from, 10, 177-87, 199, 210, 248, 252; natural explanation of, 11, 179-81, 183-4, 187
'Remartian', 43, 44, 46-7, 48, 49, 53
Rhees, R., 222, 226
Robinson, J. A. T., 230
Robinson, R., 255, 257-9, 260, 261
Runyon, D., 262

Sachsse, H., 246
saints, 13, 185-6, 189
Satan, 174, 176
Saturn, the planet, 93
secondary relations, 238-9; *see also* supervenience
sensory data, 74-7, 78-9
Sidgwick, H., 111-14
simple truth, 205, 224, 228
Smith, A., 9, 110
sociobiology, 139
Socrates, 212, 215
space-time, 75-6, 236
Spinoza, B., 81, 262
Stalin, J., 163
Stevenson, C. L., 214n
Stoics, 110
sufficient reason, principle of, 82, 84-7, 91-2, 101
supervenience, 113, 115, 116, 117, 118
Swinburne, R. G., 1, 3, 7, 11, 95-101, 115, 121-32, 134, 146-9, 162n, 215, 232, 235, 236, 243, 249, 251

teleological explanation, 86, 130, 146, 237, 243
teleology, immanent, 237
testimony, evaluation of, 16-19, 25-6
Theresa, St., 180, 185
Thompson, F., 80
Tillich, P., 230
Tolstoy, L., 179
transworld depravity, 174
Tylor, E. B., 188, 190, 191

Unification church, 259
universal properties, 151
unmediated fulfilment of will, *see* personal explanation

value, intrinsic, *see* prescriptivity, objective
veil-of-perception problem, 73–4
verificationist theory of meaning, 2–3
Virgin Mary, 181, 182
visions, 180–1, 185
Voltaire, 173
voluntary belief, 10–11, 171, 201, 213, 244, 253

Walker, R. C. S., 170n
Wallace, A., 133, 145

Weil, S., 228
Wille and *Willkür*, 170–1
Winch, P., 228–9
Wisdom, J., 228–9
witch doctors, stone age, 15
Wittgenstein, L., 190, 198, 217–19, 220
Wizenmann, T., 113–14
world-indexed properties, 55, 60, 61, 62

Yorkshire Ripper, the 180

Zeno, paradoxes of, 92